FUTURE SAC

"At this teetering moment in the story of our species, when ... just our kind but of so many other species hangs in the balance, we are massively in need of fresh ways of thinking attuned to the more-than-human matrix that holds, enables, and secretly nourishes all of our human cogitations. *Future Sacred* could not be timelier—its themes are crucial to the very prospect of a livable future."

DAVID ABRAM, PhD, AUTHOR OF *THE SPELL OF THE SENSUOUS*
AND *BECOMING ANIMAL* AND FOUNDER OF ALLIANCE FOR WILD ETHICS

"In her deeply thoughtful and wonderful book, Morley presents an engaging argument for bringing the sacred into all our world-making endeavors. She invites us to reawaken to our cosmic connectedness, reenchant our present and future, and create possibility in the face of crisis. Timely and essential reading."

DR. JUDITH ORLOFF, NEW YORK TIMES BESTSELLING
AUTHOR OF *EMOTIONAL FREEDOM*

"A richly textured cornucopia of wisdom and facts for the 21st century. Such a vibrant mixture of poetic expression and objects of fascination is rare indeed. Read and enjoy this wonderful book!"

ALLAN COMBS, PhD, DIRECTOR OF THE CENTER FOR CONSCIOUSNESS
STUDIES AT THE CALIFORNIA INSTITUTE OF INTEGRAL STUDIES
AND COAUTHOR OF *SYNCHRONICITY*

"... a richly textured investigation into where we have been, where we are going, and how and why we need to transform our society right now. Morley dives deeply into examining how unity, compassion, and collaborative creativity can reinvent our vision of the future. Exploring diverse methods grounded in complexity theory and systems thinking, Morley makes the case for a necessary healing of our planetary relationships. A wonderful contribution filled with deep theoretical reflection and challenging inquiry, *Future Sacred* presents an engaging look at the original ideas shaping the new paradigm."

RONALD ALEXANDER, PhD, LEADERSHIP CONSULTANT,
PSYCHOTHERAPIST, AND AUTHOR OF *WISE MIND, OPEN MIND*

"*Future Sacred* elegantly weaves many different threads of indigenous wisdom, philosophy, and science into a new and ancient fabric of meaning that reenchants the Earth and our co-creative role within her. This book reconnects us with the 'radical enchantment of now,' reminding us of our innate kinship with life as a planetary process and of our co-creative agency and hence responsibility for the future of life. At this time of planetary peril, Morley issues a call for embodying our sacred interbeing in all we do, so that we may heal ourselves in intimate relationship with a living planet, individually and collectively living into the future sacred now—today—through our thoughts, words, and actions."

DANIEL CHRISTIAN WAHL,
AUTHOR OF *DESIGNING REGENERATIVE CULTURES*

"*Future Sacred* urges us into a new story—a story of synergy and partnership with the cosmos. Morley's wisdom compels us to respect the intrinsic sacred sentience that underlies the interrelatedness in the web of life. This work of integrity recognizes that no true separation exists between human and planetary problems. Thanks to Julie J. Morley we are compelled to embrace sacred communion. This work requires our deepest attention."

KINGSLEY DENNIS, PhD, COAUTHOR OF *DAWN OF THE AKASHIC AGE:*
NEW CONSCIOUSNESS, QUANTUM RESONANCE,
AND THE FUTURE OF THE WORLD

"Julie Morley draws on an impressive array of sources—ancient and modern, indigenous and Western—to support a proposal that is as simple as it is profound: if we are to move toward a sacred future we must learn to live on nature's terms, with partnership rather than domination, synergy instead of mastery. She is so right to tell us that in the present planetary catastrophe we cannot afford not to act, but we can less afford to act without these deeper insights."

PETER REASON, PROFESSOR EMERITUS, UNIVERSITY OF BATH,
AND AUTHOR OF *SPINDRIFT* AND *IN SEARCH OF GRACE*

"Anyone concerned about the current environmental crisis needs to read *Future Sacred*. Inspired by indigenous wisdom and modern science, Morley combines her deep love and respect for nature with wide-ranging insights from biology, ecology, and complexity science. The result: an inspired and informed account of the intimate relationship between humanity and the rest of the natural world. The survival of our species may well depend on implementing the wisdom contained in these pages."

CHRISTIAN DE QUINCEY, PhD,
AUTHOR OF *RADICAL NATURE* AND *BLINDSPOTS*

"One thing is certain: our future is uncertain. Looking at the state of the planet today, it is hard to imagine how humanity can avoid the looming ecological catastrophe. But with enough wisdom and inspired action, we can pull through. Julie Morley's message is clear: 'We need to think differently about how we think and act.' Her book *Future Sacred,* a manifesto for the future, shows us all the way forward."

BRIAN THOMAS SWIMME, PhD,
PROFESSOR OF EVOLUTIONARY COSMOLOGY
AT THE CALIFORNIA INSTITUTE OF INTEGRAL STUDIES
AND AUTHOR OF *THE UNIVERSE IS A GREEN DRAGON*

FUTURE
SACRED

The Connected Creativity
of Nature

JULIE J. MORLEY

Park Street Press
Rochester, Vermont

Park Street Press
One Park Street
Rochester, Vermont 05767
www.ParkStPress.com

Text stock is SFI certified

Park Street Press is a division of Inner Traditions International

Library of Congress Cataloging-in-Publication Data

Names: Morley, Julie J., author.
Title: Future sacred : the connected creativity of nature / Julie J. Morley.
Description: Rochester, Vermont : Park Street Press, [2019] | Includes
   bibliographical references and index.
Identifiers: LCCN 2018027450 (print) | LCCN 2018038247 (ebook) |
   ISBN 9781620557686 (pbk.) | ISBN 9781620557693 (ebook)
Subjects: LCSH: Philosophy of nature. | Panpsychism.
Classification: LCC BD581 .M8226 2019 (print) | LCC BD581 (ebook) |
   DDC 113—dc23
LC record available at https://lccn.loc.gov/2018027450

Printed and bound in the United States by Lake Book Manufacturing, Inc.
The text stock is SFI certified. The Sustainable Forestry Initiative® program
promotes sustainable forest management.

10 9 8 7 6 5 4 3 2 1

Text design and layout by Priscilla Baker
This book was typeset in Garamond Premier Pro with Plat, Futura, and Gill Sans
used as display typefaces

To send correspondence to the author of this book, mail a first-class letter to the author c/o Inner Traditions • Bear & Company, One Park Street, Rochester, VT 05767, and we will forward the communication, or contact the author directly at **www.sacredfutures.com**.

For Chloe

CONTENTS

FOREWORD

By Glenn Aparicio Parry

Thought moves the way water moves, filtering down and pervading societies, and eventually the globe. Ideas are like droplets that pool together and circulate in streams of consciousness. Many of these streams never gather momentum and are consigned to minor tributaries that become dry riverbeds—but enough pool together into larger mainstreams that reach all the way to the ocean. This oceanic consciousness contains the ideas that have traveled most widely. Because they are so widespread, they become tacitly accepted—which is to say that nobody questions them or examines the assumptions that underpin them. These assumptions become the lens through which we view, interpret, and act in the world—commonly known as our *dominant paradigm,* which Immanuel Kant called a *weltanschauung,* or worldview.

Other ideas—sometimes our best—do not initially penetrate the mainstream, but do penetrate the soil of our consciousness. They go underground, beneath our current awareness, until the timing is right for them to bubble up to the surface of collective consciousness. By this time, they are so old and forgotten they appear fresh and new.

A key to understanding the timing of ideas—how they emerge, become mainstream, or go underground and resurface—is to realize that human thought unfolds much like the hydrological cycle.

Western science leaves humans out of this cycle, but the Hopi and other Indigenous peoples teach that the underground and above-ground waters and those held in the atmosphere are always in relationship—and that human beings are an integral part of this relationship. And why not? We are composed of 70 percent water; approximately the same proportion as the oceans that cover the surface of the planet.

When we examine the evolution of human thought, we see an even closer parallel to the movement of water. Ideas of one age grow stagnant in another, and when this occurs, the knowledge evaporates, is considered obsolete, and eventually is forgotten. But that is not the end of the process. Forgotten ideas don't just disappear; they are reborn in another form. Imagine an idea evaporating into the atmosphere, but, once there, regaining strength, like a hurricane at sea. Up in the atmosphere, the idea enlarges and recharges itself by mixing with other idea clouds—and when the time is right, returns to Earth in a brainstorm of charged energy that shakes up, breaks apart, and dissolves ideas that have outlived their usefulness. In this way (at least metaphorically), new paradigms of thought are born.

New paradigms, as Thomas Kuhn realized, are not a linear progression of new ideas as much as they incorporate the old in a new way. They are original only in the sense of being novel reformulations. They emerge from an ever-changing matrix of thought whose true source is nature. Our best thinkers realize this, and draw upon the timeless wisdom of the ages and the innate wisdom of the natural world in formulating their worldview. Julie Morley is such a thinker.

I introduce Morley in this way because she has taken on a grand mission in *Future Sacred*. Morley is both a complex thinker and modern panpsychist who sees life force and sentience everywhere. She not only challenges mainstream ideas; she dives in, dusts off, reexamines, and re-presents many of the great—and often esoteric—ideas that have circulated in human consciousness from antiquity to the present.

Future Sacred is an exquisitely erudite, wide-ranging, and important book, and one that stands outside the restrictions of linear time. Nothing escapes the web Morley weaves in *Future Sacred*—and nothing is dead or forgotten. Morley exhumes and breathes life into ancient traditions that have been forgotten or marginalized, such as panpsychism, Indigenous ways of knowing, and the ideas of Pre-Socratics such as Heraclitus and Parmenides. She also draws inspiration from romantic philosophers like Goethe, Wordsworth, and Shelley—and a wide variety of process-relational philosophers (Whitehead, Schelling, and others).

Many have tried to navigate through the labyrinth of philosophical and scientific literature, but few succeed—even fewer as well as Morley does in *Future Sacred*. Like the mythical Ariadne, Morley guides her readers out of the labyrinth by following a unifying thread—her love for Mother Earth and love for all the amazing forms and expressions that make up this radically interconnected web of life (which E. O. Wilson called *biophilia*). This includes human beings in all our various forays into understanding the Great Mystery.

Morley does all this without discounting the value, impact, or potential of modern science. She does, however, alert us to the dangers of obtaining knowledge as a victory over nature. She doesn't ask us to surrender our free will—just to choose to live in acceptance of the cosmic unfolding that is larger than (but includes) the human realm.

Morley envisions a future in which humanity establishes a different way of relating to the natural world. It is a participatory way of knowing that she describes as *communion:* something like what Thich Nhat Hanh calls *interbeing*—the realization of the radically interdependent existence of all things. Morley calls this radical interdependence *sacred symbiosis*. But this symbiosis is not merely physical; there is a mental correlate as well. This is what Buddha meant when he said, "When this is, that is. From the arising of this comes the arising of that."

To create this future, we must break out of our conditioned way of seeing ourselves as the only sentient beings, transcendent and separate from nature. This is a hard task, for, Morley asserts, it requires us not only to think outside of the box but to think outside the system that created the box.

As difficult as this may seem, it is imperative that humans do exactly as Morley counsels. The systems that created the box are not the complete picture; there are still other levels, other realms, in which humans are nested but have difficulty seeing. Morley draws upon Indigenous elders, Goethe, and modern interpreters of Goethe, such as Craig Holdrege, who understand that we must cultivate relationships and alliances with the plant, animal, and mineral kingdoms if we are to venture into their realms. Morley emphasizes the plant kingdom, and she is right to draw our attention to the sentience of plants. We could not be alive if it were not for the oxygen that plants and trees breathe out, just as they depend upon mammals to give back to them the CO_2 they need to survive. In this sacred circle, we are in a conspiracy with plants: we conspire (breathe together) with them.

As Morley knows, there are real consequences to our inability to see nature as sentient. When we deny sentience to plants and trees, for instance, we regard them as mere instruments for our utilitarian needs. Trees act as the lungs of the Earth, but are reduced to economic resources: firewood, paper, or building materials. This reductive thinking has led to rapid deforestation and climate change, which is coming back to haunt us now. We can still save ourselves from our own ignorance by changing the way we think. It is only when we revision humanity through the lens of radical interconnection that we will begin to weave a web of solutions that includes all our relations with which we share this planet.

In short, *Future Sacred* gives voice to an enormous vision—for a human and more-than-human sentient world. This vision does not deny the integrity of the human world, but recognizes that we are also inextricably interconnected with a larger whole—that we are part of a living, pulsing, willful natural world. Morley shares this vision with a growing number of philosophers and writers such as Christian de Quincey, David Abram, Joanna Macy, Lynn Margulis, Charles Eisenstein, and many others, all dreaming about the restoration—and restorying—of a more sacred, beautiful world. No vision is more important to articulate and enact than this vision, for our survival depends upon its resurgence into mainstream consciousness.

GLENN APARICIO PARRY, PHD, is the author of the Nautilus award-winning book *Original Thinking: A Radical Revisioning of Time, Humanity, and Nature* (North Atlantic Books, 2015) and the forthcoming book *Sacred Politics* (Select Books, 2020). An educator, speaker, and ecopsychologist, Parry's lifelong passion is to reform thinking into a coherent, cohesive whole. The founder and past president of the SEED Institute, Parry is currently the director of a grass-roots think tank, the Circle for Original Thinking (www.originalthinking .us). He lives in northern New Mexico.

ACKNOWLEDGMENTS

I am deeply grateful to my extraordinary daughter. She inspires me to offer something to her future and the future of this troubled but still magical world. I am also deeply grateful to my wonderful husband. He devotes his big heart to his people (human and nonhuman), supports my work in endless ways, and always challenges me to trust my own voice. I am ever grateful to my canine family member and research assistant. She devotedly curls up on the bed near my desk, offering me encouraging smiles and protection from dangerous delivery trucks. She also teaches me how to be a better person.

I could not have embarked upon this journey or navigated its passages without the editorial guidance and wisdom of mentor and friend Christian de Quincey; he is a true lover of wisdom and a wizard of the word.

I remain deeply thankful to Glenn Aparicio Parry for his inspiration, guidance, and support. His presence is a gift of synchronicity.

I am eternally grateful for the guidance, inspiration, and scholarship of the faculty at the California Institute of Integral Studies. I am profoundly thankful to those faculty members who have directly influenced my studies, my work, and this book: Leslie Allan Combs, Dan Crowe, May Elawar, Alfonso Montuori, Matthew Segall, Brian Swimme, and Peter Reason.

INTRODUCTION

This book reveals our possible future—a *sacred* future. But because every future has a past and grows from the present, the pages that follow look at our sacred future through the lens of where we are now and where we came from.

Our observable cosmos burst from a point of colossal mass and unimaginable heat, then space expanded rapidly through inflation in every direction, from every point. Our expanding cosmos cooled and formed the first stars. The residue of those early supermassive stars created beautiful webs of stellar bodies and objects strewn across vast stretches of space; the mysterious ancestral birthplace of our solar system. Billions of years later, Earth's watery surface bloomed with cellular protozoa that eventually differentiated into myriad life forms. Pangaea (Earth's primordial, connected land mass) differentiated into many lands, and diverse hominid species emerged. Fossil evidence shows that our ancestors interbred to become *Homo sapiens sapiens*. The differentiation continued as nomadic protohumans made their way out of Africa to the north. Adaptation produced genetic variations over eons, and so the Pangaeans diversified into people of different cultures and languages. They began to look, act, and speak very differently from each other, and as a result came up with different origin stories. However, they all emerged from common Pangaean ancestors, and before that, from the great ocean, and before that, from the stars.

Although we now know more than ever before about our origins, and we also know that our differences result from genetic adaptations born of nature's creativity, peoples currently find themselves enmeshed in oppositional dualities. Although we began as Pangaeans, born of the stars and Earth, today we face our greatest challenge: *How do we evolve into Pan-Gaians*—united earthlings, no longer just stargazers but also future spacefarers? The future we create will depend on how we view our past and our present.

The word *future* comes from the Latin *futurus,* the future participle of *esse,* "to be." Our future is not an outcome, but part of a process within universal unfolding—a process of becoming what we were not before. History seems to repeat itself in patterns, none of them ever exactly the same. This creates new and more complex scenarios that can seem unfamiliar and confusing, but on closer examination, we awaken to cycles and patterns that repeat themselves. In recognizing these patterns, we connect with what we were, with what we are, and with what we could be.

This book is also about the sacred—recognizing our participation in these patterns and how we participate in our own becoming. The word *sacred* comes from the Latin verb *sacrare,* meaning "to devote, dedicate." In the Western world, we tend to think of the sacred as religious or holy. However, the *embodied sacred* is about something more fundamental and primordial than religion: it is about devotion and dedication. Every being devotes and dedicates itself to some innate purpose. Single cells, microbes, plants, insects, animals—every being makes its own unique contribution. More importantly, devotion and dedication are fundamentally about connection and relationships. When we sense and honor the sacred, we devote and dedicate ourselves to other beings.

Religious devotion is often about giving something to a deity in gratitude or in exchange for benevolent care of self or our loved ones. It can even involve giving the self toward the well-being of others as a devotional act in the deity's presence. But as *embodied* devotion and dedication, the sacred becomes something different. It's about how we give ourselves to the world; it's about our relationships with other embodied beings. Relating to others in a devoted or dedicated way constitutes the essence of the sacred.

Nonhumans instinctively dedicate themselves to the embodied sacred: bees don't rely on ideologies to compel them to pollinate. Our ideologies and actions, however, interrupt the bees' sacred devotion, resulting in colony collapse. Cetaceans don't need ideologies in order to migrate. However, enacting our ideologies does interrupt their migrations (for example, through oceanic noise pollution). Our ideologies also tend to interrupt our own deep intuitive connection to the embodied sacred.

Human constructs and societal norms and narratives either support or obscure greater universal patterns, depending on the nature of the culture and government. Layers and combinations of our dominant narratives disconnect us from the deep rhythmic pulse of the universe. Ever since the Industrial Revolution, the pulse of society has become more rapid and more out of tune with the greater rhythms of nature. The grinding, clanking, rattling, and chugging of the mechanistic age obscures the deeper patterns and pulse of life. Technology that is out of touch with that deeper pulse speeds up the pace of change and intensifies complexity in ways that challenge and even imperil our next stage of evolution.

The massive explosion of information technology causes overwhelm, sensory inundation, and disassociation. Not only are we entrenched in our paradigms and hypnotized by personal and social narratives, but far too often we feel overstimulated, too exhausted to envision anything beyond the boundaries of our dominant paradigm. Being stuck in a paradigm leads to noospheric colony collapse. We compensate for the pathology of a toxic, hypercomplex world through self-numbing and self-soothing distractions—distancing us further from the deep rhythms of the cosmos. Sometimes we acutely feel this loss of connection, but mostly the alienation haunts our unconscious.

Alienation causes grief, both individual and collective. However, the depth of our grief can be so great that we suppress it and transform it into denial, rage, blame, sadness, and depression. As our world changes—with coral-reef deaths, mass species extinctions, oceanic acidification—social media overflow with memes of despair. Many are in denial, but many more feel powerless about the loss of our cosmic home and ashamed of the fact that our own species is complicit in that loss. For example, sadly, a recent study shows that in the United States most urban dwellers can no longer see the Milky Way because of air pollution—a poignant metaphor for the loss of connection to our origins and to the greater universe. Humanity's sense of wonder and cosmic connection began with our ancestors' stargazing, wondering about the universe and the meaning of it all. Loss of that wonder and connectedness leads inevitably to a loss of meaning and to the loss of a future based on sacred devotion to the embodied world.

What, then, shall we devote ourselves to? God? Science? Capital? Technology? Ideology? Everyone has a different opinion about what we should devote ourselves to, about what should be considered sacred. The complexity, the multiplicity-in-unity, of the world gives the illusion of opposites. Stuck in an endless cycle of narratives competing for dominance, society increasingly expresses itself through senseless violence. Policies vary depending on how we respond to the sacred. Many social policies express homophobic, racist, sexist, and speciesist stereotypes—the essence of oppositional ideology. Our laws and institutions emerged from a worldview that devotes itself to protecting ideology rather than promoting experience or connection between all species. The Western paradigm of governance, based on oppositional ideologies, cannot adequately support increasingly complex societies. Our sacred future depends on what we dedicate ourselves to becoming.

I offer this book as a gesture of my devotion and dedication to the future. I devote myself to examining the state of our becoming for the sake of future generations. I consider our unique (but not superior) human intelligence a sacred gift, just as all sentience creates sacred relations—from subatomic particles to atoms to molecules, cells, neural networks, and communities. Whatever our sacred gift happens to be, we honor the deeper patterns of the universe when we share it. Devotion expresses the sacred when it supports those universal patterns—the principles of life itself. We have forgotten our natural ability to live together, including with our fellow nonhumans, because we have lost the sacred collective touchstone that anchors us to the fundamental truth that our lives emerge, grow, and thrive from the same great forces and processes that drive the evolution of the universe. Our differences, born of cosmic creativity, express themselves through complexity, which, in turn, connects us to those deeper patterns and principles of the universe that created us.

I have divided this book into three parts: "Unity," "Multiplicity-in-Unity," and "Comm-Unity." "Unity" opens with the chapter "Mind in Nature: Cosmic Creativity." It addresses the ancient idea of unity and how our ancestors perceived themselves related to a larger cosmos, or ordered whole. The word *universe* comes from the Latin *unus* (one) and *vertere* (to transform, or be changed). We might say that we all transform together in this enigmatic journey full of mystery and paradox. The ancient concept of *uni-versus,* one thing transforming, conveyed the sense that humans belong to a greater whole. This transformational unity includes the intimate relationship between consciousness and matter. Our ancestors viewed nature not yet as a collection of objects, but as a growing together of related beings in a web of consciousness and energy.

In chapter 2, "Entelechy: Intrinsically Marvelous," I describe the ancient Aristotelian concept of entelechy, the intrinsic pulse of purpose driving and orienting every being in the cosmos. I expand on the nondual idea that consciousness and matter unite in the cosmic unfolding of entelechy, informing and directing the evolution of mind-matter—what the early modern cosmologist Giordano Bruno called *mater-materia.*

Chapter 3, "Metapatterns: Nature's Creative Archetypes" explores the deeper patterns that connect the two aspects of consciousness. Chapter 4, "Sentience: The Music of the Universe," traces these deeper patterns and connections through the philosophical lineage of panpsychism and introduces the concept of *ubiquitous sentience*—the idea that experience exists in the fundamental fabric of the cosmos.

The second part, "Multiplicity-in-Unity" opens with chapter 5, "Oppositional Duality: The Madness of Mastery." Here I explain how the holistic medieval understanding of the universe changed with the advent of modernity—especially following the foundations of science established by Cartesian rationalism and Baconian empiricism. I discuss how our dominant paradigm, rooted in Cartesian dualism, Newtonian mechanism, and logical positivism, has magnified the illusion of separation, oppositional duality, and the myth of mastery.

Chapter 6, "Symbiosis: The Gift of Kinship," introduces an alternative lineage, inspired by the work of Giordano Bruno, Goethe, panpsychism, and process metaphysics. It celebrates symbiosis and partnership, evolving through systemic complexity. Chapter 7, "Complexity Consciousness: Systemic Wisdom," expands on how the combination of postmodern science and a shifting societal paradigm reveals the cosmos, not as a mechanism composed of separate objects, but as a cascade of layered organic systems connected through complex relationships.

The third part, "Comm-Unity," opens with chapter 8, introducing the concept of creative synergy. It shows how, from a process panpsychist worldview, all becomings grow together in ubiquitous sentience. (Panpsychism is the view that all things, both living and apparently inanimate, possess some degree of consciousness.) This evolving sentience lies at the heart of life in the cosmos. In this chapter, I expand on the argument that intelligence and creativity exist in a continuum that composes the world we perceive.

The final chapter, "Sacred Futurism: Radical Enchantment," introduces my argument for a revision of, and reawakening to, the embodied sacred in order to create a future worth having. Previous ideas and visions of the future expressed predominantly positivistic assumptions that emerged from the Cartesian-Newtonian paradigm. I argue that purely disembodied, rational, dualistic, and reductionistic concepts cannot help us navigate a world of increasing complexity. I believe we can meet the complex future that awaits only by replacing stale reductionistic ideas of certainty and progress with complex thinking, which offers unknown possibility.

While critiquing dysfunctional mechanistic and reductionistic paradigms, this book does not promote oppositional duality. While denouncing the perils of technology, I do not advocate Luddism, nor do I repudiate science in favor of spirituality. Instead I envision an integration of multiple sources of wisdom, diverse knowledge systems, and unexpected creative collaborations—all necessary ingredients for a future worth having: a future that embraces the embodied sacred.

I see our greatest hope—perhaps our *only* hope—in the growing opportunities for creative collaboration between diverse cultures (human and nonhuman), shared intra- and interspecies experiences and alliances, and inter-, multi-, and transdisciplinary projects. Compassionate creativity, complex thinking, and a sense of the embodied sacred that connects us will enable us to guide this essential integration while respecting our wondrous diversity. In that spirit, I hope this book will inspire people to question their own oppositional dualities, as subtle as they may be, and learn to cultivate complexity consciousness: collaborative, compassionate, and deeply connected creativity. As the embodied sacred ripples out from individuals, I believe it will expand into powerful waves of co-creative potential. Sacred futurism offers us a vision beyond the narratives of certainty and progress: it offers us the expansive possibility of transformation.

Part 1
_____

UNITY

1 MIND IN NATURE
Cosmic Creativity

The question as to meaning must therefore have priority in all living beings.

JAKOB VON UEXKÜLL

Sentience was never our private possession. We live immersed in intelligence, enveloped and informed by a creativity we cannot fathom.

DAVID ABRAM

When I was a child, like many children, life's big questions preoccupied me: Where do we come from? Why are we here? When did the universe begin? What was there before the beginning? I plagued adults with these exasperating questions long before Google and was unceremoniously directed to the library, where a wealth of confusing and conflicting information awaited me. People also cautioned me not to believe everything I read. So I read everything I could, attempting to suspend belief. Still, in the midst of all the factual information, and along with my skepticism, a pervasive *feeling* remained. The feeling spread out from the center of my chest and often left me breathless and close to tears—especially when I imagined this miraculous dynamic process called *life* in all its expression.

I remember often lying on the grass at night, gazing into the great cosmic skyscape, contemplating the vastness of our universe while I was sticking to the surface of a small, blue-green planet revolving slowly around a star. As I contemplated the shimmering arm of the Milky Way, I felt a sense of uplift and wonder at its beauty and a desire to fall up into its dazzling arc, the primordial cradle of stardust. I felt embraced by the universe in all its majestic expression, from the soft grasses and flora, with their smells imbued with memory of what it is to be an earthling (the known), to the scattering of stars throughout an infinite realm of potentials (the unknown). I had a simultaneous yearning to know and a deep sense of knowing all at once.

That sense of wonder compels us to understand, to form ontologies (conceptual models of reality) and epistemologies (theories of how we can gain knowledge). Individually and collectively, we all have different ways of knowing. Empiricism (knowledge gained through sensory experience, experiment, and observation) draws us into a continual search for clues, first here, then there. Historically, however, we have embraced other ways of knowing, such as mythology and cosmology, which refer to ways of piecing together our origin stories like a detective, repeating the story with new information added, making revisions, and retrieving lost pieces. No matter how we attempt to make sense of our lives and the world, we seek to understand how this great cosmic unfolding came to be (or if it always existed).

KNOWING THE GARDEN

Our earliest ancestors still lived in the "garden," part of the wider living, growing, humming, ebbing and flowing, howling and growling wild world. It was a place full of beauty and of great struggle: the wild world could be benevolent and kind but also terrifying, both enchanted and monstrous. In their fireside gatherings, our ancestors huddled together for warmth and companionship, and for storytelling. Like us, they wondered at the mystery and magic of the world around them. They told stories based on their intuitions, sensations, and observations.

Those early stories arose out of a unified primeval form of knowing that still respected the deep and mysterious intelligence of this connected reality, what we eventually called *nature*. Our ancestors viewed this intrinsic intelligence both as a pervasive aspect of reality and as a necessary means of understanding how to relate wisely to a greater web of life. Our earliest cosmologies emerged out of an ongoing dialogue with and within that web. Indigenous worldviews value the creativity and intelligence of other animals at least as much as human intelligence; many share the understanding that all species live with meaning and purpose throughout the connected web of life. This is why more-than-human intelligence features so significantly in early creation stories, and why creatures like Raven and Coyote figure prominently as creators, sages, and tricksters.

Philosophers refer to this innate sense of meaning and purpose in nature as *teleology*—a deep intentional orientation toward becoming together. The modern scientific paradigm of materialism, disseminated through colonialism, denies any such meaning or purpose outside of the human brain. Unfortunately, the costs of such denial have turned out to be extreme. We now face what many are now calling the Anthropocene era: a time when human-created climate change and dysfunctional human systems have begun to enact the "sixth great extinction"— annihilation of many Earth species (including our own). A recent study published in the *Proceedings of the National Academy of Sciences* reveals that human systems have caused a startling redistribution of planetary biomass, drastically reducing the populations of other mammalian life forms.[1] We have rearranged the garden, and this new arrangement cannot sustain the biodiversity essential to life.

With no time to spare, scientists and philosophers have begun to awaken and expand beyond human exceptionalism (the belief that only humans possess sentience). Many acknowledge that the more-than-human world brims with creativity and sentience, as we awaken to many revelations about our nonhuman kin. One revelation that particularly interests me is recent corvid research that shows some species—especially crows, magpies, and ravens—to have complex cultures and creativity as well as the capacity to mourn and play. Coming full circle, our new sciences may ultimately help us to understand how Raven won its place as a leading character in early cosmologies.

Many indigenous cosmologies, especially those of the Pacific Northwest, place Raven at the beginning. In the Tlingit creation story, Raven, called Kit-ka'ositiyi-qâ-yît, had a son, and taught him many things, eventually giving him the strength to make a world. When Tlingit storytellers begin this creation story—which is meant to be spoken rather than read—they repeat these words of sacred, ancient knowing: "No one knows just how the story of Raven really begins, so each starts from the point where he does know it. Here, it was always begun in this way." This conveys an intuitive understanding of some truly sophisticated concepts, such as relativity and uncertainty. It also conveys an early sense of process thinking (which I will discuss more in part 3), which concentrates on unfolding through process rather than on coordinates located in Newtonian space, as we do in the West. Newton's insights are essential to us but cannot explain every aspect of causality. The paradoxical nature of reality presents complexities beyond mere classical mechanics.

Early cosmologies often included paradoxes like this. The ancient Indian *Rig Veda*'s "Nasadiya Sukta" (hymn of creation), written approximately 1500 BCE, records a similar idea:

Who knows from whence this great creation sprang? He from whom all this great creation came. Whether his will created or was mute, The Most High seer that is in highest heaven, He knows it—or perchance even He knows not.[2]

Even in our ancestors' earliest reflections on the nature of reality, we get inklings that ever-mysterious nature possesses mind. The earliest stories seem to be comfortable with the ambiguities of creative process and uncertainty. Although apparently random, these stories portray the origin of the world as a purposeful process, a manifestation of flexible and fluid teleological laws. I believe that all innate intelligence (including human intelligence) responds to some mysterious rhythm of teleology and uncertainty, expressed poetically in many indigenous creation stories. This rhythm can be felt in the art, music, dance, and stories of every culture, human and nonhuman; it is the pulse of purposeful meaning in the beat of a drum, or the clang of a crow's beak on the tin crown of my chimney early this morning. Stories happen everywhere, all the time. In *The World Is Made of Stories,* Buddhist teacher David Loy puts this well when he suggests that stories "teach us what is real, what is valuable, and what is possible. Without stories there is no way to engage with the world because there is no world."[3]

SHARED ORIGINS

Most human-origin stories begin with an event, a marker in space-time. Some begin by contrasting the premanifest world, the void, no-thing-ness, with the manifest world of Mother Earth, or Gaia. A good example of this is Hesiod's *Theogony,* composed around 700 BCE, in which Gaia is born out of Chaos (which in Greek means "void"). Many stories share this perspective: the originating void is unthinkable and unknowable; only what manifests can be imagined and known. We can think of the first origin stories as the results of humans beginning to reflect on their world, the human brain, with its unique (but not superior) structure, reflecting on the nature of nature, and eventually on the nature of mind. Our various origin stories seek to express the relationship between human minds and what we might call *nature's mind,* or what ancient people saw as the thoughts of a creator.

Materialists, who believe there is no mind in nature apart from what is found in human brains, use a method of exclusive objectivity to explain how the physical world operates. As a result, they view mind as epiphenomenal—an accidental by-product of purely physical processes in the brain. By this account, nature is for the most part mindless. Dualists, on the other hand, view mind and physical nature as two separate domains of reality that somehow interact. Idealists, by contrast, view mind as the primary source of all aspects of nature: mind creates nature.

An alternative view, which offers the idea that consciousness possesses intelligence and sentience at every scale—mind throughout nature—will remain a central topic of this book. We could say this is "mind-full" nature, meaning that matter and mind are not separate, nor does one create the other; rather they are co-creative. This alternative view draws on diverse ways of knowing the world, including ancient indigenous traditions, which consider feeling and intuition to be valid sources of data. These forgotten and suppressed ways of knowing the world provide an essential expansion of our experience. We have already seen that repudiating them has resulted in an unraveling of life itself. The reason for this is that causality does not happen only through material contact, but has a dimensional, imaginal aspect to it. We cannot suppress the imaginal—or reject diverse ways of knowing—without dropping some essential threads in life's web.

In this book, I begin with the assumption that any form of inquiry into the nature of reality must take this alternative view, along with multiple epistemologies, into account. Our society seems to prefer more dogmatic answers, because we tend to be uncomfortable with uncertainty. The human brain, which developed from our arboreal and nomadic ancestors, evolved to seek out safety (even if only in the landscape of consciousness). We look for shelter within the constructs of mind—for example, in our religious cosmologies and various ideas of "gods" or "God." Some prefer a stern, patriarchal big mind (religious dogmatism), while others prefer to use their "epiphenomenal" minds (the only mind that supposedly matters) to precisely control their environment (reductive scientism). For the past few hundred years, the latter approach has dominated.

In postmodern Western culture, the term *mind* comes loaded with layers of meaning, and it's difficult to blow away the etymological dust to reveal original meanings. Some linguists trace the etymology of "mind" to the Proto-Indo-European (PIE) *men,* meaning "thought, memory, having the mind aroused." The archaic German root *minne* refers specifically to a loving memory. This reminds me of the mythical Norse creator god Odin, who uses Raven emissaries, Hugin (thought) and Munin (memory). Again, Raven appears in a creation story as an emissary of the original creator, or Mind:

> *Hugin and Munin fly each day*
> *over the spacious earth.*
> *I fear for Hugin, that he come not back,*
> *yet more anxious am I for Munin.*[4]

While Odin fears the Raven Hugin (thought) might not return, he worries more about loss of memory if the Raven Munin fails to return. This myth expresses a deep intuition about the relevance of ancient ways of knowing, which emphasize nonconceptual memory (or wisdom) as a way to temper the reckless path of progress. I see the Raven, then, as the archetypal representation of the uncertain aspect of creation—of chaos. This Norse myth illustrates how our early associations with Creator Mind involve a twofold understanding, always moving thought in a circular pattern—that is, thought guided by memory or wisdom.

The myth tells us that the Creator fears a break in the circle of knowing. Furthermore, the myth suggests that thought and memory, in their archaic forms as flying ravens, signify movement and fluidity. Although it is dynamic, the relationship between thought and memory remains circular—each one informing the other. They move into the world and return home (to self) in a sort of dance between experience and observation, intuition and reason. We can also think of this as a spiral dance of becoming that moves forward through what we perceive as time.

Inspired by this myth, I conceive of mind as transitory, always in process, creatively expressing itself. In other words, mind in nature constantly interacts with itself through myriad experiences and creates cosmologies that express the complexity and plurality, as well as the unity, of the universe. We could think of this as a sort of cosmic dance, or creative play, that results in dazzling diversity at every scale. We have only begun to see how deep and infinite cosmic creativity really is. The human brain doesn't have the market cornered on this playful creative process. Just look through a telescope, through a microscope, or even just around you at all the other creatures that fill your world; look into the eyes of your nonhuman friends. We share more than our planet; we share deep and primordial creative connections that pervade the universe.

INQUIRY AND MYSTERY

Finding themselves embedded in a deeply mysterious universe, our ancestors began to form questions about the nature of their reality. Inheriting their legacy of asking questions to render answers, modern science tried to eliminate mystery and give us certainty, but in the process has desiccated the richness of that mysterious aspect of reality. For centuries, modern science and philosophy have separated mind from the rest of nature. As a result, we tend to inquire into nature as if we were separate from it, as if nature were out there, a mere object of study. Philosopher Gregory Bateson once said, "The major problems in the world are the result of the difference between how nature works and the way people think."[5] As we separated ourselves from nature's mind in order to develop a uniquely human mind, we created what Bateson called the *occidental schism,* a term that well describes humanity's deep, traumatic separation from nature's creativity. We are living with the reverberations of that schism.

The etymology of the word *nature* reveals that our ancestors viewed it as a complex process rather than as a static backdrop for human cultures. The root comes from the Latin verb *nasci,* "to be born, to bud, or sprout." Further back, the ancient Greek word for nature, *phusis,* derived from *phuein,* meant "to grow, to bring forth." We can also trace the etymology of *phuein* to the Proto-Indo-European root *bhu-,* meaning "to grow, or develop." Clearly the ancient associations of the word *nature* convey a sense of an expanding creative process through which every being *becomes.* In reality, we humans are just one form within a potentially infinite becoming. Ironically, this view correlates better with new scientific revelations than does the static, mechanistic view that created many of our social systems and stories.

Most pre-Socratic philosophers used *physis* to describe an ordered creative process within το ὅλον (*to holon,* the whole) or ὁ κοσμος (*ho kosmos,* the universe, world), expressing their notion of holism, process, and growth. Much like indigenous peoples, the pre-Socratics viewed mind or *nous* as part of nature. The pre-Socratic Heraclitus, with his radical view of the universe as flux or change, may have been the earliest known process-relational philosopher.

Heraclitus introduced the idea of the unity of opposites, seeing the interconnections between opposing states. He understood that the needs of one being could conflict with another, and he believed that strife was as essential to life as harmony. For example, he pointed out that fish drink seawater, though the same substance is unhealthy for humans: what sustains one being could be poison to another. Heraclitus could also be called the first complexity thinker, because he understood that chaos was a part of the order of reality.

British philosopher Alfred North Whitehead said that the history of Western philosophy is a series of footnotes to Plato. As a result, Platonic dualism has shaped the development of Western thought, most notably influencing the mind-matter split established by René Descartes in the seventeenth century. Aristotle offered an alternative to Plato's stark dualism between the realm of ideal, perfect spiritual Forms and the realm of imperfect matter. Aristotle famously brought Plato's Forms down to Earth by teaching that teleological forms existed *within* matter. This grounding of Plato's metaphysics qualifies Aristotle as a protopanpsychist, in the lineage of philosophers who believe that ensouled matter animates all living things. At this point, I believe, the occidental schism makes the insights of panpsychism essential to those of us living in the schism's reverberations.

Psychologist Carl Jung expressed the idea that a hidden order existed within disorder, which he characterized as "chaos within order." This dance between chaos and order—a creativity that thrives on paradox—suggests that some kind of intelligence operates within the natural world as an essential dynamic of nature. The Trickster archetype embodies this kind of chaos wisdom, which pervades ancient ontologies and which emerges now in complexity discourse informed by what we know about the enigmatic creativity of nature. Consciousness researcher and neuropsychologist Allan Combs describes the liminality of the Trickster archetype (such as the ancient Greek trickster Hermes) that often catalyzes transitional phases in the personal or collective evolution of consciousness. He suggests that when we are in crisis, "our psychological limits are vague, and our boundaries uncertain, we become available to insights about many things that were previously opaque to us."[6] The Trickster challenges us to expand through the uncertainty of that liminal crossroads. Physicist Richard Feynman, a trickster figure in his own right, once said, "The imagination of nature is far greater than the imagination of man."[7] The universe's imagination always remains wider than our human imaginations. No matter how our imagination expands, we can never assume that we have it all figured out. Expanding our imagination allows us to become open to the unknown.

After the European Enlightenment, when philosophy and science had split mind and matter apart, nature became "disenchanted," lacking any intrinsic purpose or meaning. This world of dead matter became a mechanistic universe created by a divine watchmaker. Following Newton, classical mechanics became the dominant paradigm for the Western world. Ironically, the further new revelations move us from that Enlightenment model, the more we seem to return to the wisdom of ancient indigenous and early Western cosmologies.

REAL MAGIC

We are looking for clues about what has gone missing, which is enchantment, what I call *real magic* in the world. This is not like the magical thinking of psychology. It means rather that when we see the world as full of meaning and purpose, we are enchanted by it. This view need not conflict with either science or spirituality, but adds dimension to both.

According to the Greeks, in the beginning, ideas of φυσις (*physis*, nature), κοσμος (*kosmos*, order), and το ὁλον (*to holon*, the whole) reigned; but following the mind-matter schism, knowledge of nature detoured into classical mechanics, where everything could be reduced to the sum of its parts. Classical mechanics allowed us to do wonderful things, like space exploration. But the mechanistic narrative that supported industrialism created dystopian blight, felt even as early as the nineteenth century, as expressed in Romantic literature. Now, as we face the perils of the Anthropocene, we recognize an urgent need to heal the mind-body split and the trauma of the occidental schism and to reenchant nature, not as something outside of us but rather as a complex process we participate in. I call this healing through a new kind of participation *radical enchantment* (I will expand on this in part 3). Nothing less than a radical shift of our awareness toward a greater understanding of and deeper respect for the complex creativity of nature will offer us the possibility of survival.

Ever since our ancestors began attempting to make sense of the complexity of an unpredictable world, humans have told stories to describe our foibles and our strengths. Some stories make us the protagonists, some antagonists; those stories continue in the Anthropocene, as we consider (or refuse to consider) how human systems have impacted life on Earth. Some stories include a primordial creator. Some stories make us humans the creator's creator. All these stories have one thing in common: they attempt to make sense of our often paradoxical experience of being human. I have no doubt that cetacean or corvid cosmologies and ontologies would be very different from ours, and I hope we will get the chance to discover nonhuman descriptions of reality when we are ready. For now we can approach the consciousness continuum only from within our current range of imagination, which occupies a narrow band on that continuum. This book seeks to expand that range by understanding our shared cosmological origins and shifting toward complex ontologies and epistemologies. This book attempts to ask different questions based upon an expanded sense of reality, questions that offer us different possibilities that are more aligned with where we are now and what really matters—not just to a few similar humans but to many diverse creatures, human and nonhuman.

If human experience occurs within a wider spectrum of all possible experiences, we might ask: how could we expand our experience and understanding of human and nonhuman forms of consciousness in ways that embrace the embodied awareness of nature's connected creativity? In other words, how can human consciousness not only inquire into its own nature but also connect with the wider and deeper consciousness that pervades nature?

Instead of seeking certainty through immediate answers, we might take another approach that is more appropriate to a hypercomplex world. Each answer always reveals another set of questions, more possibilities, and further applications. That doesn't mean we never come to conclusions, it just means that we know conclusions to be somewhat temporary and open to revision with new information.

For example, when scientists assume that research reveals something certain or final, it can lead to what French complexity philosopher Edgar Morin describes as "blind intelligence." In philosophy, such myopic finality leads to wicked environmental and sociological problems. In religion, this kind of thinking leads to dogmatism, ignorance, and intolerance. We can thank blind faith for crusades and inquisitions, and for nuclear proliferation and pollution. Perhaps these two modes intersect to produce some of our most wicked problems.

CREATIVE SYNERGY

How, then, can we use our range of conscious experience to expand our understanding of nature's creativity? More specifically, how could an expanded understanding help us participate in what I am calling *creative synergy,* the kind of flow that happens when human consciousness participates in the co-creative process that composes reality? I will address this further in part 3: "Comm-Unity."

I consider mind (memory, thoughts, sensations) to be one way in which consciousness expresses itself. Most scholars who accept scientific materialism doubt or deny that microorganisms possess any consciousness: only creatures that have made it to the top of the "selfish-gene" pile belong to the club of exclusive consciousness: that is what is called *human exceptionalism.* We consider ourselves to be exceptions in an insentient, nonconscious world. By contrast, many ancient spiritual cosmologies assume that consciousness extends to all forms of life (and even to nonliving systems, such as rivers, rocks, wind, and wilderness). Many Native American philosophies, including that of my late spiritual teacher, Suquamish elder medicine man Thomas One Wolf, assume that consciousness pervades an animate universe. According to this worldview, all beings are unified in one greater consciousness—variously known as Wakan Tanka or Great Spirit (Lakota) or Begochiddy (Diné), and many more.

In such cosmologies, universal consciousness preexists individual expressions of mind and creates the laws of nature that govern the world of matter. Every individual experience forms part of this greater, participatory consciousness, as affected by its local environment. On Earth, this local environment can be a primate's neurological system, a forest's mycelial system, or a cellular system. These conscious environments pervade life at every scale. Furthermore, because of the system's relationship to its own specific environment, each individual expression of consciousness is unique. For instance, my consciousness is different from yours because each of us occupies a unique place in the larger system. The multiplicity of perspectives and individual physical and mental expressions creates beautiful complexity and diversity in the biospheric ecosystem, and also in the ecosystem of consciousness (what Pierre Teilhard de Chardin called the *noosphere*). However, it also creates the shadow side of diversity in the noosphere—pathologies such as racism, sexism, speciesism, and many other destructive personal and collective isms. Human consciousness is part of a spectrum. When consciousness is restricted within a narrow band of awareness, it is difficult to experience anything outside that band. It is difficult to change the station, especially if we are taught that there is only one.

SACRED DEVOTION, SACRED PLACES

In *God Is Red,* Native American scholar Vine Deloria Jr. cautions that lessons of sacred devotion to sacred places must be passed through generations, lest we learn the most bitter lesson of all through "fouling our planetary nest." Although he wrote these words decades ago, they seem particularly timely now: "Sacred places . . . properly inform us that we are not larger than nature and that we have responsibilities to the rest of the natural world that transcend our own personal desires and wishes."[8] The indigenous relationship to the more-than-human world implies responsibility: the embodied sacred must guide how we respond to our relations within nature.

In *How Forests Think: Toward an Anthropology beyond the Human,* anthropologist Eduardo Kohn applies his "anthropology beyond the human" to understanding better the complex ontology and culture of the Avila Runa tribe, who dwell in the Ecuadorean Amazon. He describes how Runa cultural lives include the diverse perspectives and knowledge of the many beings who share the forest with them. Kohn suggests that encountering other species who are "radically not us . . . force us to find new ways to listen; they force us to think beyond our moral worlds in ways that can help us imagine and realize more just and better worlds."[9] Our Western minds, what I call *Cartesian consciousness,* can heal itself through the indigenous practice of thinking beyond the human and encountering other species that are very different from us with respectful curiosity.

I suggest that the success or failure of humanity depends upon saving indigenous cultures, languages, and wisdom. Animism (the idea that soul animates all nature) and panpsychism (the idea that all living beings are sentient or are composed of sentient beings) seem entirely lucid and sane compared to the modern idea that the world has no meaning or purpose, that only humans are centers of desires, needs, and agency. Laws and systems based upon such insanity cause tremendous suffering. The incorporation of new, mindful ways of understanding reality, using practices and nonordinary states that expand the bandwidth of human experience, could radically enchant our present and infuse our systems with much-needed regenerative wisdom. Embracing the teaching that meaningful mind pervades nature offers hope for better worlds.

2 ENTELECHY

Intrinsically Marvelous

In all things of nature there is something of the marvelous.

ARISTOTLE

Teleology means that in addition to physical law of the familiar kind, there are other laws of nature that are "biased toward the marvelous."

THOMAS NAGEL

Have you ever looked at sand under a microscope? You would see an assortment of tiny shells, many sharing the spiral shape known as the Golden Ratio. Countless billions of these tiny masterpieces make up what we experience as a beach. Peer into the soft face of sunflower, and you'll see the seedbeds form a similar spiral pattern. On a much larger scale, the Golden Ratio can be seen in the enduring structures of spiral galaxies. The Milky Way, for example, also forms a giant spiral, and because of gravity, inertia, and angular momentum, it retains its shape for billions of years rather than scattering off into the universe. On radically different scales, the physical laws that give structure and shape to matter create patterns we find inherently beautiful without understanding why. Nature's beauty does not need help or interference from us. We take it for granted that nature will do the job of creating shellness and beachness, flowerness, and Milky Way-ness. We delight in the beauty of these forms and patterns, and enjoy their particular blessings.

Nature uses the mathematical Golden Ratio to create forms that not only appear beautiful to us, but also serve a purpose. Shells such as bivalves or nautiluses grow in spirals because the laws of biology and physics combine to make this the most effective way for these creatures to build exoskeletons. Some flower species arrange their seedbeds perfectly according to this same mathematical sequence (called the Fibonacci series) in order to generate the maximum number of seeds at time of maturity—more seeds, more sunflowers. Nature uses the Golden Ratio as a means of guiding the development of physical and biological forms in ways that facilitate growth and stability—from potential to fulfillment.

Other shapes, patterns, and sequences also facilitate purposefulness in matter by using the laws of force and motion. Philosophy began in response to questions about these beautiful and mysterious patterns throughout our world. Our ancestors wondered about the purpose of life, its end or *telos*. They lived in a world teeming with ends and purposes, and wanted to know the *telos* (or goal) of everything that happens in nature. *Why are we here? What is our purpose? Where are we going?*

TELOS

The ancient Greek philosophers believed there must be a cosmic purpose, a reason why everything exists in the universe. As noted in the previous chapter, they thought of nature as *physis*—something that possessed intrinsic purpose, a process with a beginning, middle, and end. Humans did not have a separate *telos* from nature. Human life shared the same teleology as everything else—all transforming as one universe, or cosmos.

Early Western philosophers believed that *telos* or purpose was inherent to substance—or to some particular substance. For instance,

Thales believed water was the fundamental substance of the universe. For him, water was the *archē,* or origin, and so, like the fluid nature of water, the *telos* of the universe was motion and change. On the other hand, Thales's student Anaximander argued that no element could create any of the other elements—water could not create fire, earth, or air—and so no single element could be the fundamental substance, or *archē.* Instead he proposed a very different concept: the *apeiron,* meaning "without limit," as the origin of the universe—an infinite and unbounded substance out of which all opposites arise. The *telos* of the *apeiron* was purposeful process, such as transmutation, generation, and destruction.[1]

Plato dealt with *telos* differently, developing an idea that deeply influenced Christianity and subsequent political ideologies. In the *Phaedo,* Plato combined *telos* and *archē,* seeing both as expressions of the universal Good, separating the transcendent heaven from the mundane world. The *telos* of the material world was secondary. Even in the physical world, however, a condition, even though it was necessary, was not in itself sufficient for explaining a phenomenon:

> But to call such things "causes" is quite absurd. If you were to say that *without having such things*—bones and sinews and all the other things that I have got—I wouldn't be able to carry out my decisions, you would be right; but to say that my actions are caused by these . . . rather than simply by the choice of what is best, would be an utterly slip-shod sort of argument. Fancy not being able to see that the real cause is very different from the mere *sine qua non* of any cause! Yet that is what most people, groping, as it were, in the dark, seem to call "cause," using a name that doesn't belong to it. . . . I would very much like to learn about such a cause from someone—anyone you please; but since I have been denied this, and have not been able to find out about it for myself or learn it from anyone else, would you like me to demonstrate, Cebes, how I have busied myself with the second line of approach towards the search for the cause?[2]

In other words, the reason for existence is *metaphysical,* not physical. For Plato, it required the highest way of knowing to reveal *archē* and *telos,* origin and final cause (alpha and omega). Certainly in the natural world, all beings had *telos,* but the highest *telos* was reserved for a few men, such as the philosopher king in *The Republic,* whose *telos* was to rule with wisdom. So for Plato, *telos* was both origin and purpose. The Good made all, and all is best and most purposeful when aligned with the Good.

Aristotle too was inspired by the topic of the *telos.* In fact, he coined the word *entelechia,* which expands the concept of *telos* to include ideas about origins, causes, and meaning in the universe. He specifically used *entelechia* to differentiate between living and non-living matter. *Entelechia* comes from *en,* meaning "within"; *telos;* and *ekhein,* "to have." Hence *entelechy* means inner purpose, or the purpose within something, purpose that continues. For Aristotle, this sense of continuing-to-be was of utmost importance.[3] For instance, within the seed of a flower lies its ability (potential) to become a fully matured flower with many seeds (actualization). In his *Metaphysics,* Aristotle says, for instance, that the *telos* of an acorn is to become an oak. This challenged Plato's assertion that natural elements didn't possess *telos.*

In response to Plato, Aristotle said: "It is absurd to suppose that purpose is not present [in nature] because we do not observe the agent deliberating."[4] Where Plato called for a necessary metaphysical agent, an *external* cause for the natural world (an intelligent designer), Aristotle posited an *internal* cause (natural laws or principles). This also contradicted a pre-Socratic view, known as *accidentalism,* which rejected the idea that existence is inherently purposeful. For Aristotle, intelligence was intrinsic, not extrinsic, to nature. To him, events in nature were not accidental, random, or meaningless, but inherently meaningful.

Aristotle's entelechy complements his ideas about *hylomorphism*— the proposition that being or existence consists fundamentally of matter and form. For him, form—or, more accurately, dynamic *forming,* or in-forming—shapes matter from within; it is a kind of natural intelligence. Thus Aristotle's ideas about hylomorphism and entelechy relate to later theories known as *vitalism,* the belief that living things possess an animating life force, and *panpsychism,* the view that all life possesses some degree of sentience.

Aristotle's entelechy ties into his concept of *energeia* and *dynamis,* which roughly correspond to *actuality* and *potentiality* respectively. Some interpretations of Aristotle infer that form (soul) could be described as *energeia,* and matter (body) as *dynamis.* This indicates that when Aristotle speaks about the soul, he is talking about something fully actualized that is intrinsic to body—two aspects of one thing.[5] This nondual, ensouled interpretation remains extremely important for a dimensional understanding of life. Departure from this worldview guts nature of meaning and restricts it to human culture, casts it "out there," or makes it disappear. The occidental schism further diminished humanity's connection to meaning throughout nature, as well as the potential for connected creativity.

A series of scientific discoveries produced a model of the universe that was determined and mechanistic. The notion of universal mechanism states that everything can be reduced to motions and collisions of substances in the material world. This intellectual lineage began with the ancient Greek atomists, was carried forward by the Stoics, and was firmly set in place centuries later, when scientific evidence seemed to corroborate it. Major contributors to this worldview included Kepler, Galileo, Descartes, Hobbes, and Newton. Hobbes's *Leviathan* (1651) presented influential philosophical arguments for materialism and mechanism, later elucidated mathematically in Newton's *Principia* (1687). These contributions to philosophy and science laid the foundations of the current Western paradigm (see part 2).

THE PANPSYCHIST CURRENT

In the same era—the seventeenth through nineteenth centuries—other philosophers, such as Baruch Spinoza, Gottfried Wilhelm Leibniz, and, later, Immanuel Kant and Arthur Schopenhauer, saw things differently. Harking back to Aristotle's entelechy, they embraced a richer ontology that left room for nature's inner purpose, challenging the emerging, now dominant materialist worldview. The panpsychist current carried this dimensional worldview full of meaning and purpose from the past into the present.

For example, in 1694, Leibniz published *De primæ philosophiæ emendatione et notione substantiæ* (On the correction of first philosophy and the notion of substance), in which he described what he called the "new science of power and action." Besides presenting the laws of dynamics, he also presented an argument for a nondual, panpsychist cosmology in which entelechy played a significant part.

In his famous *Monadology,* published in 1714 (see chapter 4), Leibniz applied the laws of entelechy universally: all monads ("the true atoms of nature," in Leibniz's view) possessed an inherent entelechy responsible for the dynamism in the world. Leibniz's cosmology, then, offered a nonmechanistic alternative that inspired theologians as well as philosophers. Rather than God working on the world as an external agent, in Leibniz's philosophy the divine force operated within all monads according to a "pre-established harmony" orchestrated by God—the origin, cause, and purpose of nature: "Creation is a permanent state, thus [monads] are generated, so to speak, by continual fulgurations of the Divinity."[6]

Instead of the Cartesian concept of dead matter ensouled by spirit, Leibniz expanded Aristotelian concepts of a creative intrinsic spirit that is inseparable from matter: "And it is here that the Cartesians have fallen short, as they have given no thought to perceptions which are not apperceived."[7] Leibniz rejected the Cartesian notion that all is dead and insentient except for human souls and God.

After the Cartesian split, Western philosophy, science, and society lost touch with the ancient cosmologies of our indigenous ancestors, who viewed nature as imbued with spirit through and through. Leibniz kept this vision alive. By acknowledging the inherent sentience of monads, Leibniz offered a counterpoint to Descartes's mind-matter or soul-nature split, paving the way for reenchanting the natural world. His *Monadology* inspired many subsequent thinkers to reject Cartesian dualism, avoiding the problem of mind-matter interaction, and also to reject materialism with its inexplicable claim that mind emerges accidentally from mindless matter.

Instead, Leibniz developed a monist cosmology in which divine intelligence animates all monads. In other words, entelechy operated in nature as God's intrinsic and purposeful direction of matter. Leibniz found a way to get around the external agent while intuitively bringing the concept of divine intelligence into matter and energy. With access to the newest optical equipment—microscopes—Leibniz argued for nature's inner wisdom even at the smallest scales.

The famous German idealist philosopher Immanuel Kant (1724–1804) envisioned an intrinsic, essential force within all substances and bodies. Like Leibniz, he saw *dynamis,* force, generating the universe. In opposition to the Cartesian claim that force is only quantitative, Kant asserted that it could also be qualitative. He distinguished between Cartesian *vis mortua* (dead power) and *vis viva* (living power). The first was the product of a quantity of matter's motion, while the second was a metaphysical force—a *conatus* or "striving"—that continually generates movement and life. Echoing Newton's law of motion, Kant maintained that "a continuous action arises from a continuous force as long as no hindrance intervenes."

Kant asserted that this "living" force is an intrinsic universal quality that gives rise to all changes in the body and soul, all relationships and locations. He departed from Leibniz's idea of preestablished harmony, proposing instead that the inherent striving within matter determines outcomes in nature.[8]

Clearly Kant's *vis viva* or *conatus*—the always striving living force—essentially shares the same properties and functions as Aristotle's entelechy. However, unlike Aristotle's entelechy or Leibniz's preestablished harmony, Kant's force is not determined primordially, but is expressed continuously as the will intrinsic to force. Like entelechy, it is both origin and end—but it is not predetermined.

Arthur Schopenhauer (1788–1860) envisioned entelechy as *will,* also inherent in matter and expressed as *representation.* Inspired by Plato's Forms and Leibniz's monads, and expanding on the Kantian idea of the *Ding an sich* (the thing in itself), while rejecting the theological ontologies of German idealism, Schopenhauer converted will into pure energy—what Spinoza once called the "striving of each thing." Schopenhauer described this as "ein endloses Streben" (an endless striving), much like Kant's *conatus.* And like Aristotle's entelechy, this striving force, expressing both alpha and omega, operates within all matter and form without an external agent: "Every attained end is at the same time the beginning of a new course, and so on *ad infinitum.*"[9] This internal, inherent, ineffable, and eternal striving always expresses some purpose or aim. Will and representation, then, resemble the dual aspects from a different tradition: Buddhist monism, for which there is no external or internal agent—just an ineffable force that can be known only through reflection. Later, vitalists such as French philosopher Henri Bergson (1859–1941) and German embryologist and philosopher Hans Driesch (1867–1941) redefined entelechy as a "life force" (French *élan vital*).

Driesch, for example, proposed that the life force manifests two aspects: *das Psychoid,* or the internal mindlike director of consciousness, and *morphogenesis,* which directs the development of organic processes. In *Science and Philosophy of the Organism,* Driesch described this life force in language similar to Schopenhauer's will. However, he differentiated between primary and secondary forms of willing in order to distinguish between an organism's mental and physiological processes. Nevertheless, whether directing the unfolding of consciousness or organic development, Driesch's life force, like Bergson's *élan vital,* remained nonspatial and qualitative.

In *Creative Evolution,* Bergson challenged the two scientific and philosophical dogmas of his day: mechanism and finalism. He borrowed the idea of the *logos* (the structuring principle of conscious-ness) from Heraclitus and transformed it into the vital impulse (*élan vital*), active throughout nature, continually striving to unify opposites.

Bergson saw a third possibility between the determinism of mech-anism and the teleology of finalism. On one hand, he challenged the growing popularity of Darwinian evolution, whereby life developed according to mechanistic principles. Darwinian-inspired biology had rejected teleology (a purposeful metaphysical drive in nature) and replaced it with teleonomy (a goal-directedness of purely physi-cal evolutionary processes). According to the materialist-mechanistic view, any apparent goal-directedness in evolution had to be acciden-tal, generated solely by genetic mutations filtered through natural selection. On the other hand, finalism viewed God as an external agent that made (or makes) everything in accordance with his plan. Bergson rejected both views as limited because they removed creativ-ity from nature.

Bergson identified two main tendencies in the universe: intelligence and instinct, which balance each other through *intuition*. As he saw it, intelligence returns to instinct, and their balance activates intuition, drawing us back to our origin, the vital impulse. This ongoing process is inherently creative and cyclical, forever generating change by return-ing to the compelling force of the élan vital. In matter, the creative force is unconscious and automatic, but in consciousness, intellect combines with intuition to unify apparent complexity.

Bergson's work inspired fellow Frenchman Pierre Teilhard de Chardin (1881–1955), a scientist, philosopher, and Jesuit priest who wrote one of the most controversial and influential books of the twenti-eth century, *The Phenomenon of Man*. During his lifetime, the Catholic church censored his works because of his unorthodox cosmology. While Teilhard developed Bergson's "third way," he also revitalized the notion of the creator as origin. The scientific community criticized his science, while the church criticized his theology. Teilhard described God as a creative process (rather than agent or entity), unfolding into complexity and reaching its full potential in God consciousness—which he called the *Omega Point*.

In the tradition of Aristotle's philosophy of entelechy, Teilhard called this goal-oriented cosmic evolutionary process *orthogenesis*—the progressive complexification of matter and consciousness from the alpha of fundamental particles to the omega of consciousness uniting with the divine source, or Creator. In doing so, he reconciled Christian spirituality with evolutionary theory, combining his commitment to religion and his work as a paleontologist and proponent of Darwinism. He viewed biological processes as Darwinian, but viewed the evolution of consciousness (the noosphere) more as a Lamarckian process that involved purposeful adaptation. (Darwin's predecessor Jean-Baptiste Lamarck viewed evolution in terms of the inheritance of acquired characteristics rather than of natural selection.) In other words, consciousness (the noosphere) evolves through collective choice, or "unanimization"—a process of unification whereby all individual entelechies align with the greater cosmic entelechy, culminating in the Omega Point of blissful reunion.

The idea that all matter possesses a "within" (consciousness) features prominently in Teilhard's cosmology. He held that mind is intrinsic to matter, that everything is sentient and inherently purposeful and meaningful—expressing its unique but connected entelechy.

Aristotle thought of mind and matter as inseparable, as *energeia* and *dynamis*. Similarly, the sixteenth-century heretic Giordano Bruno defined this dual but unified whole as *mater-materia* (mother-matter). In the Western tradition, then, from Aristotle to Bergson and Teilhard, we can see versions of the third way between mechanistic determinism and teleological finalism. According to this third way, matter and mind are inseparable because mind is *intrinsic* to matter—part of its essential nature. All of these cosmologies express variations of the idea that reality consists of a unified process of ever evolving mind in matter, rather than separate substances.

PANPSYCHISM IN THE EAST

In the East, we find a similar perspective in the philosophies of Taoism and Neo-Confucianism. For example, in ancient China, at the time of Mencius, *qi* (or *ch'i*) was thought of as a vital force, an internal energy. Whereas the Taoists presented the complementarity and unity of *yin* and *yang,* Neo-Confucian philosophy developed and extended the concept of *li:* originally referring to cultural law, it came to mean a metaphysical principle. Like the Taoists with their yin/yang, the Neo-Confucians coupled qi and li. Li could be understood as the organizing law or principle inherent in qi, which can be described as matter-energy.[10] For the Neo-Confucians, qi possessed inherent li, which guided the unfolding of energy according to its own internal purpose. Thus we see a similarity between the Western idea of entelechy and the Eastern idea of qi energy, always guided by its inseparable li. One cannot exist without the other, expressed by Neo-Confucianist Zhu Xi (1130–1200): "Throughout the universe there is no *qi* wihout *li,* nor *li* without *qi.*"[11]

Zhu Xi speaks of li as the *dao* (or tao) that organizes all qi, which expresses and arranges itself in the complexity of matter: "Thus men and all other things must receive their *li* in their moment of coming into existence, and obtain their specific nature. They must also receive their *qi* to get their form."[12]

Because of their relationship to the natural world, the ancient Chinese saw humanity as a microcosm within a macrocosm. Taoism, which dates to around 600 BCE, teaches following "the Way," or tao, of nature as a "transformative process."[13] So even very early on, Chinese cosmology recognized unity and process—in other words, nondualistic, nonmechanistic universal relationships governed by universal laws inherent to being. The ancient Chinese recognized an inner purposiveness (li or tao) at the depths of matter, like Aristotle's entelechy, Bruno's *mater-materia,* Bergson's *élan vital,* and Teilhard's *within.* The inner purpose (entelechy or li) of each being interacts with that of every other being to produce the evolving complexity of the universe, from macrocosm to microcosm.

TAO AND TELOS

Although these ideas have been rejected by mechanistic science, a growing number of visionary philosophers and scientists in the West realize that in order to account for the world as we actually experience it—consisting of matter *and* mind—we need to reconsider concepts like entelechy and teleology as valid and necessary parts of our expanding interdisciplinary discourse.

New revelations in physics challenged mechanistic theories of science beginning in the early twentieth century. Physicists failed to come up with the TOE (Theory of Everything). Quantum physicist Werner Heisenberg, who gave us the famous Uncertainty Principle, later developed an interest in Taoism (which, as we have seen, aligns with entelechy). Another physicist, Wolfgang Pauli, collaborated with psychologist Carl Jung to explore the relationship between the strange facts of quantum nonlocality and synchronicity. Both nonlocality and synchronicity defy explanations in terms of causes and effects. Jung embraced the concept of entelechy, which he saw as actively guiding unconscious archetypes and somatic symptoms. Jung and Pauli believed that entelechy also guided the unfolding of quantum events.[14]

In the mid-twentieth century, physicist David Bohm developed an alternative to the standard version of quantum theory, which claimed that quantum events are inherently random. Like Einstein, Bohm rejected the idea that God plays dice with the universe. He saw creativity as deeply implicit in nature as both formal and final cause. He also said that formative cause always "implies final cause," which means: no formal cause without final cause. In his alternative, Bohm explained mathematically how quantum events are guided by a deeper "intelligence" arising out of what he called the *implicate order*. This implicate intelligence plays a similar role to Aristotle's entelechy, and is consistent with Bergson's élan vital and Teilhard's teleological Omega Point. Bohm defined entelechy as "an ordered and structured inner movement that is essential to what things are."[15]

For Bohm, at the deepest level of reality, an *implicit* wholeness contains the potentiality for all that *explicitly* manifests as apparent separateness in the physical world. Bohm's implicit wholeness took its cue from Leibniz's monads, each one of which, like the jewels in the Hindu Indra's net, reflects every other monad, and ultimately contains the whole universe. Bohm's model replaces Leibniz's preestablished harmony with the notion of quantum uncertainty. The whole contains every possibility.

Operating in the domain of implicate order, what Bohm variously called the *holomovement,* a *guiding intelligence,* and *entelechy* creates and chooses new events. He compared the universe to a giant hologram, where, again like the monads, every point in the holomovement reflects every other point. In modern digital parlance, each pixel contains the whole image.

After *Wholeness and the Implicate Order,* Bohm's fascination with creativity blossomed, and he collaborated with artists and writers to explore the creative process not only in science but in other disciplines.

Around the same time as Bohm revived teleology in physics, the transpersonal and human-potential movements in psychology also embraced the idea of entelechy. Pioneering humanistic psychologist Abraham Maslow said all organisms, including humans, have "biological wisdom." He pointed out that the Taoist way of asking, rather than telling, would convert parents to scientists—custodians of inherent wisdom and knowledge. What Maslow called *love knowledge* permits individuals to unfold according to their own entelechy or tao. It is love, rather than objectivity, that must be present in any discipline that works with living subjects. Rather than trying to force someone to fit the current paradigm, it is better to adapt or open up the paradigm to include personal knowledge. In this way, the loving curiosity of the parent, psychologist, or scientist encourages the child, client, or research subject to grow and learn by honoring the individual's own experience. This enables the creative process of discovery to unfold in a natural way. This approach accepts the universal wisdom of entelechy, recognizing that nature is inside of us, not "out there," and that each being has its inner voice connected to a deeper creativity. It also acknowledges that transformation can be hard to understand: just as a caterpillar turns into goo before it emerges from the chrysalis as a butterfly, beings and collectives *become* in sometimes perplexing and paradoxical ways. We can't always judge the goo stage of becoming.

THE GAIA HYPOTHESIS

Another expanded way of seeing our cosmological journey emerged from that potent time of new psychology, science, and experimental collaborations between disciplines in the 1960s and 70s. The Gaia hypothesis coincided with the human-potential movement and inspired many people to see their planetary home differently through the metaphor of Gaia. According to the Gaia hypothesis, developed by chemist James Lovelock and biologist Lynn Margulis, Earth forms a complex web of interrelated and self-regulating systems, integrated and stabilized by symbiotic processes. From this perspective, Earth itself becomes a living system of systems that oscillates, respirates, regenerates, and regulates, much like a living being that breathes and sweats and eats and eliminates.[16]

Lovelock and Margulis proposed that we view the Earth as a living organism in its own right, deserving of respect and regard. This revolutionary proposal coincided with a growing recognition of widespread pollution, nuclear proliferation, and climate change. Their courageous assertion that Gaia exhibits living processes—similar to how our bodies regulate their various interconnected systems—revitalized the ancient idea of nature as an inherently intelligent, living, self-directing, and self-regulating system.

Lovelock and Margulis later revised their theory to ensure that people did not take their metaphor literally. In *Symbiotic Planet,* Margulis asserted that Gaia was a metaphor—that she never meant to personify the planet. She further elucidated the idea that Earth is not an organism but rather emerges through the interaction of organisms. Margulis and Lovelock rejected teleology, but they conveyed the idea that our human systems should not interfere with the Earth's regulatory wisdom, lest we disrupt the delicate state of equilibrium that sustains us.

Though Margulis rejected teleology, she also (fortunately) rejected the neo-Darwinian dogma that evolution proceeds exclusively by random mutation and natural selection. She championed the ideas of symbiosis and symbiogenesis—the mutual cooperation of living systems—as a crucial factor in evolution. Cooperation, not competition (not "nature red in tooth and claw"), and symbiogenesis, not selfish genes, drives evolutionary progress. Changing, or expanding, these fundamental stories changes our relationship dynamics.

Symbiotic relationships qualify as examples of the biological wisdom that is inherent in all matter. Symbiogenesis suggests that nature evolves according to an increasingly complex system of cooperative organisms that interact, intersect, and nest within and without, just as nature creates connective nested systems of entelechies within entelechies. All life is a complex of systems. Some creatures perform as networks (like mycelia), some as superorganisms (like ants and bees), some as individuals that cooperate (like humans, ravens, and wolves). But all living beings, as far as we know, have some kind of subjectivity that connects them to other subjectivities. All creatures have an interior life that directs them. Have you ever watched bees closely? They seem to relish pollination; they don't just pollinate like little api-bots. Though they are part of a larger superorganism, they also possess feelings and intelligence of their own. Ever watch a snail crossing the garden path? They may be slow, but every part of them is striving. When we watch the more-than-human world around us closely, with an open mind, we intuitively feel that there is something inside each being. Our intellectual constructs tell us to ignore that feeling, but in order to feel a sense of connectedness, we must revive and trust it. That doesn't mean that we don't respect scientific knowledge, but rather that we expand it through the insight that the world is full of meaning.

MARVELOUSLY MEANINGFUL

It is easy to understand that the purpose of a sunflower's seedbed is to maximize seed distribution. As Aristotle said, the *telos* of an acorn is to become an oak. However, it is more difficult to discern the purpose of the individual within the complexity of the consciousness continuum. Why should I be aware of my own thoughts alone, and not yours? Why should each being have its own interior life or experience? Also, when we become aware of the sentience of trees, we might ask, is the *telos* of an acorn *only* to be an oak? Or could the acorn also become a parent, friend, and part of a community? Materialism sidesteps these kinds of questions by stating that all consciousness and experiential events are merely epiphenomena—simple by-products of neurological processes. But many scientists are now open to new research confirming the interiority of many creatures in the more-than-human world, and that raises many new questions about life.

What if interiority, consciousness, sentience, are ubiquitous? Then we must assume that there is meaning *within* and purpose *for* every individual's unique subjectivity. Just as billions of tiny shells and pebbles make up a beach, an infinite amount of individual experiences, each with its own entelechy, makes up the greater entelechy of the cosmos.

In *Mind and Cosmos,* philosopher Thomas Nagel recently stated that the universe makes choices, that "the consciousness, the knowledge, and the choice, are dispersed over a vast crowd of beings, acting both individually and collectively."[17] Rather than a random scattering and recombination of insentient matter into mind-boggling complexities of form and function, inherently purposeful matter directs and coordinates diverse expressions of connected creativity throughout nature. Perhaps cosmic creativity behaves like a vast superorganism of diverse entelechies.

Psychologist and transpersonal visionary Jean Houston described a visit with Pierre Teilhard de Chardin in which he explained entelechy. As they walked together, he said: "It is inside you, like the butterfly is inside the caterpillar."[18] The butterfly has always been an archetype of the soul, life force, and transformation. As noted earlier, entelechy shows up in many other guises, such as Aristotle's *energeia* and *dynamis,* Leibniz's monads, and the *li* of Taoism and Neo-Confucianism. All of these views acknowledge that matter does not consist of mindless atoms randomly bumping into each other, and life is more than blind cellular reproduction determined by mechanistic programming in the genes. That view completely rejects the reality of our experience and fails to address the ineffable mystery of life.

For Aristotle, entelechy was inseparable from the cosmos, fundamental to force, energy, and all dynamics; to him, something of the marvelous pervaded nature. Since the Cartesian split, many philosophers have challenged the principle of Occam's razor, pointing out that, in a complex world, the simplest explanation is not necessarily the best. *Marvel,* after all, is etymologically linked to the Latin *mirabilis,* or *wondrous.* As we marvel at this complex, connected, creative world full of mysterious meaning and purpose at every scale, we experience a deep sense of wonder.

3 METAPATTERNS
Nature's Creative Archetypes

Metapatterns can be thought of as those key patterns that exemplify the sphericity of the deepest forms of knowledge, the interlinking of all things and ideas in the universe.

TYLER VOLK, *ACROSS SPACE, TIME, AND MIND*

When a spider makes a beautiful web, the beauty comes out of the spider's nature. It's instinctive beauty. How much of the beauty of our own lives is about the beauty of being alive?

JOSEPH CAMPBELL, *THE POWER OF MYTH*

It has always amused me that in many cultures, displays of courtship include offering a bouquet of flowers (which are, after all, the sex organs of plants) as a token of intention to begin mating. Offering flowers to a loved one symbolizes fertility, pleasure, and flourishing life. The unfolding blooms invite the beloved to open to advances, as a pollen-heavy flower beckons the bee.

If we look a little closer at a bloom, we can see similarities to the female reproductive systems of various animal species, including humans. These cross-species similarities, both floral and faunal, didn't happen by chance. It happened because in each case the reproductive organs evolved with a *purpose:* to successfully generate life through form, function, process—and beauty. When, during estrus, the genitalia of female baboons turn red, swell, and protrude, the males, crazed with their own tumescence, aggressively turn on each other. Driven by a similar instinct, the bees in my backyard will not let me near the aromatically blissful shade of my magnolia tree in midsummer. The vulva and the flower share a kind of master form, or archetypal blueprint, for reproductive expression. Life has mastered the art of signaling readiness for sex. When we exchange flowers with a beloved, we communicate an age-old message: "I want to connect and create with you—maybe a relationship, maybe a home, maybe a child, or maybe just an enchanted evening."

Nature conveys intentions through pattern, form, and symbol. Because we are part of nature's creativity, so do we.

SACRED MIND, SACRED FORM

In the previous chapter, I talked about teleology as one aspect of nature's creative process. Nature repeats the most useful and elegant solutions. We can see evidence of these preferences, these design solutions, everywhere. When we notice nature's creative archetypes, it reminds us that we live in a world of deep and meaningful connective patterns.

Nature conveys what I call *sacred mind* through favorite shapes. In many spiritual traditions, gazing at an image of an avatar, bodhisattva, or mandala, or even creating sacred images facilitates meditative states. Observing sacred mind in nature's creativity can help us to reconnect to our own sacred mind as well. It releases a deep knowing that we inhabit a world rich with meaning—an ebbing and flowing ocean of intentionality that creates complex relationships between beautiful forms. Life itself, then, forms a mandala of complexity, layers upon layers of existence embellished with exquisite detail—all expressing nature's wise and sacred creativity.

Buddhist monks express their deep knowing of this process.

Attuned to impermanence, they express their sacred mind through the intricacies of sand paintings, which they then undo and return to nature. Just as monks wipe away the perfect culmination of their devotion and skill, intricately formed auburn leaves, which once skillfully gathered photons, decay and fall, providing nutrients for other life.

I want to point out a pattern—or, to be more precise, a pattern of patterns, a *metapattern*. First, the vulva and the flower share not only shape and form, but also function and symbolism. They partake of the same root archetype—a pattern that exhibits both physical forms and psychic meanings. These forms and meanings show up across a wide range of species—from the tumescence of desirous baboons to the offer of a vulva-shaped flower to the desired.

Archetypes express themselves through nested patterns-within-patterns, repeating a similar theme from one layer to the next. Nature's archetypes, then, form into fractals, self-similar patterns all the way down—every level an expression of nature's deep intelligence, or sacred mind.

When we realize this, we can recognize human intelligence as a subset of the world's greater intelligence. Sacred mind expresses itself in similar ways: sexual attraction and signaling repeated in similar forms and conveying similar meanings across plant and animal kingdoms— trees recycling their autumnal leaves, and Buddhist monks creating and destroying sand mandalas. Nature conveys intention through pattern, form, and symbol—expressing the same or similar meanings across all species on potentially infinite scales. These archetypes guide the unfolding of evolution as well as our lives.

If we pay attention, we can see and feel how nature speaks to us through forms that express archetypal meanings. For example:

Fallen leaves are swept away by networks of streams, rivers, and tributaries, patterned much like fractal tree branches and leaf veins— each system conducting nutrients through its networks. Trees pump water and nutrients though their trunks, branches, and leaves; rivers carry water and nutrients through the land and eventually out into the oceans—great sheets of matter and energy. This sheetlike form seems to be repeated even on the scale of the universe as a whole. Recent cosmological models suggest that such a sheetlike form might underlie the shape of our universe—a fractal pattern of self-similarity repeated at different scales. Our ocean-covered sphere, shaped to withstand great astronomical forces, revolves and orbits in an elliptical path around our sun, distributing cyclical seasonal fluctuations. Our galaxy moves its arms in a spiral shape reminiscent of the structure of DNA, ova, plants, shells, and hurricanes. Leaf, river, ocean, planet, galaxy—from the physical to the metaphysical, a mysterious universal wisdom prefers certain forms of expression.

Patterns exist everywhere. They are so ubiquitous, in fact, that lack of pattern or order is anomalous. Energy directs its movements in specific ways, and tends to organize itself according to certain rules. Systems made up of dynamic patterns within other dynamic patterns form a kaleidoscope of moving energy that creates our spatial world of form. This dynamic, complex yet organized system of systems, a great pattern of patterns, forms a universal metapattern.

THE PATTERN THAT CONNECTS

Visionary Gregory Bateson coined the phrase "the pattern that connects"—a transcontextual pattern that unifies and connects across domains.[1] Later, the brilliant biologist and systems theorist Tyler Volk expanded on this idea, extending it to convergences on many scales. "The principle of convergence in biological evolution, in which similar structures are independently evolved, is the model that can be extended even beyond biology. If the contexts of evolved systems across widely separated scales are similar, the resulting evolved systems can exhibit convergences that themselves occur at diverse scales. These grand convergences are the metapatterns." Volk suggests that recognizing these universal and transcontextual patterns takes us a step toward a "science of everything."[2]

Volk suggests that metapatterns could be broken down into eleven main categories:

- Spheres
- Tubes
- Sheets
- Borders (and pores)
- Binaries (and more complex numerical entities)
- Centers
- Layers (including hierarchies, holarchies, holons, and clonons)
- Calendars
- Arrows
- Breaks
- Cycles

Each metapattern contains, orders, and promotes conservation and transmission of energy. Metapatterns and combinations of metapatterns direct matter-energy relationships in specific ways. Volk explains that shape is to mind as the spectrum is to sight. Each shape we perceive falls somewhere on a gradient from sphericity to flatness, just as the visible spectrum appears from slower waves (red) to faster (violet). Spheres protect and contain, while sheets receive and let go. For example, think of how the receptive sheet of ocean receives and releases a diving bell, and how the curvature of the enclosed bell protects its occupants from immense pressures of deep water. Each shape in the natural world falls somewhere along this spectrum.

As a fundamental metapattern, a primordial form, the sphere shows up at the start of life. Many prokaryotes, our earliest single-celled, water-borne ancestors, adopted this shape—tiny globes of protein-and-DNA-rich jelly. In many life forms, procreation begins in the center of a sphere. Because their curvature minimizes areas of potentially hazardous contact with external forces, giving them exceptional tensile strength, spheres maximize durability and optimize containment. It's as if nature decided: "If you want to improve your chances for survival, best to curl up into a ball." As a result, this spherical metapattern organizes entities of all sizes, from micro to macro—from tiny cells to huge planets. Our cells have membranes as our planet has a crust. The sphericity of certain fruits and eggs maximizes water conservation.

Clearly, metapatterns operate across different domains—from metaphysical archetypes to physical shapes that happen to be the most efficient for maintenance and survival of organisms.

Metapatterns, then, connect existential realms on every scale of matter-energy. Their formal qualities—their ability to *in-form* matter—act like universal laws, guiding and directing the unfolding of cosmic, biological, and personal evolution. In other words, these archetypes work across both physical and nonphysical domains. Just as the sphere is a fundamental biospheric form essential for creating and sustaining life, it also represents wholeness and unity in the noosphere, the domain of consciousness.

MYSTERIOUS SPHERE

In sociological mapping and modeling, we speak about social spheres and spheres of influence. Famed mythologist Joseph Campbell once said, "God is an intelligible sphere—a sphere known to the mind, not to the sense—*whose center is everywhere and whose circumference is nowhere*" (italics added).[3] In other words, applied to spirit or consciousness, the archetype of the sphere not only transcends space and the senses, it also transcends individualized, separate Cartesian egos—forming a bridge into the transpersonal unknown, connecting domains through the rhythmic, dynamic expressions of consciousness in matter-energy.

Experience converges with environment through pattern and symbol. Directed by consciousness within matter, each pattern unfolds in time and space. If the notion of *self* seems difficult to avoid when describing the formation of dynamic complex energetic patterns, it is clearly unavoidable when we attempt to describe complex *mental* or *psychic* patterns.

In Jungian psychology, archetypes are *psychoid*—both psychic and physical. As such, archetypes exist in, and in-form, both temporal and spatial patterns. *Archetype* is derived from the ancient Greek *archetypon*, which referred to the pattern, model, or figure on a seal stamped into epistolary wax. Carl Jung redefined the word to mean "forms or images of a collective nature which occur practically all over the earth as constituents of myths and at the same time as autochthonous individual products of unconscious origin."[4] So a literal stamp becomes a metaphorical imprint held within the unconscious that manifests through myth. The word itself contains the ideas of repetition, imitation, and pattern. An archetype, therefore, could be understood as the formation of psychoid patterns.

Jung's notion of psychoid entities fits with panpsychist ontology, in which every actual, existent being consists of both subjective/mental and objective/physical elements or aspects. As Christian de Quincey has noted, every pattern is a pattern of *sentient energy*—a pattern that shows up in physical regularities correlated with a corresponding patterning or ordering in consciousness.

Scale-transcending patterns tend to repeat because of their usefulness and efficiency. As the historian of religions Mircea Eliade noted: "Whatever its context, a symbol always reveals the basic oneness of several zones of the real."[5]

Volk offers the idea of "spherituality," that the "deepest facets of sphericity are many and complex." From life's beginnings, to cosmic beginnings, to archetypal symbols, the sphere occupies many scales and zones of reality.[6]

Metapatterns differ in how they organize matter-energy (or mental contents). The sphere contains and protects, the sheet receives and transmits. As Volk points out, whereas the sphere often describes containment in various physical and mental domains, sheets and tubes also operate across "physical, biological, and cultural" domains.[7]

SYNERGIES

The way we imagine the action and interaction of matter-energy can affect the way we see our entire cosmological story. For example, a closed universe can be viewed as spherical, as open and curved (a sheet shaped like a saddle), or as simply flat (a sheet). Each description implies a different outcome. If our universe is closed and sph rical, then it could either expand eternally as a bounded sphere, or contract and expand and contract in an eternal cycle. The negative curvature of a saddle-shaped, open-sheet universe would accelerate expansion, possibly ending in a Big Rip, tearing everything apart. In fact, according to recent cosmological models, supported by Hubble data, we inhabit a flat-sheet universe. If so, the ultimate fate of the universe would be a Big Chill—eventual universal heat death.

If we roll up a sheet into a tube, we exchange surface area for structure and conductivity. As Volk puts it, a tube provides "linear stretch" as opposed to the "planar squash" of the sheet. A gossamer spider's web, made of intersecting tubes, is strong enough to catch and hold its prey, yet conductive enough to transmit vibrations—news of an imminent meal. Inside our bodies, muscles and circulatory and nervous systems form dense networks of tubes. In computers, complex digital circuits consisting of microtubes transmit signals through cyberspace. These in turn create cultural networks. A tumescent tube blasts sperm with tubelike tails into a vaginal tube on a quest to combine DNA and form new life, which starts out as a sphere. On another scale, a "space-faring tube" blasts human astronauts into space in order to land on some other sphere, perhaps to begin a new life. From the micro to the macro, tubes convey energy in many forms and make connections from sphere to sphere.

In our brains, cascades of neural dendrites closely resemble branching trees; hence their name, from *dendron,* the ancient Greek word for tree. Trees convey water, nutrients, and information through their branching tubules. Within a forest ecosystem, trees look and behave much like dendrites in a brain, communicating with each other, transmitting messages from canopy to roots, and vice versa. Dendrites carry electrochemical stimulation through a similar delivery system. Both brains and forests form highly efficient delivery systems that optimize transmission of energy and information through a larger system.

The archetypal tube occurs in many metaphysical models. The tree of life, for example, symbolizes alchemical wisdom, showing how archetypal tubes gather nourishment and direct and conduct energy across multiple realms. The rich nutrients of the subsurface earth, the atmosphere, and sunlight from the upper world converge within the tree's wisdom—mirrored in the convergence of self, spirit, and Creator. Alchemical wisdom, based on intuitions about forms in consciousness, recognized convergent three-dimensional energy patterns: *as above, so below*. In other words, guided by some deep intelligence or teleology, patterns flow from microphysical to macrophysical.

The divine conduit forms a tube that conducts information from physical to metaphysical planes. In the Hopi *kiva* (*sipapu*), an opening at ground level leads into the chamber below by way of a ladder—the archetypal conductor of matter-energy, a convergence of worlds. Just as atomic structure, made of up spheres and tubes, is part of an energetic network that creates everything we perceive with our ordinary senses, the connections between psychic patterns perceived through nonordinary knowing create everything we can imagine.

Worlds connect through openings. Just as a cell (sphere) has a membrane (border), it also has pores (breaks), which allow osmosis. An archetypal pore could be called a portal, a mystical door that permits access to another realm or another kind of knowing. The *kiva* and the *inipi*—sweat lodges of the Pueblo Zuni and Hopi and the Lakota respectively—both allow entry to another realm. Just as the uterus allows entry in order to begin the sacred process of generation, the *kiva* or *inipi* allows entry into the Mother's womb, a place of sacred regeneration for the participants. The labyrinth—a circular structure with a series of borders and breaks, doors, and portals, leading to a center—connects archetypal tubes between the physical and nonphysical realms.

Nature conveys energy and matter and mind through tubes connecting sheets and spheres—whether in the brain, a tree, or a rocket. Sheets, spheres and tubes create synergy in a world of connected creativity.

DYNAMIC DUALITIES

As a cell divides, the circle is bisected, electromagnetic energy becomes polarized, and living complexity emerges. As the magnetosphere regulates weather patterns on Earth, our heart valves create electromagnetic fields around our bodies, which in turn affects those around us. Archetypal binaries such as yin/yang, Shakti/Shiva, shadow/light help us explain the dualities in the universe and in ourselves. This chiaroscuro of creation gives our world depth.

Binary relationships, such as yin/yang or shadow/light, can serve as metaphors for balance across all domains and levels of existence. Relationships can be symbiotic or oppositional, dualities that weave life's complexities. For example, cooperation between two microorganisms can create speciation (part 2), while cooperation between two societies might create a new society. Opposition between microorganisms can generate illness, while opposition between societies can start wars.

When we realize that archetypes guide the formation of patterns throughout nature, we can see how archetype and entelechy express a similar idea: *nature consists of interactive entelechies that create the warp and weft of the cosmos.*

Symbiotic duality represents a symbolic return to the *sacred center.* Biological cells and physical atoms must constantly adapt and adjust to each other. This constant flux requires constant ceremony—the *hozho,* or "beauty way" of the Navajo, the tao of the East. In order to maintain symbiosis and harmony, we need duality. The essential sacredness of nature shows up whenever we focus our intentions on right relationships.

Mircea Eliade described the *axis mundi* (world axis) that appears in many religious ceremonies—for example, the celestial and geographical pole connecting the Earth and sky worlds, where directional spaces meet. Many temples and religious structures are built around this central point, into which a rod or pole is driven—a conduit that transforms the profane world (our finite, physical world) into a sacred world, a space within which transcendent experiences can occur.[8] At the center of the *kiva,* the archetypal womb, the primordial Mother embraces us. The ceremony takes place in sacred time, as temporality expands and slows for participants. Only when one ascends out of the *kiva* womb, returning to the surface, does the experience of time resume. One is born again into the life of circadian rhythms. Our known universe began as an unimaginably dense, hot ball (the primordial cosmic egg); the temporal universe begins with a physical/metaphysical center of experience, a self.

The center appears as the nucleus of an atom or cell, each nucleus connected by a conduit. We describe selfhood as a center, indicating a place from which we move in the world. Jung described the center as a place of origin and returning: "I saw that everything, all paths I had been following, all steps I had taken, were leading back to a single point—namely, to the mid-point."[9] Whether physical or psychoid, centers connect through exchanges of energy or through shared meaning in relationships. For example, when an atomic nucleus splits, it creates a massive explosion; when a self loses its inner compass, it tends to create destruction in its environment. Of course, destruction can also be seen as an aspect of creation, just as we understand Jung's hidden order in chaos. Dynamic, and often paradoxical, relationships create what we perceive as reality through the intersection of centers on every scale.

COMPLEX CENTRICITY

Sacred relationship can be thought of as two centers interacting through exchanges of energy and/or by sharing meaning. For example, the sun lies at the center of our solar system and interacts with the center of our galaxy through gravitational energy. The Earth, the center of our existence, interacts with the sun, another center, also through gravitational and electromagnetic energy. The Earth's gravity allowed other earthly centers to form: first cells, then fungi, plants, and animals. Interconnected assemblages of centers create complexity.

Volk defines the characteristics of centers as "spatially centered within the whole, a unique substance, singular, relatively conservative . . . tangible identity with the whole, and radiating relations to all."[10] He calls centricity a "design attractor." A center pushes energy out and receives it within a sphere. Visionary engineer Buckminster Fuller described *vector equilibrium* as a shape composed of twelve connected spheres stabilized by a thirteenth sphere in the center. Similarly, at the center of a beehive sits a queen—remove her, and the colony falls apart. In the same way, the self at the center of our being forms a mysterious inner compass that stabilizes each of us.

An ancient intuition about the dynamics of energy flow appears in the image of concentric circles, which adds layers to the center, like ripples flowing outward on a pond. The earliest examples of this archetypal metapattern emerge in the rock paintings of the Neolithic. The cup and ring mark shows up during the Neolithic at many sites around the world, including Australia, Canaan, Ireland, Mexico, Mozambique, Spain, the southwestern United States, and the United Kingdom, to name a few.

Gregory Cajete, a professor of indigenous studies, describes what the symbol represents for indigenous people:

Concentric rings radiate from every thing and every process. The concentric rings provide a visual symbol of relationship; it is a way of visualizing how all processes radiate concentric rings, which in turn affect other rings of other processes. The symbol of concentric rings is useful in seeing how one thing affects another, how one thing leads to another, and how one thing is connected to another.[11]

Cajete lists five significant aspects of concentricity:

- Processes
- Interrelationships
- Wholeness
- Systemic view of nature and universe
- Usually represented as a place or location from which myth emanated

In previous chapters, I discussed how panpsychist philosophy relates to indigenous wisdom. Process thinking aligns with many indigenous belief systems. It seems only natural that philosophers and systems theorists who have attempted to create different ontologies using alternative paradigms would opt for concentricity. Concentricity, by its circularity and layering, provides an archetypal alternative to dominator hierarchies through the description of nested, or flattened, hierarchies.

Arthur Koestler and Ken Wilber both wrote about this tendency toward alternation between hierarchy and heterarchy. Koestler first coined the terms *holon* and *holarchy* in an attempt to create a universal system.[12] Following Koestler, Wilber expands the idea that the world does not consist of parts or wholes, but of holons—parts that are also wholes. Combining many holons together into greater holons, he creates a model based on a system of nested hierarchies, which can be diagrammed as concentric circles.[13] Layers spread out from a center.

A holarchy is an example of hierarchy and sphericity interacting and converging. You could think of it as spherical layers of reality.

Volk explains that concentricity tends to be more mysterious, and perhaps this ambiguous quality makes it a better model to account for the connection between physical and metaphysical. This makes sense when we try to describe the interactions between realms. Nested holarchies, for instance, can convey the gradation of open systems from smallest to largest scales.

We can envision a panpsychist ontology, with sentience on every scale informing the sentience of every other—all the way down, all the way up. In this model, entelechies are not windowless predetermined fates, but interactive, dynamic, Escherlike fractals—worlds within worlds within worlds, holographs containing the whole in each particle. David Bohm developed a model of the implicate order in which reality, the universe, is one great dynamic hologram called the *holomovement*. For Bohm, reality is both eternally in process and intrinsically intelligent. Combined, the qualities of process and intelligence give us entelechy—the interior dynamic guiding evolution or universal process. But there is more to it: like Jung's archetypes, Bohm's holomovement swirls eternally in a dance of patterns within patterns within patterns—dynamic fractal intelligences all the way down and up. This nested holomovement is yet another version of infinite holographic concentricities that contain and manifest the whole universe.

Indigenous peoples intuited metapatterns. They observed nature closely and first used biomimicry. They also believed that nature's physical patterns expressed metaphysical archetypes. Both ancient Tibetans and Native Americans used versions of a medicine wheel (similar to the Kalachakra mandala in Tibet) that direct energy and understanding.

Spheres, borders, centers, arrows, breaks, and cycles converge and interact in the medicine wheel. The borders signify the cardinal directions. Each unit, separate from the others, and has its own meaningful attributes and power through association with an animal spirit and a color. The parts of self converge to form a unity. The cardinal directions also combine to form a unity, which points to the center. This center represents Great Spirit. As the axis mundi, Great Spirit could be thought of as a "transcendence tube" connecting our sacred mind to nature's mind.

Like the Native American medicine wheel, the Tibetan mandala has cycles, arrows, breaks, borders, tubes, centers, binaries, and layers—patterns within patterns within patterns. Both medicine wheel and mandala express the dynamic, relational processes of life. They express what Whitehead's process philosophy calls *concrescence*.

Envisioning the universe through metapatterns opens a way to sacred mind. Understanding the brilliance of nature's connective patterns helps us to simultaneously recognize our inherent unity and the fundamental necessity for diversity on every scale. From a panpsychist perspective, the unifying idea that we are all sentient matter also enables us to respect the reality of complexity—we are diverse expressions of sentient matter.

Together we co-create a potentially infinite web of diversely expressed sentient matter, forming an unfolding mandala of intricate and impermanent complexity. All forms, from quanta to cosmos, from self to collective, remain interrelated and yet truly unique. When, through sacred mind, we recognize how deeply interconnected we are in our dazzling diversity, and how impermanent those exquisite expressions are, we devote and dedicate ourselves to their care.

4 SENTIENCE

The Music of the Universe

There is one simple Divinity found in all things, one fecund Nature, preserving mother of the universe insofar as she diversely communicates herself, casts her light into diverse subjects, and assumes various names.

GIORDANO BRUNO

All things share the same breath—the beast, the tree, the man. The air shares its spirit with all the life it supports.

CHIEF SEATTLE

Awakening to a symphony of birdsong is one of life's great pleasures. On a spring morning, the variety of elaborate birdcalls often breaks through my still-sleepy awareness. Tuning into the blend of tonal signatures, I can hear nature's ever-present orchestration. Birdsong lets me know that our biosphere continues to flourish and renew itself. In one of the most important books of our age, *Silent Spring,* biologist Rachel Carson warned that a spring without birdsong signals the devastation of our fragile ecosystem. The dawn chorus, when birds once again greet the sun, reminds me that relationships sustain life, so I hear their music as a sacred call to awaken to the beauty of our world and to remember that each unique song contributes to life's sentient symphony.

Intricate relationships surround us, exchanging information in a chorus of intelligent humming, singing, chirping, shrieking, and signaling. Birds communicate about mating, territory, and food, much as we do through our language and technology. Busily feeding on seeds, worms, and insects, the avian world communicates through various sounds, vibrations, visual displays, and chemical signals. Ubiquitous bacteria and other microbes communicate chemically through various means, such as peptides, auto-inducers, signal molecules, and bioluminescence. At every scale, an invisible and complex fabric of signals and meanings arranges itself through communication, building sacred relationships—weaving the rhythmic, pulsing music of creation.

Navajo, or Diné (the word that in their language means "the people"), spirituality holds that everything is animated by *nitch'i diyin,* roughly translated to English as "holy wind," the animating breath that imbues everything with spirit. According to Diné teachings, this holy wind communicates essential wisdom, and connects every aspect of the universe.

Over time, early intuitions about a shared animating source developed into philosophical panpsychism: the view that sentience occurs throughout all levels of the universe. *Panpsychism* comes from ancient Greek words *pan,* meaning "all," and *psychē,* meaning "breath, spirit, or soul"—reminiscent of the Navajo holy wind. Life thrives in our oxygen-rich atmosphere, circulated through breathing, giving rise to the idea of one source, one creator spirit. All beings share in the universal breath and sentience of the Creator.

Contemporary Western philosophy and science reject this view. According to modern scientific materialism, sentience emerges from complex brains, which are rare in the universe. This creates a gap between humans and everything else, perpetuating vicious cycles of life-denying ecological and sociological practices. Human exceptionalism, the idea that humans are special, makes sacred relationship with the natural world impossible, leading to widespread desacralization, or disenchantment of the world.

In contemplating the Anthropocene, dystopian blight plunges us further into denial as we try to escape its frightening implications. Nevertheless, the idea of dystopia consumes us so much that most of our science fiction conveys the worst scenarios possible. Our visions of the future are pretty bleak; it seems difficult to speculate about a different possible scenario. Feminist scholar Donna J. Haraway, in her book *Staying with the Trouble: Making Kin in the Cthulucene,* says that she does not consider herself a posthumanist or transhumanist but rather a "compost humanist": in this uncertain age, extreme co-creative interdisciplinary and interspecies projects might engage in "speculative fabulation for flourishing," much like the diverse ingredients that enrich a compost heap.[1] The idea that we can co-create other possible futures across cultures, disciplines, and species also forms a major part of sacred futurism. This book attempts to speculate about how changing and expanding our ideas changes and expands our possible futures. Enriching our co-creative soil enriches our possibility.

Spiritual teacher Thomas One Wolf once said to me: "Humans lost many powers that nonhuman animals still have. Eagles can see a mouse miles away. Elk can hear the snap of a tiny twig in the distance. Wolves can smell what you're feeling. That's why we seek their guidance with respect." Our indigenous ancestors knew that human intelligence has limitations, and that attuning to the hum of intelligence everywhere is crucial for the flourishing of all sentient beings—including us humans. Their philosophy embraced asking other creatures for guidance and wisdom through connection. The Anthropocene's complex and wicked problems require that we become compassionately and respectfully curious about the knowledge systems of other species.

Eastern philosophy and spirituality avoided Western Platonic dualism by adopting forms of idealism (the belief that ultimate reality consists of pure spirit or consciousness) or panpsychism (the view that reality consists of inseparable matter and spirit). For example, Shinto, the indigenous spirituality of Japan dating from the sixth century BCE, held a panpsychist view that all things in nature are imbued with *kami,* divine beings or spiritual essence. Shintoism respects the spirit in every being.

In Navajo spirituality, *diyin din'e* refers to "holy people," recognizing natural elements and phenomena as divine beings. For instance, rain, thunder, lightning, and sun are all personified (or *sentified*), and so invite respect for nature's omnipresent intelligence. Many Native American cultures consider stones not as clumps of dead matter, but as Stone People, trees not as convenient shade and lumber, but Tree People, and ants not as destructive insects, but Ant People. Thomas One Wolf suggested to me that through these names his people have always acknowledged the essential power intrinsic to all of nature's forms. Rather than anthropomorphizing, this denotes deep respect for the personhood of other creatures. Biologist and science writer John A. Shivik suggests that we might "zoomorphize" to understand how nonhuman behaviors might teach us about our own.[2] Calling other animals *people* also acknowledges the possibility that they possess abilities we lack. Can humans echolocate? Can we see in the ultraviolet range? Can we smell each other's feelings? Can we navigate by magnetoreception? No, but other species can. Perhaps these amazing people have something to teach us. As we awaken from our Cartesian sleep, we may expand our senses and listen more deeply to the more-than-human world. Thomas One Wolf called this "listening with the heart's ears."

Earth scholar and theologian Thomas Berry noted that we humans have stopped listening, stopped conversing with the greater world: "We are talking only to ourselves. We are not talking to the rivers; we are not listening to the wind and stars. We have broken the great conversation."[3] The great conversation continues all around us and within us; being oblivious to the rhythm of that conversation alienates us, makes us out of tune. Attuning to the deep language and music present everywhere heals our world from the inside.

Only recently have Western scholars begun to wake up from Cartesian sleep. As recently as July 2012, a group of the world's leading scientists and philosophers (including famed cosmologist, the late Stephen Hawking) signed the Cambridge Declaration of Consciousness:

> The absence of a neocortex does not appear to preclude an organism from experiencing affective states. Convergent evidence indicates that non-human animals have the neuroanatomical, neurochemical, and neurophysiological substrates of conscious states along with the capacity to exhibit intentional behaviors. Consequently, the weight of evidence indicates that humans are not unique in possessing the neurological substrates that generate consciousness. Non-human animals, including all mammals and birds, and many other creatures, including octopuses, also possess these neurological substrates.[4]

This declaration stands in sharp contrast to the Cartesian delusion that nonhuman animals are simply mechanisms without feelings or emotions. Descartes was so sure of this that he justified vivisection—experimentation on live animals—attributing their screams to nothing more than mechanical reaction, like parts of a machine creaking and screeching. Charles Darwin, the father of evolutionary theory, would later revile Descartes for this legacy of cruelty.

Descartes's influence on Western philosophy created horrific research practices that have undoubtedly benefited humans. Awakening from Cartesian sleep reveals to us that many creatures possess cultures and language, the ability to create, love, and mourn. The implications of this will require transition away from animal-research models. Obviously, many of us depend upon discoveries made this way, but as we become more acutely aware of nonhuman sentience, these methods will have to change. Transformations of this magnitude always catalyze transitions.

INTELLIGENCE AND WISDOM

Medicine people, or shamans, specialize in shapeshifting: taking the form of certain animals in order to better understand the world from their perspective. I call this wanting to know what it's like for other species *perspectival wisdom*. Many ancient peoples felt that nonhuman intelligence often surpassed human intelligence. Raptors, for instance, can see much farther than humans, and the olfactory sense of canines reveals information about the world we cannot fathom. Indigenous peoples respect the superior senses of other beings, and spend time learning by studying their unique gifts.

Norse myths and Native American creation stories portray ravens and crows as exceedingly clever tricksters who symbolize ingenuity and connections between worlds. Scientists, for their part, have recently discovered that corvids, such as crows and ravens, have enlarged forebrains and intricate neural networks, making them capable of complex logic, emotions, and play.[5] Crows and ravens hold a special place in my heart because of their creativity, curiosity, and playfulness.

In ancient Greece, dolphins were considered sacred, and by law dolphins had the same rights as humans. Killing a dolphin was a capital offense. According to legend, the god Apollo assumed the form of a dolphin when creating his most sacred temple at Delphi. Dolphins show up in many mythologies around the world as divine beings with superior intelligence and telepathy. Sacred sites dedicated to dolphins dot the Australian coastline. Aboriginal medicine men in northern Australia were thought to possess telepathic connection with bottlenose dolphins that maintained the flourishing of the tribe.[6] The Tlingit of the Pacific Northwest and the Maori of New Zealand both revere the orca as a powerful ally. Ancient indigenous peoples related to cetaceans as beings of great intelligence—something modern science has just begun to acknowledge.

We now know that cetaceans use tools, have linguistic ability, and possess self-awareness. Some researchers now argue that they meet the social and cognitive requirements for having cultures.[7] The Helsinki Group, founded in 2010, released the Declaration of Rights for Cetaceans: Whales and Dolphins. India's government recently announced that dolphins should be considered "nonhuman persons" and banned their use in theme parks.

Lori Marino, a neurobiologist and president of the Whale Sanctuary Project, argues for the personhood of cetaceans. Her research suggests that the cetacean cerebral cortex evolved along a different evolutionary trajectory than that of other mammals, and that the structural complexity of cetacean brains indicates social-emotional sophistication greater than that of other mammals, including humans.[8]

Octopuses have lately made news as possible aliens that made it to Earth through panspermia. (Panspermia is a theory that life on Earth, or at least some of it, was essentially transplanted here through microbe-bearing asteroids, comets, meteors, and other vectors.) We don't know enough to confirm panspermia (though it is a fascinating theory), but whatever the case, genetic studies show that octopuses have "alien" DNA, meaning it is unlike any other on Earth. In 2015, a study published in *Nature* suggested that what makes cephalopods, especially octopuses, unique is the rapid evolution of large and complex nervous systems.[9] Octopuses have developed many unique adaptations, including cromatophores, which are cells that allow them to camouflage themselves instantly and perfectly. They possess a unique neurology, a large brain, and ladderlike ganglia that distributes their "thinking" into their eight arms. Their arms literally have minds of their own.

Octopuses, aside from being "alien" earthlings, are also clever, creative, curious, and playful. Naturalist writer Sy Montgomery recently shared engaging stories about her emotional experiences with her fascinating cephalopod friends in *The Soul of an Octopus*. She unfolds her story of connection with a few octopuses (possessing very different personalities) over time, and the gift of deeper understanding they gave her of "what it means to think, to feel, and to know." She points out that octopuses, and many other creatures, possess similar hormones to those of humans: "Whether a person or a monkey, a bird or a turtle, an octopus or a clam, the physiological changes that accompany our deepest-felt emotions appear to be the same."[10] Perhaps a great lesson that encounters with diverse nonhuman souls teach us is that we are deeply connected by our shared feelings.

Encounter, or experiencing the more-than-human world through shared feeling and meaning, means that we connect to other beings as fellow subjective centers through interspecies intersubjectivity (I will expand this idea in chapters 8 and 9), rather than through supposedly neutral objective empiricism.

Indigenous people have always associated intelligence with plant life as well. Many non-Western cultures believe that plants hold "spirit wisdom" that humans can access in altered states of consciousness for medicinal and spiritual knowledge. Renowned for their life-giving qualities, many plants serve as teachers and guides. By contrast, science rejects any notion of plant intelligence and views our photosynthesizing kin merely as a means to human ends—such as food or sources of pharmaceuticals. This view is changing with new research and revelations.

A group of visionary plant neurobiologists now recognize that plants communicate through intricate webs of electrochemical signals, similar to what happens in the nervous systems of animals. "This system includes long-distance electrical signals, vesicle-mediated transport of auxin in specialized vascular tissues, and production of chemicals known to be neuronal in animals." In other words, something comparable to nervous systems and brains govern decisions and communication in plants, as well.[11] (See chapter 8, "Creative Synergy.")

The scientific community generally dislikes and discourages applying neurobiology to plants. One well-known plant physiologist stated that scientists who compare plant systems to brains are guilty of "over-interpretation of data, teleology, anthropomorphizing, philosophizing, and wild speculations."[12] These watchwords appear whenever scientists react to a paradigm shift that redefines our place in the universe. If we assume that nature teems with sentience and intelligence, the scientific community dismisses such ideas as a return to what they consider the dark ages of animism. However, it seems to me that before we can reenter the cosmic conversation, and remember how to sing the song of *sacred relationship,* we need to acknowledge the widespread presence of intelligence in the universe. Environmental critic Bruno Latour suggests that one of the great enigmas of Western history is not that there are people "naïve enough" to believe in animism, but rather that people still naively believe in a "deanimated 'material world.'"[13] Animism turns out to be saner than mechanism; not a naïve return to superstition, but rather, a mature re-integration into the intrinsic wisdom present throughout an entirely animate world.

Before we search for nonhuman intelligence, we need to ask, what is intelligence? *Intelligence* derives from a Latin compound of *inter,* meaning "between," and *legere,* meaning "to select" or "choose." The ancient roots of the word imply the ability to make choices. Intelligence at this time is generally defined as the ability to learn and apply that learning to different situations. With this understanding, we can see that intelligence operates at different scales in nature. For example, recent discoveries reveal that even microscopic single-celled organisms such as paramecia employ strategies to search for food. Quorum sensing among some species of bacteria and insects are other examples of intelligence at even the smallest scales of life. Given discoveries like this, some scientists are rethinking previously held positions on intelligence and communication in other species. This perspectival wisdom has been practiced by indigenous peoples for many thousands of years. Instead of assuming that other beings think as we do, it makes more sense to consider what it might be like to *be* them, and how we might be expanded by a more dimensional understanding of other intelligence as fascinating as—or perhaps more fascinating than—our own.

As humans begin to awaken to an animate and sentient universe, our attitude toward reality will change accordingly, and so will our systems. Humanity's assumed priority and dominance will give way to the recognition that our particular form of sentience is just one evolutionary choice among many. It is up to us to make it a good choice by contributing to the overall flourishing of our shared world.

By positing sentience "all the way down," panpsychism could inform and sustain our survival by encouraging a respect for the intrinsic sentience and interrelatedness of all species. Panpsychism, especially process-oriented panpsychism, which I will discuss below, gives primacy to the sacred relationships that regenerate the great conversation, the deep music that resonates through our animate world.

Donna Haraway calls this new world of interspecies relations Terrapolis and describes it as "ripe for multispecies storytelling."[14] Multispecies storytelling means that our story is one of many, a song of many songs. Humans are not special; rather, every species, and every individual in that species, has its unique personality and voice in the great conversation. Every being has its special instrument to play. If we listen deeply, we understand when and how to play our part, and how better to improvise together.

ANCIENT PANPSYCHISM

The panpsychist lineage goes all the way back to the pre-Socratic philosophers. For example, Thales (624–546 BCE), founder of the Milesian school, believed that all matter including stones, had "life" or "soul."[15] His student, Anaximander (610–546 BCE), proposed that a fundamental organizing principle or *archē* imbued all matter with sentience. In turn, his student Anaximenes (585–528 BCE) identified this fundamental source as air. Much like the Navajo holy wind, this air pervades and constitutes everything. Anaxagoras (510–428 BCE), credited with bringing philosophy to Athens, rejected pre-Socratic materialist monism. Instead he envisioned motion or process, rather than substance, as the *archē,* the first organizing principle: "The seed of everything is in everything else." Much like modern physicists, he realized that the universe possesses a fundamental principle of organization.

Empedocles (495–430 BCE) envisioned love and strife as the twin fundamental forces organizing matter. Strife led to chaos, while love acted as an attractor, harmonizing elements. According to Empedocles, love acts as an intrinsic unifying organizing principle, implying universal sentience. In short, the presence of love as a fundamental force means that nature as a whole possesses *selfness.*

Plato's student Aristotle rejected his teacher's metaphysical dualism (of transcendent Forms and immanent matter), instead embracing a version of naturalistic panpsychism or *hylomorphism*. As noted earlier, Aristotle brought Plato's Forms down to Earth by insisting that matter itself possessed an intrinsic in-forming entelechy, guiding the development of all matter from within. For Aristotle, no transcendent Platonic Forms existed; all forms resided naturally within the earthly world. Aristotle's hylomorphism proposed that *ousia,* or being, consisted of both matter and form. I discussed his concept of *entelechia* in the second chapter, where I described it as the intrinsic and purposeful dynamism of matter-energy. Like li and qi in Neo-Confucianism, *morphē* (form) and *hylē* (matter) constitute an inseparable unity. The inherent principle of entelechy shapes matter from within, directing its energy.

Plotinus (204–70 CE), an enigmatic philosopher, transformed Plato's idealistic dualism into a version of theological monism, which emphasizes the universal significance of *nous,* or mind. While ubiquitous, and more developed in higher-order beings, *nous* constitutes the ultimate level of being, the transcendent One—a primordial, omnipotent creator that orients itself within matter in order to return to the One. According to Plotinus, everything is ensouled and a divine unity because of this "world soul." He says of this,

> By the power of the Soul the manifold and diverse heavenly system is a unit: through soul this universe is a God: and the sun is a God because it is ensouled; so too the stars: and whatever we ourselves may be, it is all in virtue of soul.[16]

MODERN PANPSYCHISM

Giordano Bruno (1548–1600), a Dominican friar, philosopher, astronomer, mathematician, and poet, strongly advocated Copernicus's doctrine of a heliocentric solar system, rejecting the Ptolemaic Earth-centered

cosmology that was accepted by the church at the time. Bruno also bra-
zenly proposed an acentric universe—the radical idea that the universe
is infinite and has no center. He also proposed that stars are distant
suns with planets, some of which could sustain life (a view known as
cosmic pluralism). The church accused Bruno of heresy. But most scientists (and theologians) today accept the strong likelihood of a universe
teeming with life and sentience, so Bruno's cosmic pluralism was centuries ahead of its time.

Besides propounding the idea of an acentric universe, thereby con-
tradicting geocentric cosmology, Bruno angered the church authorities
by proposing a panpsychist view of nature. In fact, more than anything
else, Bruno's panpsychism fatally marked him as a heretic. He argued
against the notion of God as an external agent ruling over the Earth
and humankind. Instead, his panpsychist teachings placed God wholly
within the natural world. In *The Expulsion of the Triumphant Beast,*
he made his most famous and dangerous statement: "*Natura est deus
in rebus*" (nature is God in all things).[17] His panpsychist views under-
mined the need for any church hierarchy to mediate between God and
humans. Not surprisingly, the church authorities did not like this. They
tried him for heresy, finding him guilty on multiple counts—including
expressing "wicked words," for which a vise was clamped to his mouth
before he was burned alive at the stake (without the mercy of strangula-
tion). Rather than condemning him as a heretic, I would prefer to can-
onize him as an intellectual visionary for his prescient revelations: the
universe is infinite, unbounded, and matter and mind (which he called
mater-materia) are one.

As recently as 2000, the Catholic church defended its treatment
of Bruno. Panpsychism, the notion that all of nature possesses sentience, contradicts the tenets of many Judeo-Christian forms of religion
(though not all), based upon dualism's separation of body and soul. If
everything, including us, consists of *mater-materia,* then religious lead-
ers cannot mediate the relationship between humanity and creator.

In his dialogue *Cause, Principle, and Unity* Bruno makes it clear that sentience is not the same in all beings, but that everything has a "soul," a "vital principle":

> I say, then, that the table is not animated as a table, nor are the clothes as clothes . . . but that, as natural things and composites, they have within them matter and form [soul]. All things, no matter how small and miniscule, have in them part of that spiritual substance. . . . For in all things there is spirit, and there is not the least corpuscle that does not contain within itself some portion that may animate it.[18]

Radical stuff in an age long before quantum physics. Essentially, Bruno proposed that all matter is sentient to some degree, without claiming that everything is alive or aware in the same way as humans, other animals, or even plants. In other words, centuries ago, Bruno had insightfully distinguished between what some modern philosophers call "heaps and wholes." A table or a rock, for example, is a "heap," an aggregate of sentient parts (molecules and atoms), but tables or rocks per se do not possess "table consciousness" or "rock consciousness." Different levels of complexity and self-organization produce different qualities of sentience. For Bruno, matter is sentient all the way down and all the way up, reaching its apex in Cosmic Mind. He describes this ontology in terms of a triadic monad—God, souls, and atoms. His philosophical genius influenced the works of later philosophers, including Leibniz, and continues to echo in the revelations of modern physics.

In his most famous work, *The Monadology,* Leibniz described a panpsychist ontology. He described monads as the only beings endowed with "true unity." Unlike Plato's idealism, in which the ideal Forms are true and eternal contrasted with the imperfect emanation of matter, Leibniz's physical world is an aggregation of pure monads. He refuted the Cartesian assumption that bodies were separate from souls. Bodies, according to Descartes, were not animate except by means of the soul— hence his mind-body dualism. Leibniz, on the other hand, explained that all substances consist of monads organized into aggregates or complex living systems. He identified four types of monads: humans, animals, plants, and inorganic matter.

Leibniz considered the physical world an expression of divine intelligence, the source of the preestablished harmony among the multitude of monads. His monads self-organize throughout the universe into nested systems, networks, and aggregates. Each monad occupies a unique place in the cosmic web, and each one mirrors all the others in a dance of infinite complexity. This cosmic "mirroring" resembles the Vedic image of Indra's net:

> Every portion of matter can be thought of as a garden full of plants, or as a pond full of fish. But every branch of the plant, every part of the animal, and every drop of its vital fluids, is another such garden, or another such pool. . . . Thus there is no uncultivated ground in the universe; nothing barren, nothing dead.[19]

Leibniz understood monads as centers of creative force, possessing awareness and intentionality. In other words, Leibniz's monads anticipated by hundreds of years a panpsychist view of sentient fundamental subatomic entities. For panpsychists, quantum particles such as photons, electrons, and protons—fundamental units of all matter—consist of bundles of sentient energy, capable of intention and choice. A unit of sentient energy, then, fits the description of a Leibnizian monad.

Leibniz described all monads as having perceptions in the sense that they have internal properties that express external relations. Leibniz's panpsychism accounts for an infinite distribution of life and the unity of sentient energy on a fundamental level. He distinguished between *little perceptions* and *apperception*. Simple substances possess little perceptions, while only animals and humans possess apperception.

Leibniz described different levels of interiority. Simple monads possess a basic interiority, and complex organisms have complex interiority or minds. In Leibniz's era, philosophy placed God at the top of the hierarchy of being; and, consistently with this Christian theological view,

Leibniz presented a hierarchy of monads with God as the prime and ultimate causal agent.

Leibniz also found a way to reconcile entelechy with complexity. Not only does everything possess some kind or degree of interiority, but everything also expresses some deep internal cosmic plan. The organic nature of Leibniz's cosmos of monads differed significantly from the mechanistic worldviews and theories of his contemporaries. Most enlightenment philosophers saw God as the watchmaker who set the gears of the universe in motion. Leibniz saw the divine as intrinsic to the entire cosmos, not beyond it. In this way, Leibniz anticipated the visionary philosophies of Bergson and Teilhard de Chardin, both of whom posited a creative intelligence directing motion and evolution throughout nature.

Schopenhauer's idea of *Wille* (Will) as entelechy fits panpsychism: he made *Wille* intrinsic to all mind—in humans, other organisms, and objects alike. *Wille* sparks all beings, on every scale, into action. As I noted in the chapter "Entelechy," I referred to this spark as the *endloses Streben* or "endless striving." Schopenhauer's vision of endless striving, an unrequited yearning, could result in distinctly pessimistic ontological assumptions. If all we could ever look forward to were striving and more striving, what a depressing and terrifying world that would be! But Schopenhauer also offered us a palliative perspective on a world full of endless striving through his articulation of *aesthetic perception*. His aesthetic way of viewing the world's shimmering archetypal nature provided enchantment to remedy eternal longing and striving. This expanded perception would influence the development of phenomenology.

Johann Wolfgang von Goethe (1749–1832), one of the most famous poets of the Romantic era, was also a scientist and philosopher. He made significant contributions to many areas of knowledge, from the humanities to science. In an 1828 essay, "Nature," he described spirit and matter as fundamentally inseparable: "Since, however, matter can never exist and act without spirit [*Seele*], nor spirit without matter,

matter is also capable of undergoing intensification, and spirit cannot be denied its attraction and repulsion."[20] He believed that raw sensory experience, the most valid part of scientific inquiry, would lead to the development of methodologies based on what the American philosopher and psychologist William James would later call *radical empiricism*. Goethe's *delicate empiricism* would contribute to the development of participatory theory.

THE DAYLIGHT VIEW

Gustav Fechner (1801–1887), founder of psychophysics—a study of mind-body interactions—rejected Cartesian dualism and, instead, felt all nature was *beselt,* or "ensouled." In an Aristotelian-Brunian vein, he attributed mind to nature as a fundamental property of matter-energy. As part of his theory of psychophysics, Fechner presented an *identity hypothesis*—whereby mind and matter are two sides of the same coin, one manifesting as subjective mind, the other as objective body.[21] In this way, Fechner believed he had a solution to the perennial mind-body problem that had mystified philosophers ever since Descartes had split them apart.

According to Fechner's vision, the universe abounds with interconnected life. In his later work, *Life after Death,* he compared the "night view" of materialism to the "daylight view" of panpsychism. For Fechner, the "daylight view" revealed and described an ensouled universe, full of sentience, which he also extended to the afterlife. He believed that by the laws of conservation, nothing is ever lost (including our minds or souls), just transformed. He contrasted this with the sense of isolation and separation wrought by materialism.[22] Fechner, much like Empedocles, regarded love as the ultimate organizing principle that harmonizes the cosmos. Panpsychism, then, offers philosophical and cosmological daylight by recognizing an intrinsic, loving, universal principle. Beyond philosophy, Fechner was more interested in applying psychophysics as an experimental approach to studying the mind.

Seeking a scientific method to study consciousness, he created the foundations for quantitative experimental psychology.

Physicist Ernst Mach (1838–1916) studied supersonic motion and contributed much to later developments in aviation and space travel. Rejecting the works of Schopenhauer and other German idealists, and inspired by Fechner, he identified the fundamental "substance" of reality as "sensation."[23] He concluded that sensation creates consciousness and matter, consequently sensation is ubiquitous, giving his idealism a flavor of what de Quincey calls *consequent panpsychism*.[24] Later on, this radical panpsychist assertion would develop further in the hands of William James and other process theorists.

Although a committed Darwinist, Ernst Haeckel (1834–1919) used his knowledge of biological science to promote a panpsychist ontology. In *The History of Creation* (1868), he rejected the commonplace idea that the data of science support materialism. Instead, he said, modern science and evolutionary theory actually point toward a nondual, panpsychist ontology.

In *The Science of Mechanics,* Haeckel presented chemical affinity as an argument for panpsychism.[25] He recognized that all organisms, even microorganisms, possess sufficient sentience to direct relationships and thus contribute to the evolution of order and complexity. The concept of chemical affinity also influenced later work, such as the endosymbiotic theory of Ivan Wallin, which in turn influenced biologists such as Lynn Margulis and Jan Sapp and the theory of symbiogenesis.

William James (1842–1910) drew inspiration from the works of Fechner, Mach, and Goethe. James wrote that Goethe "had a deep belief in the reality of Nature as she lies developed and a contempt for bodiless formulas. Through every individual fact he came in contact with the world and he strove and fought without ceasing ever to lay his mind more and more wide open to nature's teaching."[26]

Recognizing that reality consists of more than whirling masses of matter and energy, James proposed that an adequate science or cosmology would need to take account of the fact of experience, of subjectivity, of minds, of consciousness—of *sentience*. For this, he insisted, science would need to develop what he called *radical empiricism*. In other words, science would need to acknowledge as valid, not only data gathered through the five physiological senses, but also the data of *any* experience—including, for example, feelings and intuition. These other extrarational and nonsensory ways of knowing require the knower to *participate* in what is known. There can be no separation between the scientist and events he or she studies in the natural world.

In this way, James offered a severe critique of and alternative to the myths of objectivity and reductionism that underlie scientific materialism. For him, as a panpsychist, experience pervades the natural world, so, when an observer studies nature, both knower and known share experiences mutually. Knowledge arises from *intersubjective relationships*.

Recognizing a problem in explaining how multiple "little minds" (e.g., in cells) could combine into a unified mind of the whole organism (a human), James opted for a diluted form of panpsychism called *neutral monism*.

He described consciousness as an ongoing "stream" rather than a succession of states—paving the way for Alfred North Whitehead's elaboration of process-relational ontology. By the end of his life James had concluded that, much like Mach's sensation, reality hinges on experience.

Philosopher Ferdinand Schiller (1864–1937), a pragmatic humanist, contributed significantly to the development of panpsychism. He echoed the work of Schopenhauer and Mach by granting even inanimate objects some sort of interiority—a way of experiencing force. In his great work *Riddles of the Sphinx,* Schiller described a universe alive with dynamic processes and experiences on every level, at every scale: "The notion that 'matter' must be denounced as 'dead' . . . no longer commends itself to modern science," he wrote.[27]

Schiller believed that advances in science enabled both philosophers and scientists to see and acknowledge the aliveness of matter on every scale. In this way, his philosophy offered an antidote to the deadness of Cartesian matter.

PROCESS: POSTMODERN PANPSYCHISM

Alfred North Whitehead (1861–1947) stands out as one of the most influential modern panpsychist philosophers. In his major work, *Process and Reality* (1929), Whitehead developed the idea first presented by Heraclitus that reality consists of "events" not "entities"—process, not substance. This road less taken in Western thought aligns with the cosmologies of many ancient Eastern and indigenous peoples. The Diné concept of the holy wind that blows through and animates everything seems a deeply intuitive understanding of nonlocality and process-oriented ontologies.

Whitehead scholar Christian de Quincey summed up Whitehead's cosmology in three succinct points: First, the "essential nature of reality is not material substance, but organisms in *process*." Second, "universal process is necessarily sentient, unfolding by *feeling*." Third, "all events are mutually co-creating. They interfuse and interpenetrate each other . . . it is a fallacy to speak of the reality of any actuality as an isolated, self-contained entity."[28]

In other words, reality consists of interdependent *experiential embodied events*. Every event has two aspects: mental (sentience) and physical (embodiment). This reminds me very much of the indigenous understanding of synchronicity and nonlocality—all is connected (related) and everything feels and perceives. The universe hums and brims with sentience, unfolding through relationships on every scale. Indeed, nothing or no one could ever *not* be in relationship. This is a very different view from the typical Western notion of a separate self, which has created so much alienation and loneliness.

Despite the immense complexity of Whitehead's philosophy, key elements can be identified easily enough. For instance, the relationship between "actual entities" (studied by science) and "eternal objects" (possibilities studied by philosophy): at every moment, every actual existing thing or event comes trailing clouds of possibilities. The subjective "pole" of every event "prehends" or perceives its range of possibilities and chooses one to "collapse" into the next moment of experience—contributing to the ongoing process that creates novelty in the world by instantiating a new possibility into a new actuality. And so the universe's "creative advance," as Whitehead called it, flows from actuality to possibility to new actuality in a never-ending process. Furthermore, both process and relationship involve interiority—an ability to prehend, or feel, possibilities and actualities. For Whitehead, therefore, nature's processes always involve an element of *choice*—selecting possibilities to embody in the next moment of experience. This was what he called "prehension."[29]

For Whitehead, experience emerges from processual connections within the cosmic organism. "The philosophy of organism is the inversion of Kant's philosophy. . . . For Kant, the world emerges from the subject; for the philosophy of organism, the subject emerges from the world."[30] This inversion radically changes ontology and epistemology, expanding the scope of empiricism.

Sentience, then, exists on every scale, and relationship is the means by which it appears to me. For example, I am sitting here looking up at a mountain. Rather than seeing it as a stationary lump of earth, I see its formation as the result of continuing relationships that create changes that are not readily visible to me. The mountain and I have a relationship, not just because I see it from my desk and I find it beautiful, or because I love to wander through its winding trails, but also because we have both developed out of the same universal processes into a cosmological sea of complexity and motion.

Viewing the mountain with these eyes helps me to respect its life and value it as an ancestral relation. From this perspective, we see nature consisting of a complex web or network of relationships—a beautiful, fluid fabric woven of entelechies, rather than parts in a great mechanism. Awakening to the importance of relationship, and to how relationships create life, offers us a sacralized reality. Instead of seeing matter as deanimated, or even as substance, to be used, controlled, and measured, we choose the radically enchanted perspective that matter is sentient and connected at every level.

Humans do not exist at the top of a meaningless hierarchy—rather, we occupy one strand in the complex and dynamic web of life. The ancient intuition that sacredness requires sacrifice—all life feeds on some other life—echoes Whitehead's concept of "concrescence," the process by which each moment of experience "collapses" a new possibility. In this way, sentience and choice participate in the ongoing flow of reality, as the past flows into the present moment. Nature, a complex, co-creative process, depends upon offerings and exchanges that take place over time—and, as such, can be considered a sacred process.

PANPSYCHISM'S PRESENT

Contemporary panpsychists vary in their explanations for the mind-matter relationship. However, most begin with the assumption that matter possesses an inherent self-organizing capacity that creates order and direction in otherwise random or determined systems. Panpsychism, then, implies inherent entelechy—just as Aristotle had taught.

Author David Skrbina summarizes nine core arguments for panpsychism, which I paraphrase:

Indwelling power. All objects exhibit certain powers or abilities that can be plausibly linked to noetic qualities.

Continuity. A common principle or substance exists in all things.

First principles. Mind is posited as a fundamental and universal quality, present in all things.

Design. The inherent self-organizing capacity of physical processes suggests the possibility, if not the likelihood or necessity, of some purposeful intelligence (entelechy) active throughout the physical world.

Nonemergence. It is inconceivable that mind should emerge from wholly mindless matter.

Theology. Omnipresent God, understood as universal "mind" or "spirit," exists in all things.

Evolution. A combination of continuity and nonemergence arguments. Certain objects (e.g. plants, the Earth) share a common dynamic or physiological structure with human beings, and thus possess mind. This points to the continuity of composition between organic and inorganic substances.

Dynamic sensitivity. Living systems, like all physical systems, respond dynamically to changes in their environment. This inherent responsiveness implies "sensitivity"—an ability to feel and be aware of its surroundings.

Authority. Major intellectuals have expressed an intuitive or rational belief in some form of panpsychism.[31]

Skrbina adds two further arguments from process philosopher David Ray Griffin:

Naturalized mind. Panpsychism "truly naturalizes mind" because it integrates mind deeply into the natural order of the world.

Last man standing. In light of "the terminal failure of approaches built on the Cartesian intuition about matter," panpsychism stands as the most viable alternative.

Skrbina's list provides good reasons for rejecting materialist teleonomy in favor of an active teleology at work throughout nature—in line with a key theme in this book: the intrinsic and ubiquitous presence of sentience in matter. As a result, nature flows with intelligence and meaning.

Skrbina's reformulation of Aristotle's hylomorphism (being results from compound of matter and form) into hylonoism (enminded matter) also beautifully contributes to participatory theory. Skrbina suggests, "My mind is . . . a function not just of the brain, body in environment, but literally the entire universe."[32] His panpsychist participation articulates the quantum-scale connectedness of our minds to the cosmos, and to every other expression of cosmic creativity in the cosmos. It also suggests that we might reenter the great conversation at a higher level of consciousness than before. Participatory theory (especially in its panpsychist formulations) offers us the insight that reconnection to cosmic creativity with new insights about the more-than-human world are crucial to our becoming.

The participatory way of knowing was first elaborated by Goethe and later expanded by Polish ecophilosopher Henryk Skolimowski. Cultural historian Richard Tarnas describes this way of knowing as *participation mystique*, "mystic participation," an idea first proposed by French philosopher Lucien Levy-Bruhl. Tarnas suggests that mystic participation offers a reenchanted understanding that the *anima mundi*, or animate world, "in all its flux and diversity" are "articulated through a language that is mythic and numinous." He describes *participation mystique* as "multidirectional and multidimensional, pervasive and encompassing."[33] Because everything at every scale of the cosmos is always fundamentally complex, connected, creative, and intrinsically meaningful, we can always engage with it through this participatory way of knowing. Coauthor (with Hillary Bradbury) of *The Sage Handbook of Action Research,* Peter Reason applied this "dialogical" way of knowing through what has become known as Participatory Action Research (PAR). Reason has referred to this dialogical form of research as "lived inquiry." Through participation with research subjects as co-subjects, researchers remain open to the transformative quality of shared experience. The transformative aspect of dialogical participation begets new insight, which adds dimension to research.

Ecologist Stephan Harding also expanded the discourse of participation through his descriptions of *encounter*. Harding relates his experience as a young researcher at Oxford University studying the muntjac deer of Britain. While collecting data in the field, he would at times allow his mind to temporarily relax; rather than collecting data, he would just sit among them. This kind of experiencing informed his senses with an unfamiliar but intensely pleasing "contentment." He felt that his "sensing organism" may have informed his work more than his data collection and analysis.[34] Participation does not replace scientific empiricism; rather it informs it. Since that time Harding has touched others with sharing his experience of the more-than-human world through encounter. He offers a way to relate to diverse species on many scales and also many temporalities. His work teaches us that our deep cosmological connection to the cosmos avails us of the experience of communion with other beings if we open to it; that experience offers us not only connected contentment but also a more dimensional view of reality.

In her important book *For Love of Matter: A Contemporary Panpsychism,* panpsychist philosopher Freya Mathews describes encounter as a way of knowing that offers us something different from traditional knowledge: "Knowledge seeks to break open the mystery of another's nature; encounter leaves that mystery intact." Encounter is "open-ended, allowing for spontaneity and entailing vulnerability."[35] Encounter enchants reality through connection to, intimacy with, and the inexhaustible mystery of the *other*. Mathews's sense of encounter teaches us that being solely objective often takes the magic out of our world, whereas viewing reality as an animate, sentient, creative cosmos full of mystery allows us to love the world. We need to see the real magic present in reality so that we can fall in love with the world again.

NATURE'S EXPRESSION

Christian de Quincey says, "We are constantly sharing messages with the world around us, picking them up in our bodymind, processing or metabolizing them, and expressing some residue back. We call this process 'life.'" The significance and meaning of these expressions occurs at every scale—for without those infinite expressions, life could not continue.[36]

The most meaningful times of my life defy description, because they have been experienced in nonordinary consciousness. What secular Westerners see as the most evolved and valuable state of awareness—

ordinary waking, rational consciousness—is a tiny bandwidth on a continuum of consciousness that hums with diverse expressions of meaning. As philosopher David Abram has noted, the absence of human language does not indicate the absence of meaning—actually, it's the other way around. He describes this beautifully:

> The ability of each thing or entity to influence the space around it may be viewed as the expressive power of that being. All things, in this sense, are potentially expressive; all things have the power of speech. Most, of course, do not speak in words. But this is also true of ourselves: our own verbal eloquence is but one form of human expression among many others.[37]

This spectrum of expression creates the dynamic process of nature, full of open systems communicating at every level—a matrix of relationship and communication, a song of many songs.

Many contemporary Westerners have forgotten how to listen to the speech in all things—the deep communication—the dawn chorus of birdsong, and the nonverbal language all around us. The insights of panpsychism and participation offer us a renewed ability to listen to the humming, thrumming, barking, buzzing, flapping, quacking, roaring music of the universe. Mozart said music exists in the silence between the notes. If we are silent enough to listen deeply, not only with our ears but through a participatory way of knowing, we can experience communion with deep and sacred sentience—the music of the universe.

Part 2

MULTIPLICITY-IN-UNITY

5 OPPOSITIONAL DUALITY

The Madness of Mastery

Do you not see what damage has been done to science through this: . . . pedants wishing to be philosophers; to treat of natural things, and mix themselves with and decide about things Divine?

GIORDANO BRUNO

Perhaps Descartes would have been closer to the mark and could have saved Western civilization from four-hundred years of epistemological and ontological dualism—not to mention the pathological consequences of the mind-body split—had he declared, instead of cogito, ergo sum *(I think, therefore I am),* sentio, ergo corpus sum *(I feel, therefore I am embodied).*

CHRISTIAN DE QUINCEY

These days it seems like news and social media alternate between horror and absurdity. Texas cheerleaders and Midwestern dentists pay large sums to trophy-hunt and kill endangered and protected animals. Teen violence and suicide have risen for several decades,[1] while legislators largely prevent death with dignity for the ill and elderly. Antidepressants proliferate in our water supply, along with dangerous toxins. A reality-TV star archcapitalist known for his misogynistic and racist narratives reigns as the forty-fifth president of the United States, delegating power to those who repeatedly prove that they value profit over the well-being of people and places. Their decisions and policies have shown little respect for minorities and indigenous communities, and even less respect for the larger community of nonhuman life. Though scientists overwhelmingly agree that human-caused climate change speeds us toward catastrophe, we continue to drill, frack, mine, and pollute irresponsibly. Patriarchal religious fundamentalists and neofascists engage in brutal hate crimes, targeting minorities and women's rights and violating their bodies. Meanwhile artificial intelligence (AI) and genetic-engineering technology advance faster than our ability to truly understand its ethical implications. The Anthropocene challenges us with many—some old, some new—complex and wicked problems.

This reality seems increasingly dystopian. Many of the science-fiction scenarios once predicted have come to pass. Margaret Atwood, Aldous Huxley, and George Orwell, to name a few, predicted some of the dismal scenarios humanity has wrought in just a century. I wonder how long before this uncomfortably real science-fiction scenario will become the new normal—a long-term existential fact. When we realize the arc of this tragedy begins in a flawed ontology, we understand that only a radical shift in our worldview offers us real possibility.

Science is a simultaneously wondrous and dangerous gift that our species contributes to evolution—one that we must monitor with care. Through science, we can diminish suffering in our world and we can explore the vast universe. However, the shadow side of science causes more suffering than we could have previously imagined. Recent history reminds us that this "objective" way of knowing comes with great responsibility. The word *science* comes from the Latin *scire*, which means "to know, to understand." The Proto-Indo-European root, however, is *skei*, "to split or cut." Reductionism lives within the very origins of the word. Reductive ontologies and the destructive technologies they created have radically and rapidly changed the face of our world. Fossil-fuel consumption and deforestation have disastrously altered the balance of our biosphere—right down to the foundation of life itself: water. Our lakes, rivers, and oceans are increasingly contaminated by chemicals and other pollutants, clogged with plastics. The oceanic circulatory system slows, and lakes and rivers dry up.

In the midst of overlapping ecological crises, we face equally extreme sociological crises as polarized ideologies clash and fight for supremacy. Fundamental religious fanaticism and dogmatic scientism both suppress humanity's best quality—empathy. Materialistic consumerism distracts an anxious or apathetic society plagued by trauma and cognitive dissonance. Ideologies and fantasies comfort us when reality challenges us. Francis Bacon famously declared: "Knowledge is power," and two millennia earlier Plato quoted Socrates: "The measure of a man is what he does with his power."[2] What, then, is the measure of humanity, given how we have applied scientific knowledge in the service of immense technological power?

In the previous chapter, I mentioned Thomas Berry's great conversation. He called the current age, so heavily dominated by humanity, the Anthropocene era. He hoped we would transcend the "mental fixation of our times expressed in the radical division we make between the human and nonhuman." He articulated the need to heal that division and rejoin the great all-species conversation, beginning a new cosmological age that he called the *Ecozoic era*. Berry spoke of our need to experience the universe as composed of "subjects to be communed with" rather than "objects to be exploited."[3] The need is then for communion, or intersubjectivity, rather than extreme subjectivity or objectivity. Knowledge must be balanced by wisdom.

The oldest story could be called *oppositional duality,* which reaches back into prehistory. Whenever unity becomes duality, a relationship begins. It takes at least two to form a relationship. The dynamic exchange between participants generates novelty and creativity. But different kinds of relationships produce radically different consequences. Symbiotic duality *creates* mutual growth and harmony, while oppositional duality *destroys* mutuality by instilling conflict. In nature, *create* and *destroy* do not imply morality. We can, perhaps, view them as impersonal—or transpersonal—consequences of nature's complex processes. Similarly, growth and decay do not involve moral awareness; in nature, nothing is ever good or bad—*it just is what it is.*

Morality requires a minimum of self-reflexive and intersubjective awareness—of values, of goals, and purposes, of what is good or bad for the individual and for the community.

When sentient matter evolves to a sufficient level of complexity, it develops self-awareness. At this point, as participants in relationship negotiate choices in order to sustain or nurture mutual harmony and balance, morality emerges. A smooth evolutionary transition occurs— from comparatively simple relationships in the *physiosphere* to complex organic relationships in the *biosphere* that inform, and then transform into, higher levels of complexity in the *noosphere.* Complex matrices link the noosphere to the biosphere and physiosphere.

By its very nature, any relationship between self-aware participants inevitably raises awareness of *other* as well as *self.* How subjects negotiate this dance between self and other can make the difference between symbiosis and opposition. Every relationship contains the seeds of both. However, when our beliefs and ideologies lean toward opposition and conflict, our relationships reenact and reexpress an ancient and fundamental oppositional quality. Unchecked, the dormant pathology grows in various forms.

Plato's thought created a huge oppositional duality—between perfect, divine Forms and imperfect mundane matter: the ideal Forms alone are real, and all manifestations of the material world are nothing but imperfect reflections or shadows of them. His philosophy heavily influenced later Christianity, which during the Inquisition devolved into brutal dogmatism and reprehensible acts—all rooted in a fundamental dualism. Platonic idealism continues to influence philosophies that view human consciousness as real, while regarding the physical world we inhabit as either an emanation or an illusion.

Perhaps the most destructive idea to emerge from Western consciousness was Descartes's *Cogito, ergo sum*. The Cartesian mind-body split created a new dualism between the domains of the church (soul, mind) and of science (body, matter). By focusing exclusively on the matter half of the split, science rapidly advanced unimpeded by religious dogmas. Furthermore, the Cartesian split not only divided reality in two (creating an ontological dualism), it also split apart different ways of knowing (creating an epistemological dualism). The new science celebrated reason and either marginalized or pathologized other ways of knowing, such as feeling or intuition. The intellect focused its power on knowing the objective physical world, and rejected any knowledge of other worlds, accessed in other modes of awareness beyond reason and intellect.

The Cartesian split separated nature from humanity, with consciousness presiding over creation from deep within the human cranium. Embodied feeling was to be ignored in favor of intellectual thought and analysis. The split also left us with subjective mind outside the external, objective world. Only reason could match the nuance, complexity, and precision of nature, with measurement, calculation, and logic. Descartes had used his method of radical doubt to arrive at his eureka moment: *Cogito, ergo sum*. With that, he launched Western philosophy and science on a course of inquiry and a relationship with the natural world solidly based on *skepticism*. In time, this gave rise to the strong dialectical strain in Western society, the idea that only through strife and conflict—through *opposition*—could progress be achieved and new ideas and inventions come into being.

HOW FAITH BECAME DOUBT
(AND VICE VERSA)

The roots of skepticism can be traced to ancient Eastern idealism. Pyrrho of Elis (360–270 BCE) studied with the gymnosophists (naked philosophers) of India, ascetics who denied the world of matter and the body. These naked philosophers believed that sensory apprehension was faulty, because the world was essentially a product of consciousness. Consequently, the Pyrrhonian school, remained in a perpetual state of inquiry, withholding belief (*epochē,* meaning "check" or "cessation" in Greek). The Stoics, Epicureans, and Skeptics refined Pyrrhonian ideas, including their radical rejection of sensory knowledge, into new expressions of skepticism and antidogmatism.

Fast forward to the Renaissance: appalled at the atrocities of the Inquisition, humanists such as Michel de Montaigne incorporated skepticism as an antidote to religious dogmatism. Montaigne's humanism devoted itself to free enquiry, concerning itself with ethics and morality—the human condition. Though a Catholic dualist, he advocated skepticism of both theological and scientific abstraction and dogmatism. Montaigne, like Bruno, rejected "pedantism." Ahead of his time, Montaigne presaged the dangers of scientism and the isolation of philosophy from the concerns of lived experience. Like other humanists, he concerned himself with the struggles of embodied life and attempted in his essays to imagine the experience of others, human and nonhuman. He famously said, "When I play with my cat, who knows if I am not a pastime to her more than she is to me?"[4] Montaigne was certainly limited by the prejudices of his time but saw clearly that issues of lived experience should remain vital to philosophy and science.

Accepting that doubt and skepticism must be counterbalanced by some possibility of knowledge, classical skeptics embraced more than one kind of epistemology. Even the Pyrrhonists realized that an epistemology based exclusively on doubt could not be sustained. When physiological needs kick in, the body responds instinctively with its own intelligence—expressing an implicit form of *embodied* knowledge. The naked philosophers repudiated embodiment through asceticism. Rather than going to such ascetic extremes, however, the Greek skeptics simply cultivated the practice of *epochē,* suspending all judgment about the external world—similar to the Buddhist concept of *samatha-vipassana,* or "tranquility insight." By practicing *epochē,* the Skeptics learned to live in the world, but not of it. They cultivated a pragmatic *epistemological* attitude that involved suspending rational judgment about the world in favor of direct embodied experience. In the hands of Descartes and his followers, the Skeptics' *pragmatic* mind-world distinction became an *ontological* mind-body, subject-object, split. Whereas the Skeptics had cultivated tranquil minds through a balance of positive regard and non-attachment, the Cartesian split later led to inevitable mind-body conflict and to an attitude of detachment plus objectification—separating the knower from the known. A new oppositional duality arose right at the foundations of modern science.

Unlike Bacon and other humanists, Giordano Bruno rejected dualism. Whereas the church claimed that the "two books" of nature and God were separate, Bruno claimed that the book of nature *is* the true book of God. In other words, God could be found more readily in nature's revelations than in biblical doctrine. In the eyes of the church, neither nature nor human feelings could be trusted. At best, both were corrupt; at worst, they were the devil's playground. This distrust of nature and feeling later gave rise to secular ideologies and to the notorious Cartesian split. By rejecting Bruno's panpsychism in favor of Descartes's dualism, Western scholarship and society broke the human covenant with nature, disrupting our embodied, symbiotic relationship with the natural world.

René Descartes scampered about as a toddler in the Loire region of France as Bruno was being tied to a stake in the Campo de' Fiore in Rome and burned alive for heresy. In the days leading up to this, his tongue and jaw had been clamped into a wooden vise for "holding opinions contrary to the Catholic faith and speaking against it and its ministers."[5] As mentioned in chapter 4, Bruno's beliefs in many worlds, ensouled matter, a heliocentric solar system, and an infinite, acentric universe—assured his death sentence at the hands of the Inquisition. (However, his belief that Mary was not a virgin might have been the proverbial final straw.) Bruno's teachings ran afoul of church dogma and challenged the idea that priests and bishops mediated between sinners and salvation. Defending their power, the church authorities could not let Bruno's teachings go unpunished. Bruno's naturalistic monism, pantheism, and panpsychism threatened the ideological religious dualism that entrenched the power of the church.

Because the church violently suppressed Bruno's work, Western philosophy and science developed from a foundation in Cartesian dualism, rather than Brunian panpsychism. I cannot help but wonder what our world today would be like had Bruno lived and influenced modern philosophy as profoundly as Descartes had.

Descartes's philosophy sparked the Age of Reason, in which radical doubt replaced blind faith. The Age of Reason repudiated the idea of knowledge based exclusively on faith. Renaissance thinkers rejected the idea that skepticism could open a path to truth. Prior to Descartes's method of radical doubt, Bruno had warned that pedants would become philosophers.

Descartes qualifies as a modern visionary in a literal sense: During a fever (possibly due to carbon monoxide poisoning from a wall stove he huddled beside to keep warm), he experienced several visions. As a result, he developed analytical geometry and his famous *cogito,* which confirmed his assumption that everything outside subjective experience should be met with extreme doubt—the position known as *philosophical solipsism.* Cartesian subjectivity also established the subject-object split, which held that everything beyond the human mind lacked sentience. The human ego, therefore, exists alone and apart in a world of insentient objects to be measured, categorized, and observed. In an uncertain world, Descartes elevated doubt to the level of a new faith.

VEXATION SCIENCE AND THE MYTH OF MASTERY

But we cannot single out Descartes as being solely responsible for the consequences of overzealous reason and the scientific method. Others featured prominently in the history of science—such as Galileo, Bacon, Newton, and Hobbes—who likewise excluded mind from the natural world. All the above-mentioned "natural philosophers" promoted the idea that nature and man are separate, the natural world lacks sentience, and that only enlightened Christians had the right to shape the future.

Descartes's contemporary, Francis Bacon, the father of British empiricism, launched a new experimental science that I call *vexation science,* because he describes his approach to science as *vexationes artium,* or "vexation of the arts." Philosopher of science Carolyn Merchant suggests that Bacon was attempting to "intervene" in nature.[6] This kind of vexation, or intervention, pervaded the new science of "mastery." This mastery over nature meant that European Christian men of science felt progress could design a better world.

Bacon's *New Atlantis* inspired utopian visions of a world controlled by science for the benefit of humans (and, in seventeenth century Europe, that meant *Christian* humans). Examples include Thomas Moore's *Utopia,* Tommaso Campanella's *City of the Sun,* and Johannes Andreae's *Christianopolis,* in which humans triumph over nature through science and technology. Andreae's utopia, for instance, presented an orderly picture of Christian brotherhood carving an orderly society from the natural world by application of a relentless, punitive scientific method: "Here in truth you see a testing of nature herself; everything that the earth contains in her bowels is subjected to the laws and instruments of science."[7]

Baconian utopianism asserted that nature might be measured, mapped, and plumbed in the interest of human progress. Subjected to "violent impediments" and transformed by the art of man, nature would render up the best possible world for humanity. Bacon's humanism expressed the radical skepticism of his time. Combined with intrinsic patriarchy, skepticism shaped Bacon's vision of science as an orderly, masculine force to subdue the feminine chaos of nature. In the preface to *The New Organon,* his language emphasized violent treatment of nature as a way to unearth her secrets: Men should "conquer" and "penetrate" nature when attempting to access her "inner chambers."[8] Ecofeminist philosopher Val Plumwood refers to this as "a model of domination and transcendence of nature in which freedom and virtue are construed in terms of control over, and distance from, the sphere of nature, necessity and the feminine."[9] The myth of mastery over the "sphere of nature" justified the many atrocities of colonialism in the name Christianity, reason, and science, creating a utopian vision for the few and a virtual hell on Earth for the many.

Control, domination, transcendence of nature, and the myth of mastery loom large in the Western cultural etho that created the Anthropocene; modern utopian ideas mutated into many current and potential dystopias. I call this phenomenon the *utopian paradox,* which states that for any one utopia there must be potentially infinite dystopias. If sentience composes reality at many scales and temporalities, and diverse centers of desire pervade the cosmos, then one small section of sentience cannot build a world according to its own preferences without harming many others. Heraclitus's proverbial insight that sea water is sustaining to fish but lethal to humans remains particularly relevant. What seems palliative to some may be poison to others. World building must include many voices, or it will always create untold suffering.

Baconian empiricism—vexation science—led to unethical scientism, as colonialism and imperialism (the myth of mastery) led to unethical expansion, exploitation, and enslavement of people (human and non-human) and their places. The terrible triad of colonialism, industrialism, and scientism disseminated the culture of mastery throughout the world; progress became the utopian clarion call that exponentially increased dystopias for many cultures. The madness of mastery manifests in the barbaric spirit of slavery—a possession of the human mind by insanity that harms supposedly separate bodies marked as *other.* But cognitive dissonance inevitably emerges from the fact that deep down, our fundamental connectedness remains the reality. Justifying or legitimizing atrocity through legislation doesn't erase the reality of its deep generational trauma. Frederick Douglass, the abolitionist father of the civil rights movement, once said, "No man can put a chain about the ankle of his fellow man, without at last finding the other end of it fastened about his own neck."[10] Of course, the harm done to enslaved people, nonhuman and human, is always far greater than harm to the oppressor, but that harm remains fastened to a toxic idea that creates and perpetuates a toxic society.

PROGRESS AND PERSPECTIVE

In the preface to *The Great Instauration,* Bacon called for a new form of human understanding to ensure our domination of nature:

> The state of knowledge is not prosperous nor greatly advancing, and [. . .] a way must be opened for the human understanding entirely different from any hitherto known, and other helps provided, in order that the mind may exercise over the nature of things the authority which properly belongs to it.[11]

In this passage, Bacon made his intentions clear: the "state of knowledge is not advancing" and the way forward lay in the exercise of "authority" over the physical world. In the eighteenth century, French philosopher Voltaire described this "advancement" as *progress.*

This future-oriented perspective (which in modern times has morphed into an obsession) not only rejected traditional wisdom, it also instilled a view of time and causality very different from that experienced in indigenous societies. Cartesian clock time pushes Westerners onward, driving them forward into the future—an anxiety-producing experience of time. Western causality rejects any metaphysical understanding of causality, which rips the mystery from being. Our views of time and causality make life into an empty march to the relentless drum of progress. No wonder many young people are tragically opting out of this meaningless march into the void.

Many other cultures view time and causality very differently than we do—as full of dimension and mystery. Ancient Akkadians saw the future behind them and the past in front of them.[12] Likewise, the ancient Greeks believed that the future must be behind them because they could not see it. They inferred that the future must come around from behind, enveloping them.[13] One could only move forward by looking back. Janus, the most powerful god in the Roman pantheon, controlled the unfolding of time. With his two faces, he could look backward and forward simultaneously.

Both indigenous and classical Western philosophies viewed time as cyclical. Oral traditions often begin with an invocation of ancestors and an honoring of ancient wisdom. Like indigenous peoples, the ancient Greeks did not view time as a string of linear causality. Instead, they related to time as recurring in patterns, often involving acausal synchronicities. The ancient Greeks also distinguished between *kairos* (qualitative time) and *chronos* (quantitative time). Beyond mechanistic causality, *kairos* fits modern notions of synchronicity as well as the indigenous idea of sacred time—the idea that time is not linear, but cyclical. Glenn Aparicio Parry says, "An indigenous sense of time . . . includes both *kronos* [sic] and *kairos* and then maybe something more." He points out that indigenous concepts of time developed an "intuitive awareness . . . that recognizes the time to act within a given cycle."[14] To ancient people, time was pattern, cycle, and synchronicity.

By the Renaissance, not only had the concept of time radically changed, so had conceptions of space—and of the relationship between space, time, and self. In the fifteenth century, inspired by geometry, Italian artist Filippo Brunelleschi (1377–1446) developed linear perspective. As a result, the idea that the self looks out on the world from a point in space eventually pervaded Western consciousness. Whereas ancient people saw themselves as a part of the landscape, the new linear perspective made the eye the point from which the future unfolds. My forward-looking self projects itself ever forward into time. The discovery of perspective during the Renaissance, and the associated notion of the self as a dimensionless point, laid the foundations for the Cartesian notion of the ego. The mind did not exist in space, but observed space and its contents from a transcendent point of view. "Progress," then, could be graphed according to a set of coordinates through space (representing linear movement through time).

Our word *progress* comes from the Latin *progrediri,* meaning "to go forward." Following the Renaissance discovery of perspective, the self (and the society of collective selves) "looked forward" to progress. By the early modern period, progress had come to mean *advancement*—specifically, the betterment of humankind. Whereas Cartesian coordinates mapped space, Cartesian subjectivity mapped perception. Although it was not located in space, the dimensionless Cartesian ego-mind existed in time, and time could be mapped according to geometric spatial coordinates. In this way, the Cartesian mind-world split set the scene for the mechanization of time—opening the way for the development of clocks. Beginning innocently enough with Christian Huygens's pendulum clock, the spatialization of time reached its peak with Einstein's notion of space-time. Time devolved into measurements of motions in space (e.g., hands moving on a clock face), governed by universal laws of motion and force. The break with indigenous cyclical time could hardly have been more acute, as time inevitably moved forward like the gears in a clock, and the universe became a perfect celestial machine.

Kepler, for example, who influenced Newton, described how he arrived at his laws of planetary motion: "I am much occupied with the investigation of physical causes. My aim in this is to show that the celestial machine is . . . rather a clockwork."[15] Mechanization took hold in our understanding of life as well. Descartes had famously described animals as soulless machines; humans differed only because the machines of our bodies were animated with souls.[16] In essence, this clockwork ontology described the subjective self as a dimensionless entity moving forward through Euclidean space—a geometric space that could be charted and predicted by the rigorous application of mathematical calculation.

Modern philosophers came to view the universe as a mechanism, populated with entities designed and calibrated by an omnipotent external agent. At the turn of the nineteenth century, theologian and philosopher William Paley described this agent as the "watchmaker."

Many Enlightenment thinkers, including Isaac Newton, believed that in order to understand the mind of God, one must understand the laws of the physical world. Empirical observations seemed to confirm that the laws of nature operated the same everywhere; therefore, accurate calculations could be applied throughout the universe. In his *Essay on Man,* Enlightenment poet and satirist Alexander Pope expressed this intrinsic ordering of the universe.

> *All nature is but art, unknown to thee;*
> *All chance, direction, which thou canst not see;*
> *All discord, harmony not understood;*
> *All partial evil, universal good.*[17]

Pope's poetry echoed Leibniz's idea that God had preordained the best of all possible worlds. However, if God had preordained the universal mechanism—including all submechanisms within it—how, then, would understanding universal laws deliver us from evil? Right/wrong, good/bad, God/Devil, light/dark . . . Christianity delivered a theological cosmology filled with *oppositional,* not symbiotic, dualities.

The problem of evil loomed large during the Enlightenment. At that time, Europe suffered from high infant-mortality rates (as well as high rates of maternal deaths during childbirth). Poor hygiene practices accelerated the transmission of disease and infection. Archaic medical practices (such as bloodletting) killed or maimed more than healed. Child labor tilled the fields. Public executions were held in most towns, often leaving corpses to rot and smell.

In early Enlightenment society, how could people reconcile faith in God with the pervasive presence of evil and the atrocities of everyday life? With the emergence of Cartesian subjectivity, free will had become a controversial subject, plaguing philosophers, scientists, and theologians.

Modern philosophers developed the idea of *nomological determinism,* the idea that the past and present create the future by rigid natural laws, that every event can be traced to some prior events—a logical assumption in a mechanistic, insentient universe.

In England, Hobbes proposed *compatibilism,* the idea that necessary causes (determinism) and voluntary actions (free will) do not exclude each other. In *Leviathan,* Hobbes identified the first link in the universal causal chain as "God Almighty," and claimed that free will forms part of this causal chain. In other words, although God preordains everything, predetermination includes human choices. He challenges the reader to consider: "If a man determine himself, the question will still remain, what determined him to determine himself in that manner?" Ultimately, of course, causality can be traced back to God.

Hobbes famously declared that the natural state of man was "solitary, poor, nasty, brutish, and short." The desire to avoid pain and seek pleasure forced humans to live in community—an extension of the mistrust of the natural world. Just as nature needed to be conquered and subdued, man's natural state was believed to be flawed and in need of rigid control. Human cooperation did not happen naturally, but had to be imposed by society. Echoing Empedocles's notion of universal strife, Hobbes characterized the lot of humankind as "a perpetual and restless desire of power after power, that ceaseth only in death"[18]—amplifying the oppositional duality between love and strife.

OCCAM'S RAZOR AND HUME'S GUILLOTINE

Isaac Newton (1643–1727) wrote the *Principia* trying to understand the "mind of God" in ways consistent with causal determinism. For example, his Third Law of Motion stated: "For every action, there is an equal and opposite reaction." This billiard-ball view seemed to explain why things are the way they are: God wound up the clock; once released ("created"), the clockwork mechanism took over, determining everything that happens in the universe. The billiard ball view also fit well with the scientist's creed based on Occam's razor.

Scholastic philosopher and Franciscan friar William of Occam

(1287–1347) famously asserted his razor-sharp logical principle "Entities are not to be multiplied beyond necessity." This was taken to mean that when you have two competing theories that make exactly the same predictions, the simpler one is the better. For mechanistically minded thinkers, the billiard-ball view seemed an elegant and simple ontology. Euclidian space, mapped by Cartesian coordinates and ruled by Newton's laws, provided the simplest explanation for the way of things. Using Occam's razor, many post-Enlightenment philosophers rejected metaphysics in favor of the certainties of classical physics. We can trace a trajectory from Occam's razor through Descartes's reason-based subjectivity and Bacon's sensory empiricism to the rise of positivism in the twentieth century. Positivism claims that only objective scientific knowledge counts as real—and should be applied to all problems, including psychological and sociological issues.

Applying Occam's razor, British philosopher John Locke (1632–1704) denied that our senses could detect causation; nevertheless, he accepted that causality appears to be the simplest and most logical explanation. A determinist and compatibilist like Hobbes, he attributed the billiard-ball effects of mechanistic causality ultimately to God, and assumed that causes were unknowable.

Unlike Hobbes's pessimistic view of humanity, Locke proposed that because the human mind begins as a *tabula rasa* (blank slate), people could be trained or educated to cooperate, rather than fight and compete in "nature red in tooth and claw." Locke's philosophy, presented in his major work *An Essay Concerning Human Understanding*, argued in favor of human autonomy and, with that, the ability to design one's own life by choosing which experiences to inscribe on the *tabula rasa*. Among his many memorable catchphrases, his defense of human rights to "life, liberty, and property" influenced the authors of the U.S. Declaration of Independence.

Locke believed that we learn how and what to think about the world only through experiences of "primary qualities, such as solidity, extension, motion, number, and figure." He argued that subjective qualities, such as color, taste, smell, and sound do not provide objective knowledge and cannot yield accurate knowledge of the natural world.

Taking a cue from Locke, Scottish philosopher David Hume (1711–1776), in *An Enquiry Concerning Human Understanding*, forcefully argued that our senses never perceive a cause in itself: all we ever see are sequences of effects—one thing happens after another, but we never see an actual thing that we can call a cause. Hume concluded, therefore, that causes cannot be truly known. He famously used the example of a billiard ball moving in a straight line toward another. We can observe the balls collide and ricochet off each other, but we don't see one ball *causing* the other to move. We see a sequence of *effects*—one ball moves, strikes another, both balls move away from each other, but at the moment and point of contact, we don't ever see the first ball *causing* the second one to move. Hume called causes "matters of fact," arguing that "matters of fact" cannot be derived through induction (which involves sensory evidence).

Hume's critique of causality alarmed the scientific world, because all science relies on these two elements of scientific knowledge—sensory empiricism and the concept of causality. Hume had pointed out that these two elements cannot fit together. In short, our senses cannot ever reveal causes. Yet all of science is sense-based and assumes the universality of causality. Hume's critique effectively pulled the foundations out from under science: if we can never know any causes, science loses its power of explanation. For the first time since Descartes and Bacon, the entire scientific enterprise seemed in doubt.

Hume also applied skepticism to morality. Whereas Occam gave us his razor to cut through tangles of competing explanations, Hume gave us a guillotine that severed morality from science by arguing that you cannot deduce an *ought* from an *is*—you cannot use reason to get moral conclusions from nonmoral premises. Not only did Hume throw the entire body of science into question, he also raised doubts about the power of reason to arrive at certainty or moral judgments.

ENLIGHTENMENT'S SHADOW

Enlightenment-era thinkers did not all agree on the way forward. Clearly, a paradigm shift—in philosophy, art, and science—had produced many more challenging questions about the nature of reality and human society. The early empiricists had trusted reason and logic to solve the world's problems. But Hume had cast a great shadow over science by pointing out the unscientific nature of causality. He also applied his guillotine to moral philosophy. Nevertheless, science marched on relentlessly, more and more dominating the consciousness of post-Enlightenment Europeans. The order of things as ordained by the church progressively gave way to empiricism, rationalism, and science.

German philosopher Immanuel Kant (1724–1804) confessed to have been "awakened from his dogmatic slumber" by Hume's critique of causality. Kant's ingenious and novel solution involved a new dualism, this time between *appearances* (phenomena) and *reality* (noumena). This split had (and continues to have) a decisive impact on Western philosophy—effectively sidelining metaphysics in favor of epistemology; Kant has been called the first postmodernist. Reality—Kant's noumenon, *das Ding an sich* (the thing in itself)—transcended our modes of perception and, therefore, we could know nothing about it. Instead, all we ever know—and *can* ever know—are the ways reality shows up or appears in our consciousness (Kant's phenomena).

Kant agreed with Hume that we never perceive a cause in itself. But he rejected Locke's idea that we are born with blank, clean-slate minds. Instead, Kant proposed, consciousness comes with inbuilt mental *categories* right from the start. These categories act like mental lenses or filters shaping what we perceive. Kant included causality among these innate categories. In other words, we can't help but overlay the idea of causality onto the world. It's automatically part of our mental equipment.

Because our minds come with ready-made lenses—the categories—we can never perceive or *know* the world or reality as it is *in itself.* Knowledge, therefore, remains confined to the *appearances,* to whatever shows up in consciousness (phenomena). And because we cannot know *reality,* the business of science and philosophy is to explore the *nature of knowledge* (epistemology), not the *nature of the world* (ontology and metaphysics). After Kant, most Western philosophers regarded metaphysics as pointless. Why spend time speculating about what we can never know anyway? (Whitehead stands out as a major exception to the Kantian tradition, because of the inversion mentioned in chapter 4).

Pierre-Simon Laplace (1749–1827), "the French Newton," applied scientific empiricism to the clockwork universe. He believed that science could restore harmony to society. Given sufficient knowledge about the details of the current universe, and by using the right calculations, we could, at least in principle, know and predict everything yet to come—including events in human society:

> Let us apply to the political and moral sciences the method founded upon observation and calculation, which has served us so well in the natural sciences. Let us not offer fruitless and often injurious resistance to the inevitable benefits derived from the progress of enlightenment.[19]

These "inevitable benefits" seemed obvious to Enlightenment intellectuals, including: the invention of telescopes by astronomers Christian Huygens and William Herschel; the universal laws of Newton and Laplace; Robert Hooke's discovery of the cell; Anton van Leeuwenhoek's discovery of microbes; advances in medicine and surgical technique. Given these and other remarkable successes, the path of Cartesian subjectivity, bolstered with Bacon's empiricism, seemed to validate the march of the Enlightenment and modern science. Given the apparent triumph of the individual ego, rugged individualism seemed the way into a brighter future. We know in hindsight that a shadow cast by that "brighter" rational future looms as the Anthropocene. Every great invention has had a dark side: antibiotics and superbugs, plastics and plastic pollution, nuclear energy and nuclear proliferation—the list increases exponentially.

FAUST AND FRANKENSTEIN

Despite the successes of Enlightenment science (or perhaps because of its success), leading to the invention and development of industrial technology, many philosophers, artists, and writers reacted to the widening gap between human society and the natural world. Motivated in part by nostalgia for the loss of a wild, pristine nature, Romantic scholars challenged the rise of reason, science, and technology as the saviors of humankind. In 1802, the English poet William Wordsworth wrote:

> *Getting and spending, we lay waste our powers:*
> *Little we see in Nature that is ours;*
> *We have given our hearts away, a sordid boon!*
> *This Sea that bares her bosom to the moon;*
> *The winds that will be howling at all hours,*
> *And are up-gathered now like sleeping flowers;*
> *For this, for everything, we are out of tune,*
> *It moves us not—Great God!*[20]

Romantic-era thinkers lamented the impact of urbanization and reckless progress on the environment. Shipbuilding had deforested much of Europe, and the mining and burning of coal devastated landscapes and polluted cities. Urban sprawl had rapidly transformed small towns into cities. By the 1820s, London had earned the nickname "The Great Wen" (a wen is a sebaceous cyst). Industry had replaced heart with profit. Wordsworth's "we are out of tune" foreshadowed Thomas Berry's "broken conversation" between humans and nature. Even as early as the late eighteenth and early nineteenth centuries, people feared the impact of human technology on the natural world—and that the devastation might be beyond repair.

In 1808, Goethe published the first part of his most famous work, *Faust*. In the previous chapter, I mentioned Goethe's panpsychist orientation, his influence on the philosophy of William James, and his early articulation of participatory knowing. Goethe emphasized feeling and experience in his research, especially experiences of the natural world. A polymath and visionary, he contributed profoundly to the humanities, the sciences, and philosophy. Subsequent research—especially in biology—confirm Goethe's early intuitions that *knowing* the world means more than measuring it.

Goethe felt strongly that modernity's endless categorizing, specializing, and analyzing led to fragmented knowledge. He saw hyperspecialization as limiting, and recognized that humanity could integrate knowledge across disciplines even as seemingly disparate as science and poetry.[21] One might say he was an early inter-, multi-, and transdisciplinary thinker. He also cautioned that the mechanistic account of reality led ultimately to materialism and nihilism. He saw progress as humanity's Faustian bargain.

Goethe's *Faust* criticizes modernity's dubious promise of happiness through progress. Faust laments that rationalism failed to give him true wisdom or joy:

> *Alas, I have studied philosophy,*
> *the law as well as medicine,*
> *and to my sorrow, theology;*
> *studied them well with ardent zeal,*
> *yet here I am, a wretched fool,*
> *no wiser than I was before.*[22]

Romantic scholars made feeling rather than reason their dominant epistemology. For Goethe in particular, intensity of feeling revealed true human nature. Romantics, whether philosopher, poet, or scientist, regarded feeling as a requisite for any valid ontology. In general, the Romantic movement celebrated individual resistance to and revolt against overbearing social pressures. The German phrase *Sturm und Drang* (storm and drive) evocatively expressed this sentiment.

Goethe argued that the inevitability of subjective experience in every scientific project prevents true objectivity. He also cautioned against the danger of scientism:

> I would venture to say we cannot prove anything by one experiment or even several experiments together, that nothing is more dangerous than the desire to prove some thesis directly through experiments.[23]

Goethe also critiqued the limitations of the standard scientific method:

> We often find that the more limited the data, the more artful a gifted thinker will become. As though to assert his sovereignty he chooses a few agreeable favorites from the limited number of facts and skillfully marshals the rest so they never contradict him directly.[24]

Foreshadowing philosophers of science Karl Popper and Thomas S. Kuhn, Goethe argued that science cannot establish certain proof, only confirm or disconfirm hypotheses. He recognized the danger of this scientistic closed loop of validity. Goethe predicted that Cartesian solipsism and mad objectivity would lead to eventual disenchantment and nihilism.

As *Sturm und Drang* rippled through Germany's philosophical and literary circles, poet Lord Byron and literary couple poet Percy Bysshe Shelley and author Mary Shelley formed a Romantic literary circle in England. The two poets often wrote about the sublime natural land-scape and the depth of human feeling, the necessary oneness of nature and humankind. Both inspired by Wordsworth, they conveyed the deeper meaning of life represented by the forces of nature.

In 1818, Mary Shelley portrayed science's hubris and humanity's disconnection from nature in her novel *Frankenstein,* a macabre tale of a scientist obsessed with reanimation and the source of life after the death of his mother. Frankenstein's monster clearly represented the shadow of modernity's lurking scientism, the reckless pursuit of knowledge. The title, *Frankenstein: The New Prometheus,* harked back to the Greek myth of Prometheus, who stole fire from the gods of Olympus. Prometheus's hubris cost him dearly: eternal bondage and torture. Shelley's tale echoed the growing Romantic forebodings about technological advancement, and the increased perception of humans as separate from nature. As Frankenstein's monster wanders the bucolic landscape, all of nature's creatures revile him, and he finds love nowhere. While acknowledging the undeniable benefits of modern science and medicine, the Romantics intuited the shadow side of technological progress, the horrors of vexation science, and the arrogance of mastery.

I perceive another prescient message in Shelley's story: a cautionary tale for transhumanism, the belief or philosophy that human-enhancement technology (HET) will help humans evolve. When we have this greater power to alter and create new forms of life, such as cyborgs and hybrids, we have a greater responsibility. As we said before, knowledge-power comes with caveats and requires consideration. When we become technology-enhanced, what will that make us? Will we still be human? More-than-human? Better-than-human? Do human-enhancement technologies offer a truly better world? For whom? How might nonhumans benefit from enhancement? Sacred futurism parts ways with transhumanism when it fails to think beyond vexation science and the myth of mastery. The value of technology must primarily be its compassion. Compassion must become technology's touchstone. So I would ask, can HET make us more compassionate, connected, and creative? To return for a moment to Montaigne's prescient warning toward those who would love knowledge more than wisdom: "Any other knowledge is harmful to a man who has not the knowledge of goodness."[25]

Science became the benefactor of humankind during the nineteenth century. Much like Prometheus's fire, science greatly benefits society when contained by compassion and ethics. Knowledge indeed brings immense power, as Bacon put it; but without compassion, knowledge-power turns sinister. In the search for superobjectivity, knowledge-power denies subjective error and dismisses ethical concerns in the name of progress. This extreme form of positivism amounts to what I call *mad objectivity*.

Goethe rejected the possibility of a truly objective science, cautioning: "The observer never sees the pure phenomena with his own eyes, rather, much depends on his mood, the state of his senses, the light, air, weather, the physical object, how it is handled, and a thousand other circumstances."[26] He insisted that observers, rather than attempting to remove themselves from the object or experiment, must assume they are part of the observational process. Goethe's method offered an alternative to the cold, detached scientific method that concerned many Romantic thinkers. Removing scientists, or anyone, from direct participation within the connected creativity of nature generates observations and ideas removed from that creativity. As Bateson reminded us earlier, the "difference" between human thoughts and nature's works create some of our greatest problems; we are not separate but think as if we are. Goethe's method, *delicate empiricism* (chapter 8), forms another way of understanding phenomena that avoids the madness of hyperobjectivity. He offers us a way of thinking *as* nature.

PROMETHEUS UNCHAINED: POSITIVISM AND UTILITARIANISM

The nineteenth century exploded with invention and innovation. Science made huge leaps that launched the Western world into the age of industrial technology. Charles Darwin proposed his theory of evolution; Louis Pasteur developed his germ theory, and invented antibiotics and vaccines; and James Clerk Maxwell proposed the theory of electromagnetism—taking physics beyond Newton's billiard-ball mechanics. The invention of steel, electricity, the internal combustion engine, the telegraph, and the telephone, along with the massive construction of railroads, wove together a net of commerce and communication that changed the world—a Western world of unbridled progress that expanded throughout the world through colonialism. To the rising middle class, who benefited greatly from these developments, the utopian promise seemed to be coming true.

Discoveries that drastically improved health and reduced mortality rates looked like undeniable evidence that science had cracked the code of nature. After all, wasn't the world becoming a better place? Europe abolished slavery; industrious individuals could profit and gain upward mobility; and diseases could supposedly be treated effectively with a pill or a needle. Science seemed poised to solve nature's great mysteries. According to Pasteur, microbes or germs caused all illnesses: eradicate germs, and eventually we eradicate all illness. Growing awareness that we live surrounded by invisible germs motivated educated people to pay much greater attention to hygiene. Increased hygiene practices helped to prevent the transmission of disease. Maxwell and Michael Faraday unveiled the hidden world of electromagnetism and gave society a new source of power to transform daily life. The ever-advancing successes of science and technology inspired millions to believe that scientific innovation could solve all of the world's problems.

However, Maxwell cautioned overconfidence and criticized the assumption that "in a few years all the great physical constants will have been approximately estimated, and that the only occupation which will then be left to men of science will be to carry on these measurements to another place of decimals." Even Maxwell, a great paradigm-changing physicist (Einstein credited him as a foundation for relativity), acknowledged that the "unsearchable riches of creation" lay beyond the reaches of science in the "mind of God."[27]

Positivism and Christianity played well together in a clockwork universe. However, the success of science increasingly made religious teachings seem obsolete and archaic—certainly as descriptions or explanations of the natural world. The faults of religious morality had been obvious to humanist philosophers, and scientific empiricism highlighted these shortcomings.

Philosopher Jeremy Bentham (1748–1832) in the early nineteenth century, and John Stuart Mill in the middle of that century, sought to improve the world through *utilitarianism*—the philosophical position that the greatest happiness for the greatest number should be the guiding principle of conduct and consequences. Bentham's "felicific calculus" proposed to measure the amount of happiness our actions are likely to cause. Like Hobbes, Bentham believed that pleasure and pain underlay human motivation:

Nature has placed mankind under the governance of two sovereign masters, *pain* and *pleasure*. It is for them alone to point out what we ought to do, as well as to determine what we shall do. On the one hand the standard of right and wrong, on the other the chain of causes and effects, are fastened to their throne. They govern us in all we do, in all we say, in all we think: every effort we can make to throw off our subjection, will serve but to demonstrate and confirm it.[28]

Bentham's positivism and utilitarianism attempted to replace the need for religious morality. Society would flourish through the correct calculation of the most pleasure for the most people. In his view, science rather than religion could solve the problems of humanity—and so the social sciences began. An early proponent of animal rights, Bentham also championed gender and race equality. He believed that religion gave us a flawed and dogmatic morality that led to more pain than pleasure. To him, quantification of morality seemed a rational solution.

John Stuart Mill (1806–1873) expanded Bentham's work to include internal motivations for happiness, such as conscience and self-esteem. Like Bentham, Mill believed that religion could not solve humankind's problems and actually hindered true progress. He advocated sweeping legislative reforms to address slavery, gender inequality, and child abuse. He contributed much to social reform in an age when most children did not have access to education and worked long hours in factories.

Unions did not yet exist to protect workers' rights, and women could not vote. Many of Mills's ideas led to positive changes. However, the application of purely rational, empirical science to social problems had its own inherent dangers and philosophical traps.

Utilitarianism refuted Locke's social contract theory, and other theories of the Enlightenment, which inspired libertarian doctrines such as the U.S. Declaration of Independence. In Victorian England, Bentham's and Mill's philosophy seemed a welcome alternative to religious indoctrination. Utilitarianism seemed a perfect social complement to scientific principles. Ironically, in intellectual circles, faith in doubt (the scientific method) swiftly replaced faith in God, leading to polarization between the lay public and intellectual elites in Victorian England. Before that time, the church reigned over all—educated, rich, uneducated, poor. Empiricism and skepticism seemed to provide a superior epistemology aligned with the new political and economic ideologies.

Charles Darwin contributed to this radical political, ideological, and sociological movement (chapter 6). Darwin published his landmark *On the Origin of Species* in 1859, at the height of the Victorian age. His theory of evolution broke new ground by offering an explanation for the origin and descent of species without the involvement of a supernatural agent. In his theory, design happened purely as a matter of natural "descent with modification" over eons. A deeply religious man, Darwin himself felt disturbed by the implications of this radically new secular ideology. Later, positivists and utilitarian philosophers saw evolution as an obvious example of natural algorithmic processes that, if understood, could be applied to social problems. Many in the scientific community saw Darwin's theory as an argument for atheism, positivism, and materialism. Darwin himself, who wrestled with the implications of his own theory, remained more ambivalent than most of his champions, who became ardently polarized across sociopolitical lines.

The religious equated Darwinism with atheism and the death of absolute morals. Scientists disagreed, but many viewed Darwin's theory as freedom from religious dogma, heralding the advent of a rational, secular society governed by sensory empiricism. Politicians used Darwinism to push their agendas. Society in general, not just the scientific or religious communities, reeled from the implications of Darwin's "dangerous idea" that the great chain was not linked from above, but from below. In a society that still viewed races as different species, the radical suggestion that the entire human species evolved from a single common ancestor met strong resistance (and still does today in fundamentalist religions).

In 1874, fifteen years after Darwin's *Origin*, John Tyndall, physicist and president of the British Association for the Advancement of Science, gave a keynote speech that drew a clear line between science and religion. Before this, in 1872–73, he toured the United States, giving a series of lectures about the promise of science. Tyndall later printed a series of pamphlets on agnosticism, written for the general public. He also lectured about the cultural importance of science for everyone, not just for universities. Tyndall translated science into language lay people could understand and, as such, qualifies as one of the first advocates of popular science.

Biologist T. H. Huxley (1825–1895), known as "Darwin's Bulldog" for championing the theory of evolution, promoted science and agnosticism:

> Agnosticism, in fact, is not a creed, but a method, the essence of which lies in the rigorous application of a single principle. That principle is of great antiquity; it is as old as Socrates; as old as the writer who said, "Try all things, hold fast by that which is good"; it is the foundation of the Reformation, which simply illustrated the axiom that every man should be able to give a reason for the faith that is in him, it is the great principle of Descartes; it is the fundamental axiom of modern science. Positively the principle may be expressed: In matters of the intellect, follow your reason as far as it will take you, without regard to any other consideration. And negatively: In matters of the intellect, do not pretend that conclusions are certain

which are not demonstrated or demonstrable. That I take to be the agnostic faith, which if a man keep whole and undefiled, he shall not be ashamed to look the universe in the face, whatever the future may have in store for him.[29]

The milieu of gentleman scholars that surrounded Darwin, men of reason and science, defied the superstition of the church. They felt a sense of solidarity in the promise of scientific progress, believing that it should prevail over ignorance at all costs. They felt confident that the benefits of science to humanity would eclipse any detriments. Meanwhile, the cultural lives of those same men of reason and science were steeped in sexism, speciesism, and racism. They often used their scientific theories to support vertical hierarchies and societal inequalities. Scientific progress didn't necessarily align with social progress.

MALTHUSIAN STRUGGLE AND SOCIAL DARWINISM

The ancient understanding of the universe was as a unified whole. Parmenides described the universe as a single, unified block of being. Then Plato split apart this unity with his ontological distinction between Heaven and Earth. Descartes's mind-body dualism further removed humanity from nature by excluding consciousness from the natural world. Following Descartes, the major unresolved philosophical and scientific mystery has hinged on explaining the relationship between the fact of consciousness and the assumed insentience of nature.

The third schism occurred after another paradigm shift: empiricism and the rise of scientific materialism threatened both Platonic and Cartesian dualism.

Today, secular materialism views humans as natural products of evolution and places our species at the top of the great chain. Human exceptionalism and opposition remains, carried into a secular modernity through social Darwinism.

Thomas Robert Malthus (1766–1834), cleric and scholar, influenced social Darwinism more than Darwin himself. The "Malthusian catastrophe," named after him, stated that famine and disease check the growth of populations. Malthus repudiated the popular utopianism of his contemporaries, predicting instead a theory of eternal struggle—ordained by God to teach virtue to humanity.[30] In *An Essay on the Principle of Population,* he calculated that humanity's drive to procreate would eventually outstrip available resources. He opposed the Poor Laws—the original welfare system—blaming it for an increase in taxation. He believed that "moral constraint" would most effectively prevent overpopulation and resulting lack of resources. Malthus-inspired hardline policies on poverty and population control showed up in the works of Charles Dickens, which portrayed the bleak poverty rampant in industrial Victorian England. Echoes of Malthusianism reverberate throughout our current political policies.

Meanwhile the characterization of nature as "eternal struggle and competition for resources" influenced Darwin's theory. He acknowledged that Malthus's inspired *On the Origin of Species:* "The doctrine of Malthus [applies] to the whole animal and vegetable kingdoms."[31] For Malthus and Darwin, this "endless struggle" characterized the dynamics of nature—reminiscent of Empedocles's strife and Schopenhauer's endless striving. The struggle, strife, and competition of *Origin of Species* had a greater influence on subsequent biologists and sociologists than the cooperation documented in Darwin's other great work, *The Descent of Man.* Indeed Darwin's later work portrays a more cooperative story of evolution (chapter 6).

Huxley, a staunch advocate of Darwinism, viewed morality through the lens of secular science. He noted: "Science commits suicide when it adopts a creed," hinting at the looming shadow of scientism. Huxley regarded humans as complicated, "unsociably sociable" animals. Inspired by Kant, Huxley believed that humans, compelled to live separate from nature in a civilized world, had to suppress our natural instincts, leaving us with ever-warring internal states.[32] Following Descartes's mind-matter split and Darwinian notions of evolutionary struggle for survival, Huxley saw competition as nature's imperative.

Herbert Spencer (1820–1903), a polymath philosopher, biologist, anthropologist, and sociologist, developed social Darwinism—a theory that supported his liberal political ideas. He presented his synthetic philosophy as an alternative to Christian morality, believing that universal scientific laws will eventually explain everything. He rejected vitalism and intelligent design, as well as Goethean science and everything transcendental. Whereas Huxley elevated agnosticism to a secular faith, Spencer sought to knock the wind out of any remaining teleology.

Independently of Darwin, Spencer saw evolutionary changes as a result of environmental and social forces rather than of internal or external agents, proposing that life is the "co-ordination of actions." In his *Principles of Biology* he proposed the concept of "survival of the fittest, . . . which I have here sought to express in mechanical terms, is that which Mr. Darwin has called 'natural selection,' or the preservation of favoured races in the struggle for life."[33] He famously said that life's history has been "a ceaseless devouring of the weak by the strong."[34] His political and sociological ideas, derived from his evolutionary perspective, deeply influenced postmodern America—in particular, the idea that the fittest in society will naturally rise to the top and create the most benevolent society. Assuming this evolutionary trajectory, Spencer predicted a future of benevolent harmony for humanity.

Spencer's sociological theories ran into paradoxes. Although Spencer believed that "sympathy" inhered in human nature, he saw it as a recent evolutionary development. As in biology, he regarded *struggle* as central to his political ideology, which celebrated laissez-faire capitalism. He even described "cupidity," or greed, as a virtue, exemplified in our times by the Wall Street avarice of Gordon Gecko's "greed is good" slogan.

In 1884 Spencer argued in *The Man Versus the State* that social programs to aid the elderly and disabled, the education of children, or any health and welfare went against nature's order. In his opinion, unfit individuals should be left to perish in order to strengthen the race. His was a cruel philosophy that could be used to justify the worst impulses of human beings. Unfortunately, Spencer's sinister ideologies influence much of our current government's worldview and policy.

Taking its cue from Hobbesian-Malthusian views on nature, social Darwinism justified cutthroat, competition-based sociopolitical ideologies. Many of the isms that plague today's Western consciousness began here, taking a slightly different form. Darwin, Spencer, and many of their contemporaries classified humans into different evolutionary categories. Darwin clearly supported the view that all humans have the same simian ancestors, but that intelligence evolved differently according to sex and race. Although Darwin came from a family of abolitionists, and openly detested slavery, he saw evolution as support for the idea that different humans were better suited to different purposes. In *The Descent of Man*, Darwin cited comparisons of the cranial size of men and women as an indication of men's intellectual superiority. Spencer originally argued for gender equality in his *Social Statics*, but he too attributed different evolutionary characteristics to the sexes and races.

Scientific justifications for racism and sexism seeped into secular society. Christian-based racism focused on the idea of the "heathen savage" contrasted with "noble" and "civilized" Christians, assuming that God had given the Earth to European Christians. This entitlement combined with a fear of otherness to create the belief that other races or ethnicities were not human, further justifying conquest and genocide. Evolutionary racism codified those superstitions, elevating them to supposedly logical assumptions. The dangerous creed of scientism has long since poisoned Western consciousness. In *The Chalice and the Blade*, Riane Eisler says: "Justified by the new 'scientific' doctrines . . . social Darwinism . . . economic slavery of 'inferior' races continued."[35] Not only did scientific assumptions about race and gender create a new kind of slavery but, combined with mad objectivity, they generated a new level of inhumane and hostile policies toward people of color, women, and the more-than-human world. Science "justified" not only exploitation of resources but of humans and nonhumans. Scientism and positivism found justification in social Darwinism, magnifying the myth of mastery through dogmatic materialism.

Following Darwin, Huxley and Spencer advocated a Malthusian view of life as a struggle. Huxley characterized the animal world as a "gladiator show," and asserted "the Hobbesian war of each against all was the normal state of existence."[36] If nature operated on the principle of incessant struggle and competition, then the same logic should be applied to human society. Spencer's lecture tours in the United States inspired archcapitalism, a culture of avarice benefitting the "fittest" in society.

Darwin, Huxley, and Spencer lived in a world barely awakening from the bondage of church dogma. Revolutions in Europe had empowered new leadership based on industry and ability rather than on family title and inheritance. Science promised to solve many problems through a secularized, egalitarian society. But Victorian assumptions about race, sex, and the relationship between humans and nature emphasized progress of the "fittest," justifying runaway capitalism and blind innovation, including a medical industry that places profit before public safety. These problems have been magnified in the United States, dominated by the ideal of rugged individualism. Meanwhile, the split between humans and nature, boosted by archcapitalism, has accelerated the destruction of the global ecosystem. Author Charles Eisenstein observes, "With few exceptions, modern human beings are the only living beings that think it is a good idea to completely eliminate the competition. Nature is not a merciless struggle to survive, but a vast system of checks and balances."[37]

Others reading Darwin rejected the pervasive idea of struggle and survival of the fittest. For example, Peter Kropotkin (1842–1921), a geographer, zoologist, economist, and general polymath, accused Huxley—and to a lesser degree Spencer—of incorrectly interpreting Darwin and his evolutionary theory. In a thorough study of his own, Kropotkin pointed to the ubiquitous presence of cooperation throughout the natural world, including humanity. His great work *Mutual*

Aid rejects the Malthusian conclusions in social Darwinism, and the assumption that natural selection results from competition within species. He describes a world of widespread interspecies and intraspecies cooperation. This alternative reading revived the idea that *mutual aid,* as much as or more than struggle, characterizes life (chapter 6).

HEALING CARTESIAN FRAGILITY

Buddhist teacher David Loy succinctly summarized the pathology of the Cartesian paradigm: "our most problematic dualism is not life fearing death but a fragile sense-of-self dreading its own groundlessness."[38] He describes this fragile sense of self looking for something to fix itself to rather than surrendering to its groundlessness. Cartesian fragility arises from lack of grounding in a relational, living, breathing, feeling web of life. Somewhere between solipsism and objectivity lies the lost self, abandoned in a primeval landscape. Whether religious or secular, Western consciousness suffers from abandonment of self and our connection to the more-than-human world.

This vital consciousness/matter inseparability brings us back to the central tenet of panpsychism. As de Quincey notes, matter "tingles with sentience" in an inseparable unity. Intentions and choices ultimately affect what happens to matter. Indigenous people have long known that what we think affects what is, so their philosophies emphasize prayer and gratitude. Likewise, Eastern spirituality emphasizes balance between critical, deliberative thought and meditative contemplation. The quality of our thoughts creates the quality of our world. This doesn't mean that we can magically think ourselves into the best world. But we must radically think ourselves into a better world. As Donna Haraway puts it, "It matters what thoughts think thoughts."[39] How can we think compassionate, connected, co-creative thoughts toward possible futurity?

Healing Cartesian fragility (the lack of resilience that pervades a rigid, oppositional paradigm) and the struggle paradigm will require us to embrace a different paradigm—based on *the embodied sacred* and *symbiosis*. If nature is a complex, connected creative process in which we always participate (through feeling, thinking, and doing), then *how* we participate matters. How we participate ripples through reality.

Awakening from the trance of mad objectivity, the myth of mastery, and the struggle story, we might face the perils of the Anthropocene through applying nature's connected creativity.

6 SYMBIOSIS
The Gift of Kinship

We are symbionts on a symbiotic planet, and if we care to, we can find symbiosis everywhere.

LYNN MARGULIS

Kinship with all creatures of the earth, sky, and water was a real and active principle. In the animal and bird world there existed a brotherly feeling that kept the Lakota safe among them. And so close did some of the Lakotas come to their feathered and furred friends that in true brotherhood they spoke a common tongue.

CHIEF STANDING BEAR

Symbiosis lies at the heart of the intricately complex web of life. It continuously creates everything we perceive in the living world around us. When we embrace a human or nonhuman loved one—spouse, partner, child, or friend—and feel our hearts fill with care and compassion, our bodies erupt inside with cascades of collaborations—unions and mutual alliances between organs, hormones, nervous, cardiovascular, and other vital systems. This inner dance of cooperation deepens our sense of belonging. *We experience our profound interdependence.*

Our hearts generate strong electromagnetic fields that interact with, and can even regulate, each other. In one moment of love, hearts exchange feeling, energetic fields interact, and a symbiotic ripple moves through the sentient web of life. Our interdependent, embodied sentience connects us with the rest of the ever-dynamic, mutually sustaining environment. Our offerings and gifts to others matter because these deeply felt exchanges compose reality. The more love ripples we make, the better our world gets. That doesn't mean struggle doesn't pervade life for many, if not most, as well. To deny that would be naïve. But it does mean that sharing love ameliorates even the toughest challenges in life.

Even science has moved beyond a simple reductionistic view of life. In the last decade or so, science and society have awakened out of Cartesian sleep to the reality of a microbial world that forms the basis for, and supports, all life. Informed and honest people can no longer deny that biodiversity and cooperation support the ongoing complexity of our biosphere.

Our ancestors intuited this fundamental interdependence, recognizing that humans are just one of many societies on Earth that must support each other for mutual flourishing. Ancient indigenous people always practiced ways of life consistent with the knowledge that all beings exist as systems-within-systems. Lakota Sioux chief Standing Bear described this as our kinship with all beings. Indigenous people have always understood symbiosis—or *sacred kinship*—as the beating heart of nature's connected creativity.

In the previous chapter, I described how this human-nature schism created a deeply problematic oppositional duality that I call the *struggle paradigm*. In an insentient world, the Darwinian struggle of survival of the fittest produces successful species; and in Spencer's social Darwinism, competition leads to personal and organizational success, establishing a vertical, stratified social hierarchy, placing the "fittest" at the top. All of this, so the story goes, comes without a cost because nature doesn't feel anything and has no intrinsic value, and the misery of human masses is considered a necessary sacrifice to capitalist-industrialist progress. The struggle paradigm, a cruel-world narrative, "legitimizes" cruelty and domination, paving the way for rich industrialists to convert the natural world into products designed exclusively for human comfort—especially the comfort of the elite few.

Every sentient being feels the damage and destruction, the dwindling biodiversity, the pollution, because each of us remains inextricably and inevitably connected to nature's process. We not only share a planet but also share the grief and urgent vulnerability that comes of its destruction. We are kin by way of a shared cosmological origin, shared DNA, Earth's water and carbon cycles, and much more. We share the many perils of the Anthropocene, whether we are aware of it or not.

Epigenetic studies reveal how much our own actions as well as the environment contribute to evolution over many generations. DNA mutates in response to radiation, hormones in response to chemicals, and our experience alters dramatically as these inner/outer relationships form and transform our genes. Our relationships, both local and global, form our experience and in turn shape the world. In the social realm, our beliefs and ideologies shape our actions toward one another and the natural world. Kinship serves as an epigenetic preservation strategy; the wisdom of understanding ourselves as related to all beings on many scales, in many temporalities, and through many generations. Indigenous philosophy has always done things with generational wisdom, taking generational kinship seriously. Research shows that generational kinship requires our consideration of what we think, how we relate, and what we do. Our choices ripple through generations on many levels and scales, as inner and outer environments connect through epigenetics. Intergenerational kinship wisdom respects those connections.

The Anthropocenic state of planetary systems shakes us out of our Cartesian sleep, and we must face the volatile aspect of Gaia. Bruno Latour describes the impossibility of our continued indifference, "From now on, *everything is looking at us.*"[1] Christian de Quincey writes that nature "has a mind of its own,"[2] and it fights back in the form of natural disasters such as frequent and immense storms, droughts, floods, and climate change in general. The indigenous prophecy—which says that either we quickly assume our rightful place in the natural world, or we will perish—turns out to be alarmingly accurate. As Lynn Margulis once put it, living species on this planet will "continue their cacophonies and harmonies long after we are gone."[3] If we want to continue to be a part of this magnificent world, we have no option but to cultivate kinship through thinking and acting symbiotically.

At the height of social Darwinism, many different ideas about progress and evolution emerged. Two very different readings of Darwin's evolutionary theory implied different paradigms: one based on struggle and survival of the fittest, the other on cooperation and symbiosis. Cooperation-based models asserted that success or survival did not depend on ruthless competition, but on living cooperatively within complex, interdependent symbiotic systems. These alternative theories held that evolution unfolds through the ability to adapt to change, cooperate, and combine resources.

Peter Kropotkin gained fame for his influence on the development of communism. Just as we can trace many modern Western pathologies to social Darwinism, we can also trace some Eastern European pathologies to Kropotkin's genius, presented in *Mutual Aid*. If we look closely enough, however, buried beneath the ideologies that shaped totalitarian communism, we can find healing philosophies that are shared by many indigenous peoples—in particular, the idea that symbiotic relationships constitute existence. Kropotkin points out that Darwin himself was concerned that his idea of the struggle for existence would be misconstrued. Kropotkin clarified Darwin's intentions, stated plainly in *The Origin of Species,* that the phrase should be understood in a "large and metaphorical sense including dependence of one being on another, and including (which is more important) not only the life of the individual, but success in leaving progeny."[4] Kropotkin argued that mutual aid and cooperation appeared in nature, and that Darwin stated this frequently in his writings.

Naturalists at the time were split by their political and cultural affiliations. Darwin's travels on the *HMS Beagle* greatly influenced his theory of evolution—for instance, when he visited Tierra del Fuego, and encountered the Yaghan people. From his cultural perspective, the indigenous people seemed to him "miserable creatures." Anthropological scholarship reveals that the Yaghan were actually a relatively prosperous and happy people, with a complex language of more than thirty thousand words. Continuous attacks on their herds by European ranchers, along with the introduction and spread of European diseases, decimated their ancient way of life, and eventually the tribe vanished. Darwin's European prejudice led him to view their way of life as uncivilized, which he interpreted as a sign that the descent of man (evolution) coincided with the ascent of culture.

Darwin believed that at the social level, natural selection progressed toward a more Western way of life. Goethe, by contrast, pointed out that every scientific theory includes the observer's mood, and so can never be truly objective. He also cautioned:

> It is easy to see the risk we run when we try to connect a single bit of evidence with an idea already formed . . . such efforts generally give rise to theories and systems which are a tribute to their author's intelligence. But with undue applause or protracted support they soon begin to hinder and harm the very progress of the human mind they had earlier assisted.[5]

In hindsight, we can perceive that Darwin's original thesis as set forth in *The Origin of Species* proposed a biological, not a social theory. Unfortunately, many interpretations of his landmark book focus on just one aspect, leading to various Darwinian sects and variations of social and neo-Darwinism that are reminiscent of religious sects. If we set aside for a moment the privileged, Victorian gentleman-scholar Darwin, with his prejudices and beliefs, the heart of his thesis beats with a reverence for many forms of sentience, and the wish to understand nature's creativity. Darwin's *Descent of Man* focuses on emotions in both humans and animals; this conveys his deep interest in how feeling expresses itself in many creatures. It seems poignant that Darwin spent his last years devoted to the study of earthworms. After years of research he observed, "they deserve to be called intelligent; for they act in nearly the same manner as would a man under similar circumstances."[6] Darwin's later works offer us an understanding of his reverence for many intelligent and sentient beings. He was even known to have publicly reviled vivisection.

Systems scientist David Loye, in *Darwin's Lost Theory,* noted: "We are looking at the theory that most importantly gives rise to and shapes the story of who we are, and how we got here, and what it is reasonable to expect of us and the human future." Loye points to the seed of Darwin's underlying theory buried in his early notebooks: the "evolutionary basis for all we know today as love, including . . . what eventually became *moral sensitivity*."[7] Loye argues that Darwin would have been aware that positing sex as the seed of morality would have been too radical for the Victorian age. In an era that blushed at the legs of chairs and tables, covering them with fabric, sex was not an acceptable topic of conversation. In an era of strict adherence to Christian cultural norms, sex became the original sin, an aberration rather than a natural expression of desire or love.

Loye also points out that in the second-to-last chapter of *Origin,* the words "Mutual Affinities of Organic Beings" appear at the top of every page. He further notes: "Key to the process of evolution, Darwin tells us, is 'the mutual relation of organism to organism' . . . Darwin was already talking about . . . the complementary and eventually transcendent bedrock drive of mutuality, or the cooperative relationship of organism to organism."[8] The leap from one to two, and then to three, began the evolutionary thread of symbiosis, involving a quality of sentience that evolved into the evolutionary imperatives of empathy and mutuality. Loye calls this sentient choice to cooperate as a dyad *organic choice.* Animal morality provides evidence for this tendency toward altruism as organic choice developed through the evolutionary path of many species.

Kropotkin's *Mutual Aid* gives examples of mutuality across, between, and within species. Both Darwin and Kropotkin made the idea of moral sentiment central to their theories, but each approached the topic through a different cultural lens. Unlike Darwin, a member of the industrial upper class of Victorian England, Kropotkin came from exiled nobility, with a princely title but anarchist ideas. Though he was born into a land-owning family, he supported the emancipation of the serfs in 1861. Kropotkin developed a lifelong interest in the lives of peasants that grew during his expeditions to Siberia. Among his peers, he earned the epithet "the Anarchist Prince." His ideas, influenced by Pierre-Joseph Proudhon, opposed growing centralized authority in Europe. Kropotkin believed in restructuring societal systems and redistributing wealth. Like many Russian intellectuals, he believed that capitalism created false scarcity and the desire for privilege. Contrary to the Hobbesian-Malthusian notions of brutish nature and constant struggle, he believed that humanity could organize not only for the purposes of addressing dire needs, but also for the common goal of mutual benefit. Several previous and contemporary scientists in Russia proposed alternative theories that recognized symbiosis as the basis for evolution and life itself. Their theories influenced and supported Kropotkin's ideas of mutuality, and even raised the idea of mutuality to the status of an ontological imperative.

In 1860, before *Origin* was translated and published in Russian, Andrei Nikolaevich Beketov (1825–1902), the premier botanist in Russia, published his essay "Harmony in Nature." In a manner reminiscent of the Buddhist notion of codependent arising, Beketov characterized nature's harmony as "a manifestation of the law of universal necessity . . . the mutual dependence of all the material parts and phenomena of nature." He proposed a positive mechanistic view of interrelated species, using the metaphor of harmony in contrast to Darwin's struggle. Although Beketov strongly disagreed with Malthus, calling his law a "statistical abstraction," he defended Darwin's metaphorical use of "struggle," interpreting it to mean "complex relationships" in nature.[9]

Sergei Ivanovich Korzhinskii (1861–1900), a well-known botanist in St. Petersburg, proposed an alternative evolutionary theory called *heterogenesis*. He sought to explain the perplexing transitional leaps in fossil records that remained unexplained by Darwin's theory. Proposing a form of vitalism, Korzhinskii insisted that these leaps (or "saltations") could be explained only by an intrinsic force that he called "life energy." Much like Aristotle's entelechy, Bruno's *mater-materia,* and French vitalism, Korzhinskii proposed that internal energy creates variation. "Morfoma," the external characteristics, combine with "biont," the "true essence," to produce evolution. The idea of interactive external pressure and internal essence resembled Bergson's and Teilhard's evolutionary theories.

Instead of the Darwinian idea that human progress requires annihilation of the weak by the strong, Kozhinskii promoted the idea that unstable and mutant forms serve as prime agents in evolutionary progress. In his model, the weak also survive because they have an important genetic contribution to make in the future.[10] This implies entelechy, a directive and purposeful force in nature, an idea that remained anathema to many; indeed because of this, Darwin took great care to avoid teleology in his thesis. However, some early supporters of *Mutual Aid,* with its central idea of cooperation, continued to view teleology as compatible with naturalism.

K. F. Kessler (1815–1881), a zoologist instrumental in the Russian naturalist lobby in St. Petersburg, began his career in ichthyology, the study of fish. This led him to believe that despite the appearance of struggle in searching for food, the reproductive life and family ties of fish rely on cooperation. Based on observations, he extrapolated that species who cooperate "proceed further in developing and improving."[11] In an 1879 lecture, "On the Law of Mutual Aid," Kessler described the organizing principle of evolution as "unity and aid to those near." Although he had no objection to the idea of competition and struggle in nature, he argued that they did not form the underlying principles of evolution.

Much like Kessler, Kropotkin held that mutuality took precedence over any other operating principle driving evolution, and took Darwin at his word when he described the use of struggle as metaphorical:

> No naturalist will doubt that the idea of a struggle for life carried on through organic nature is the greatest generalization of our century. Life is a struggle; and in that struggle the fittest survive. But the answers to the questions "by which arms is the struggle chiefly carried on!" and "who are the fittest in the struggle!" will widely differ according to the importance given to the two different aspects of the struggle: the direct one, for food and safety among separate individuals, and the struggle which Darwin described as "metaphorical"— the struggle, very often collective, against adverse circumstances.[12]

Kropotkin described what Loye considers to be the most important of Darwin's considerations, presented in *The Descent of Man*—the evolutionary necessity of mutual aid, or what Darwin calls *virtuous habits:* "We may expect that virtuous habits will grow stronger, the struggle between our higher and our lower impulses will be less severe, and virtue will be triumphant."[13]

Instead of emphasizing competition and survival of the fittest, which put the brute victors at the top of a hierarchy, here Darwin reads more like Kropotkin's description of the fittest as those that cooperate and support each other:

> If we . . . ask Nature: "who are the fittest: those who are continually at war with each other, or those who support one another?" we at once see that those animals which acquire habits of mutual aid are undoubtedly the fittest. They have more chances to survive, and they attain, in their respective classes, the highest development of intelligence and bodily organization.[14]

Kropotkin and his contemporaries sowed the seeds for the idea of organic symbiosis, what Loye calls "organic choice." These "seeds," however, failed to germinate in the "soil" of the dominant competition-based evolutionary theory.

A century later, Lynn Margulis revived the idea of evolutionary cooperation in her endosymbiotic theory, which, like mutual-aid theory, differed radically from the dominant evolutionary and genetic theories.

With the rise of industrialism and plutocracy, theories involving survival of the fittest grew in popularity. Just as centralized government formed the basis for society, the nucleus of the cell with its selfish genes formed the basis for life.

In the late nineteenth century, biologists largely denied the possibility of symbiosis as a factor in evolution. Jan Sapp, professor of biology at New York University, suggests: "The symbiotic interpretation of the cell confronted an overwhelming belief in the nucleus as 'the ultimate court of appeal' in cellular activities." Whereas Darwin's theory seemed to lend support to the struggle view of biological and sociological evolution as a struggle, the hereditary theory of Gregor Mendel reinforced the idea that "cytoplasmic structures were differentiations formed by the nucleus."[15] Very few scientists bothered to explore the nonnuclear cellular material as possible factors in evolution: "The concept of symbiosis continued to oppose an amoral view of cosmic processes."[16] In the early twentieth century, the notion of evolutionary mutualism did not support the late-modern commitment to progress, conquest, and increasing militarization that led up to the First World War. As a result, the idea was relegated to obscurity, except for a few renegade researchers.

In the early 1900s, Russian biologists A. S. Famintstyn, K. Mereschkowski, and I. E. Wallin first hypothesized the symbiotic basis for life by studying cell parts outside the nucleus. Toward the end of the century, Lynn Margulis followed their example, intuiting that those extranuclear parts were "remnant forms of once free-living bacteria."[17]

Andrei Sergievich Famintstyn (1835–1918), a botanist, first proposed the theory of *symbiogenesis,* derived from his study of algal cells. After his work separating algae from lichens, he discovered the symbiosis of algae cells and radiolarias. In his 1906 paper "Symbiosis as Means for the Synthesis of Organisms" he proposed that all organisms emerged as "consortiums."[18]

Konstantin Mereschkowski (1855–1921) also proposed a theory of symbiogenesis in 1910, in *The Theory of Two Plasms as the Basis of Symbiogenesis: A New Study or the Origins of Organisms*. Mereschkowski based his theory on the idea that cellular evolution involved the development of complex cells in symbiotic relationships between less complex cells. He rejected Darwin's natural selection as the basis for speciation, and instead proposed that complexity arose from microbial symbiosis.

Ivan Wallin (1883–1969) collaborated with Mereschkowski, and together in 1927 they published a more complete theory called "Symbiogenesis and the Origin of the Species." Mereschkowski's work suggested that plastids originated from symbionts. Wallin went further, suggesting that eukaryotic cells (ones with nuclei containing genetic material) began as symbionts composed of less-complex microorganisms, such as mitochondria. Wallin's and Mereschkowski's endosymbiotic theory met with ridicule and rejection until the invention of the electron microscope revealed DNA within mitochondria—clearly showing that mitochondria have their own genetic material, and that they once lived independently as individual organisms, which later combined through symbiosis to form more complex organisms.

Modernity largely rejected symbiosis as a primary evolutionary principle, opting instead for the selfishness model aligned with the struggle paradigm. David Loye discusses this, saying that the neo-Darwinists and "super-Darwinists" described several versions of the same basic underlying premise, never fully diverging from the selfish-gene ideology. A continuum of evolutionary models emerged from the paradigm of selfishness and struggle.[19] At the far end of that spectrum, biologist Richard Dawkins proposed his famous selfish-gene hypothesis: that competitive genes drive evolution. In most neo-Darwinian theories, selfishness plays out through blind mechanism, algorithmically driving life's evolutionary processes, devoid of any intrinsic meaning or sentience.

Of course, biologists such as Dawkins don't mean that genes or nature act with literal *selfishness*; these theorists deny any self to nature. Instead, Dawkins and others on that continuum describe nature as indifferent, meaning that there's nothing in nature's processes that cares (or could care) about what happens one way or another.

Use of the terms *indifference* and *selfishness*, popular in current neo-Darwinian circles, reveals a disenchanted view of nature. David Loye calls this *pseudo-Darwinism*. He points out that Darwin himself constantly returned to descriptions of "moral sensitivity" and "love," evidenced in the behavior of many species. He speaks of these qualities as ubiquitous among the nonhuman world, and extends this logic to include man's "instinctive love and sympathy for his fellows."[20] Whereas Darwin acknowledged the presence of emotions such as empathy ("moral sensitivity") and love throughout the natural world, neo-Darwinians ripped the emotions out of nature and replaced them with blind, algorithmic calculations—a pathologically reactive position that turned ideas into ideologies, science into scientism.

Although we cannot reverse the damage done by the widespread objectification of nature and the struggle-for-survival ideology that came with it, we can still choose a different perspective, different thoughts (because it matters how we think), and a different set of metaphors for describing the advance of evolution—such as *cooperation* and *connected creativity*.

The greatest insight offered by ideas of symbiosis and kinship is that evolution has different aspects to it: evolution happens through material contact, but there is an inner life to it as well, full of meaning. Creatures do not co-create on potentially infinite scales simply from blind algorithms; rather, a dimensional world of beauty, meaning, and purpose takes place within these myriad exchanges and offerings.

SACRED SYMBIOSIS AND KINSHIP

Teilhard de Chardin rethought evolution on the basis of Darwin's "other theory," more noticeable in the *Descent*. In *Phenomenon of Man*, Teilhard states:

If there were no internal propensity to unite, even at a prodigiously rudimentary level—indeed in the molecule itself—it would be physically impossible for love to appear higher up, with us, in hominised form. . . . Driven by the forces of love, the fragments of the world seek each other so that the world may come into being.[21]

Much like Empedocles, who said that love creates the world, Teilhard, expanding the positive face of Darwin's theory, pointed to the molecule and to life forms at a "prodigiously rudimentary level" as originators of what we know as love. Rather than indifference or Bertrand Russell's "blind collocation of atoms," we find feeling, sentience, right down at the fundamental level of matter.

Scientists have just scratched the surface of understanding the microbiome that accounts for the greatest planetary populations; we find that we are not only systems within systems, but that systems of microbiota live lifetimes within our bodies and influence who we are. We are only beginning to understand that evolution—including us—has resulted from countless bacterial mergers, and that bacterial cells outnumber human cells ten to one in the average human body. We can no longer deny the intelligence of the superorganism or the creativity of the ecological assemblage (chapters 7 and 8). Sentience, we now realize, does not require brains, certainly not human brains.

The phenomenon of *microchimerism* also holds significant implications for how we understand our interconnectedness. During pregnancy, some of the fetus's cells and mother's cells transfer to one another. This means that the mother and child literally contain each other's cells. And if you are the youngest child, you receive your older siblings' cells as well. That means that close kin actually compose each other. I am a chimera (an organism composed of cells with distinct genotypes) made of not only my mother and my child but also my older sibling's cells. Biologist Margaret McFall-Ngai suggests, "Thus each one of us is a chimera of sorts, our bodies containing the cell-lines of others."[22] This reflection changes the conversation; in many cases, we literally are made up of each other.

Learning more about the intelligence of our planet's many ecosystems begins with becoming students to the most widespread intelligence on our planet: *microorganisms*. They teach us symbiosis and the profound lesson that kinship creates life inside us and all around us.

Endosymbiosis offers us a way to rethink neo-Darwinian models of evolution through bacterial mergers. When Lynn Margulis published her groundbreaking paper "On the Origin of Mitosing Cells" in 1967, she radically changed the conversation by presenting endosymbiosis as a basis for evolution. Margulis took the work of Wallin, Merezhkovsky, and Famintsyn to the next step. She suspected they were correct that "nonnuclear cell parts, with their own peculiar heredity, were remnant forms of once free-living bacteria." This intuition had huge implications: "double inheritance systems inside cells." She expanded her theory of "serial endosymbiosis" by emphasizing the evolutionary importance of "bacterial mergers."[23] Her understanding of life, of evolution, shifted radically:

> I remember waking up one day with an epiphanous revelation: I am not a neo-Darwinist! It recalled an earlier experience, when I realized that I wasn't a humanistic Jew. Although I greatly admire Darwin's contributions and agree with most of his theoretical analysis and I am a Darwinist, I am not a neo-Darwinist.[24]

Margulis argued that "natural selection eliminates and maybe maintains, but it doesn't create," and she argued that symbiosis was *the* major driver of evolutionary change. In *Symbiotic Planet,* she calls serial endosymbiosis theory (SET) a theory of "coming together"[25]—a very different story than the "selfish gene."

Where the reductionistic linear account of the universe failed to envision the incredible complexity of evolutionary processes, Margulis and her transdisciplinary colleagues began to ask different questions, and different answers began to emerge. Margulis and colleague Richard Guerrero stated: "In the arithmetic of life, One is always Many. Many often make one, and one, when looked at more closely, can be seen to be composed of many." Complexity arises from relational processes, and in the case of evolution, new life emerges through symbiosis.[26]

Viewing life from this perspective, relationships form the basis of everything; nothing exists on its own. Nothing is ever one thing only. Our cells carry traces of ancient DNA from primitive single-celled organisms. Our mitochondria, for instance, important structures inside our cells that provide fuel for the operations of life, have their own DNA—remnants of a time when bacteria cooperated by *coming together* to collaborate and form more stable, longer-living composite organisms. When Henri Bortoft says, "Everything is in everything," he speaks a biological truth as well as a metaphysical idea. Each of us forms an ecosystem and a microcosm, and within that microcosm lies another. Interdependence, then, forms the basis of all life. Instead of descending or ascending, life expands into complexity through relational processes. If we view evolution in this manner, humans do not qualify as the pinnacle of complexity. Margulis: "Humans are not the center of life, nor is any other single species. Humans are not even central to life. We are a recent, rapidly growing part of an enormous, ancient whole."[27]

Our significance, then, in this "ancient whole" depends upon what our species offers to the whole. I call this *sacred symbiosis*. When a species evolves from relational processes and mergers, we see nature's connected creativity in action. This usually serves a purpose; for example, symbiosis forms collaborations that serve the whole. And when a species cannot sustain "sacred offering," its creative license may be revoked. Without such sacred kinship, survival of the species in relation to its ecosystem would fail. Many indigenous cosmologies contain the seeds of this fundamental wisdom; that *right relationships* sustain and regenerate the web of life.

In *Animate Earth,* British ecologist Stephan Harding poetically conveys the idea that bacterial mergers essentially transform struggle into cooperation. He asks us to imagine going inside a liver cell to visualize a mitochondrion:

> Savour the recognition that, long ago, the ancestors of this very mitochondrion tamed their aggressive instincts and began to cooperate with the very cells they had once destroyed. Feel the beauty and dignity of this 2-billion year old cooperative association. . . . The mitochondria teach us that independence is impossible—that we all depend on each other.[28]

Harding offers us a way of encountering the more-than-human world on many scales and in different temporalities that we might learn from them.

In this wonderful vision, we discover how the essence of life arises from a choice to cooperate. David Loye's "organic choice," and the endosymbiotic theory of Lynn Margulis—symbiosis, also called *affinity, desire,* and *love*—reflect choices made by multiple organisms on many scales to unite, for one night or for billions of years, to co-create something beyond themselves. Harding offers us a way to experience the meaning held in these bacterial mergers and cosmological unions.

GIFTS AND GRATITUDE

In *The Gift,* poet, essayist, and cultural critic Lewis Hyde discusses how anarchist worldviews, such as Kropotkin's, and gift-exchange systems typical of many indigenous societies "share the assumption that it is not when part of the self is inhibited and restrained, but when a part of the self is given away, that community appears."[29] So by offering a "part of self" we take our place as a natural part of the greater relational web— the "intercentric" exchange. This intrinsic inclination to care opposes Hobbes's idea that selfishness, a tendency to accumulate rather than share, lies at the heart of human motivation.

In *The Old Way: A Story of the First People,* Elizabeth Marshall Thomas describes the gift culture of the Ju/Wasi people inhabiting the Kalahari desert. She describes their concept and practice of *xaro:* "Almost every object in Nyae Nyae was subject to *xaro,* received as a gift from someone else, to be given as a gift to another person later." She enumerates many aspects of this practice embedded in their society. Social upset occurs, she notes, when people "might begin to cite failures of xaro as they cited failures of sharing." Xaro has to be authentic. For example: "A return gift made too soon would seem like a trade, not like a gift made from the heart, and thus would not strengthen the social bond, which was its purpose." In other words, the social bonds formed by xaro grew from an authentic desire to be tied together, and benefit to one was seen as benefit to another. "In a social fabric as tight and thick as that of the Ju/Wasi, what happens to one happens to all."[30]

Western modernity inverted this idea that we exist, first and foremost, as intersubjective social beings. Unlike the embodied, connected proverbial Nguni wisdom of *ubuntu,* articulated by Bishop Desmond Tutu, "My humanity is caught up, is inextricably bound up, in what is yours,"[31] Western hyperindividualism emerged out of the disembodied Cartesian ego. When hyperindividuality rules, we reject the gift of kinship that blossoms through intersubjectivity. Celebrating individuality at the expense of interbeing (as Buddhist teacher Thich Nhat Hanh called it) leads to social systems dominated by a few powerful individuals and to the cruel ideology of trickle-down economics. The reality is that not much trickles down in a rigid, stratified, vertical hierarchy.

By contrast, in gift-sharing and kinship societies, individuals do not win at the expense of society, but rather consider society's shared win as theirs. Riane Eisler referred to this as "linking rather than ranking," typical of the partnership paradigm, and the antithesis to the dominator paradigm.[32] Instead, "empowerment of self and others" characterizes the partnership model. We win together.

James Haywood Rolling Jr., chair of the art education department at Syracuse University, describes the pathology of what Paulo Freire, in *Pedagogy of the Oppressed,* called the "banking model" of education. Rolling presents an alternative *palliative model* that expands on Freire's insights. In his recent paper, "Pedagogy of the Bereft," Rolling suggests that many "profitless exchanges" in modern society include some of our "greatest shared energy resources." Challenging zero-sum capitalism, which emphasizes knowledge as wealth or power and produces "winners" and "losers," Rolling asks: "What if we are each so latent with convertible assets that it is possible to cast off any oppressive condition through self-actualizing . . . emphasizing complex conversation and altruistic transmissions over dialogical exchanges, common purpose over informed praxis, and the deterritorialization of prior boundaries and limitations over the mere awakening of local consciousness?"[33]

We don't just *have* gifts to offer; we *are* gifts—intrinsically so. Rather than solely judging our worth by what we can offer materially, we might nurture the gifts within each being. Humans and nonhumans are not just cogs or commodities in the great corporate wheel but centers of connected creativity. Persons released from their enslavement in a struggle paradigm have the possibility to become a dimensional self. Relationships freed from the enslavement of struggle dynamics, what Eisler and epistemologist Alfonso Montuori call "power over," have the possibility to co-create through "power with."[34] An objectified world of static identities and commodification leaves little room for the dimensionality of intersubjective "profitless exchanges." In sacred kinship, however, we enter into symbiotic exchanges, in which we offer gifts, including our dimensional selves, to one another.

The indigenous people of the Pacific Northwest used potlatch and symbolic wealth-killing ceremonies to prevent the glut of private accumulation that dominates industrial societies. They abhorred too much private accumulation as potentially destructive to the more valued gifts of kinship and symbiosis. The flow of abundance through community supports right relationship and generational longevity. Gifts circulate through the system as a common benefit. In *Silent Theft,* David Bollier says of this, "once a gift is treated as 'property,' once it can be exclusively owned and withheld from the community—its power as a gift begins to wane."[35] Sacred symbiosis and sacred kinship means that we perceive of the immense power in shared gifts. It also means that gratitude for those shared gifts animates our thoughts with desire to always give back, supporting the longevity of our kinship and the integrity of our interdependent systems.

Sharing gifts often implies connected creativity. When we engage in sacred kinship with many diverse beings, we open to new forms of participation. Sacred futurism enacts possible futurity in the Anthropocene through these new forms of participation instead of relying on the stale dynamics of the struggle paradigm. Interspecies intersubjectivity offers us a way to share gifts across species, and to learn lessons from many other creatures. Sacred kinship offers us many lessons toward futurity, from microbial mergers to interspecies creative collaborations (chapter 8).

Scientist and systems theorist Fritjof Capra clarified the importance of symbiosis in our evolutionary destiny: "All larger organisms, including ourselves, are living testimonies to the fact that destructive practices do not work in the long run. . . . Life is much less a competitive struggle for survival than a triumph of cooperation and creativity."[36] Eisler also notes: "By the grace of evolution, we humans are equipped with a neurochemistry that gives us pleasure when we care for others."[37] We are each other (made of the same stuff) and we also need each other. We always remain "symbionts on a symbiotic planet" in the words of Margulis.[38] Thinking as symbionts helps us stay in the practice of offering our gifts with gratitude in recognition that we are deeply and inescapably kin. We might ask: *How can I be a better symbiont today?*

The deep evolutionary drive to connect composes what we perceive as reality. On every scale, beings seek each other, desire and require each other, and reach out to each other in diverse ways; the great conversation takes place through many languages, verbal and nonverbal. Atoms form bonds; bacteria merge; most invertebrates and vertebrates seek contact at least to mate, and often to commune and co-create. We are not singular, atomistic selves, but rather walking cosmoses within the cosmos that contain cosmoses relating to other cosmoses within cosmoses. We also exchange bits of our cosmoses constantly; we are chimeric, made up of the stuff we exchange. We are participating in nature's complex creative process. When we participate through the lessons of symbiosis and kinship, we share our gifts and view each other as gifts.

It is worth asking ourselves, what symbiotic gifts can we contribute to others (human and nonhuman)? What symbiotic gifts are we grateful for, that others (human and nonhuman) contribute to us? When we think beyond commodified gifts, we think in terms of what flows from the self—creativity, intimacy, presence, and love. A future that emerges from the sacred practice of symbiosis and kinship offers diverse people, both human and nonhuman, a more dimensional gift than progress: *possibility.*

7 COMPLEXITY CONSCIOUSNESS

Systemic Wisdom

Reality is therefore as much in the connection (relationship) as in the distinction between the open system and its environment.

EDGAR MORIN

A finite living being partakes of infinity, or rather, has something infinite within itself.

JOHANN WOLFGANG VON GOETHE

When I began to think of the universe as a system, I had a radical awakening. Previously I viewed the world through a Cartesian lens, believing that my consciousness existed separate from everything else. When I began to see myself as an emergent, meaningful cosmos within a plenum of other sentient beings (cosmoses), I suddenly felt a deep connection to all life. I understood that each of us lives inextricably connected to the greater cosmos, and that each of us constitutes a cosmos, a home to countless beings, just as our universe undoubtedly harbors countless other living beings. We can think of ourselves as multiscale, multilayered, and multidimensional, made of stardust and joy, water and tears, part of an infinite unfolding of creative evolutionary forces. As

Goethe put it, we "partake of infinity" while simultaneously serving as home to the "infinite within." Beyond that, we need to recognize and respect the cosmic depth, the infinity, within every being.

Systems thinker Edgar Morin attributes this dynamic process of partaking of infinity and containing infinity—of being both cosmos and cosmic—to the fact that all systems are "insufficient wholes."[1] In other words, living systems are *open systems* that remain both autonomous and dependent throughout their existence. Unlike the modern view of humans living in closed systems, as autonomous wholes in a mechanistic void, our postmodern understanding of complexity reveals a world of open systems—layers of relationships in process.

INSUFFICIENT WHOLES

In the previous chapter, I discussed the concept of symbiosis. I also discussed Riane Eisler's concept of dominator and partnership paradigms. The dominator paradigm, combined with the Cartesian-Darwinian worldview, has magnified the tendency toward anthropocentrism and exceptionalism. The perils of the Anthropocene reflect a deeper and more fundamental pathology in human consciousness, and confront us with the need to address it, lest we become merely part of a stratum in the Earth's crust—fossils to be found, perhaps, in the distant future by other life-forms. Those life-forms might wonder at how quickly we annihilated ourselves. Instead of leaving it to them to wonder, we might begin to wonder now about our brief journey to possible self-annihilation. Unlike the dinosaurs of the Cretaceous era, wiped out by the infamous asteroid Chicxulub, Anthropocene humans face the strange reality of a futureless existence that is self-created. Certainly near-Earth asteroids and plagues have always threatened life on this planet. But the complexity of Anthropocene reality sometimes has us longing for the simplicity of an asteroid. At least we wouldn't feel so confused, so implicated, so inundated with ecological factoids that seem so removed from our daily lives.

As the combination of paralyzing shame and overwhelming information throws us into deeper despair, I suggest stepping back for a moment into the deep wisdom of systems and the possibility of connected creativity. We cannot afford not to act, but we can less afford to act without these deeper insights.

Edgar Morin describes the cosmos as *"unitas multiplex*—multifaceted oneness."[2] Like an ever-turning kaleidoscope, our universe produces infinite variations of complexity. This multifaceted quality gives dimensionality to our world, and yet we recognize that everything in the universe began as elemental, undifferentiated soup. Although we began together, the process of emergence, combining and diverging, generation and dissipation—all these paradoxical life processes, cycles of impermanence—have created multiple levels of cosmic expression. This same fundamental complexity finds expression in Lao Tzu's *Tao Te Ching*:

> *The Tao begot one.*
> *One begot two.*
> *Two begot three.*
> *And three begot the ten thousand things.*[3]

Initially the universe consisted of explosive plasma and radiation, which then condensed into subatomic particles such as electrons and protons. About 380,000 years after our universe began, the first element, hydrogen, formed, followed by the emergence of helium and other heavier elements. (Hydrogen atoms consist of one electron orbiting a single proton.) All matter that exists in our universe fourteen billion years later came into being from combinations of these elements. When we recognize that the shimmer of sentience pervades matter on every scale, we realize that we are all facets of this dazzling cosmic dance of sentient matter. All beings remain inextricably linked to each other—expressions of the universe interacting with itself. I call this *complexity consciousness*.

Complexity consciousness helps us view ourselves linked in a great multiscale matrix of being, in which each being conducts energy and information back and forth between all levels in the living system. In other words, we cannot simply evaluate the importance of any life-form merely by its place in the web of complexity, because nothing exists by itself. All beings depend on each other in an ecology of interconnections, and when we behave as if we are separate, we get into serious trouble. We need to adopt the humility of Morin's insufficient whole; we need to cosustain what has created us. Nor can we simplistically conceive of a being as a mere part in the whole. Every being is a cosmos, an infinity partaking in infinity. We are open, and infinite, wholes.

In previous chapters, I discussed the problems with dualism, reductionism, and materialism. I also discussed an alternative third path, based on the premise of nonduality, symbiosis, and the assumption that sentience exists on every scale. In this chapter, I will expand on how this alternative path dates back to the beginning of philosophy and resurfaces throughout history. I believe that this *third way* offers a path to futurity: complexity consciousness—an expanded awareness that embraces and embodies fundamental interdependence through connected creativity. Faced with what Morin calls "hypercomplexity,"[4] humans need radical new ways of thinking, relating, and acting. Viewed from the perspective of cosmic time, our species has just arrived on the scene. And now, even in the short time we've been around, we face the prospect of, even the *need* for, an evolutionary leap—perhaps before we are ready. Visionary technologist Buckminster Fuller once called this humanity's "final examination." Some think of the Anthropocene as a trial by fire (literally), a wake-up call for our species, or an initiation rite through which we enter maturity. Even these views may still hold the residue of human exceptionalism. Is it really all about us? Another perspective beyond human exceptionalism, held in Bucky's prescient metaphor: unless organisms learn to connect in creativity, they fail the cosmic examination and cease altogether. Co-create or die.

In order to understand how to be creative collaborators in a world of hypercomplexity, we need to embrace complex ontologies and epistemologies that value the co-creative potential of diverse knowledge systems. Pioneering systems theorist and biologist Ludwig von Bertalanffy

(1901–1972), creator of general systems theory and a member of the Vienna school of philosophers, said: "We are seeking another basic outlook: the world as an organization. This would profoundly change categories of our thinking and influence our practical attitudes. We must envision the biosphere as a whole with mutual reinforcing or mutually destructive tendencies."[5]

Complexity consciousness includes the metaparadigmatic viewpoint to avoid the built-in traps of rigid ideologies and cultural agendas. Systemic wisdom avoids such traps by recognizing that every living system—from individual organism to ecosystem—remains both open and closed, always subject to transformational processes.

FLUX AND TAO: ANCIENT SYSTEMIC THOUGHT

The origins of systemic thinking appear in indigenous oral traditions, conceivably dating back to the beginnings of language itself. I have already discussed the Diné concept of *nilch'i,* or holy wind. The sacred hoop of life appears repeatedly in Lakota Sioux and many other ancient indigenous philosophies—indicating an intrinsic understanding of life as a connected system of systems. Written systemic philosophies also appear in both Western pre-Socratic philosophy and Eastern Taoist philosophy as early as the sixth century BCE. In the *Cratylus* (chapter 1), Plato quotes Heraclitus as saying, "all things flow" and "you cannot go into the same water twice."[6] Similarly, Lao Tzu also mentions flow and change many times. Both philosophers examine the paradoxical and process-oriented nature of life.

Heraclitus refers to the paradoxical nature of life as the unity of opposites, intuiting a systemic worldview: "Collections: Wholes and not wholes; brought together, pulled apart; Sung in unison, sung in conflict; from all things one and from one all things."[7] His notion of "wholes and not wholes" predicted an important insight of systemic thought, fully elaborated only in the 1920s: the idea that interdependence forms the basis of life and that each organism constitutes a cosmos in its own right.

COMPLEX SYSTEMS
AND IRREVERSIBLE PROCESSES

Ludwig von Bertalanffy described systems theory as a "general science of wholeness." Von Bertalanffy believed that in order to understand biological and sociological evolutionary processes, scientists would have to take a more holistic, transdisciplinary approach. He also believed that scientific collaboration must replace the extreme specialization of science, which both fosters and derives from an ideology of reductionism.

Classical science focuses on mechanism and reductionism, presenting a clockwork picture of reality governed by determinism and causal interactions. For example, the second law of thermodynamics states that, over time, natural processes composed of complex systems irreversibly and progressively degenerate into disorder (increased entropy). By contrast, von Bertalanffy developed the idea of *open systems,* perhaps his greatest contribution to systems theory. As more powerful microscopes revealed the layered complexity of the world, including networks of molecules and cells, von Bertalanffy suspected that as open systems, complex biological structures escape entropic decay. He knew that life does not work like a clock, always winding down, but as a self-creative, self-sustaining system that defies the second law because creativity injects new order into complex systems, fighting off entropy and producing its opposite: *negentropy.*

Mathematician and engineer Norbert Weiner (1894–1964) formed a transdisciplinary group at MIT where he originated the term *cybernetics* from the Greek word *kybernētēs,* meaning "steersman." Weiner used the example of a steersman to describe the concept of feedback loops present in all systems, mechanical or organic. Cyberneticists' studies of feedback loops in engineering had profound implications and wide applications in many fields. After World War II, Weiner collaborated with the young Gregory Bateson and many other scientists, mathematicians, philosophers, and sociologists. As the benefits of transdisciplinarity became clear, the small but innovative group of cyberneticists welcomed many other disciplines into their research. For example, neurologists used cybernetic concepts to understand neural networks, producing the important revelation that nonlinear feedback governs living systems. Systems theory expanded to incorporate these ideas of feedback, self-organization, self-regulation, and nonlinearity—concepts that helped to build a theoretical bridge from mechanism to organism.

Physical chemist and Nobel laureate Ilya Prigogine (1917–2013) developed the theory of dissipative structures and elal rated the role of self-organization in living systems. His work on self-organization sought to unify general systems theory and thermodynamics, continuing the work of von Bertalanffy and expanding on the work of cyberneticists.

Prigogine faced the problem of the inconsistencies between laws governing biological and physical systems—a topic that remains controversial today. He envisioned the arrow of time as a nonlinear, irreversible trajectory that creates the novelty, diversity, and complexity of life: "We have learned that it is precisely through irreversible processes associated with the arrow of time that nature achieves its most delicate and complex structures."[8] Prigogine described the tendency for living systems to generate new order out of disorder (negentropy). Processes that tend to dissipate not into states of disorder, but that reorganize into higher orders of complexity, he called *dissipative structures*. He envisioned how negentropy prevailed in living systems, and he elaborated on the difference between theoretically reversible systems and observably irreversible processes in the natural world.

Prigogine rejected Cartesian mind-body dualism and the idea that some supernatural soul or mind interferes with or interrupts the natural flow of physical events to produce novelty and new order. Instead, in living systems, creative novelty happens not because of some "frictionless spirit" but because complex dynamic systems involve nondetermined, *nonlinear* processes that spontaneously generate new order. At "bifurcation points," complex processes can either spontaneously fall into chaos or flip the other way and release disorder and entropy, building up new order, more complex structures.

Dualists assumed that the appearance of new order in complex systems had to be caused by the action of some frictionless mind. Prigogine rejected this. Instead, his theory of dissipative structures explained how even purely physical systems, if complex and dynamic enough, could spontaneously generate new states of order (negentropy). Living systems stood out as paradigms of such complex self-organizing processes.

Prigogine rightly rejected Cartesian dualism and the notion that some separate mind could interact with physical matter. Instead he identified the processes of self-organization that naturally arise in complex dynamic physical systems "at the edge of chaos." As a physicalist, he avoided any reference to mind, consciousness, or sentience. For him, self-organization had nothing to do with any self, but referred to the natural spontaneity of complex dynamic systems to generate new order.

Many people in New Age circles who heard about Prigogine's breakthrough work, showing how natural processes can produce novel forms (countering entropy), assumed (incorrectly) that the Nobel-winning chemist had discovered soul or mind in matter. Not so. Prigogine was not a panpsychist who believed that mind or consciousness goes all the way down to the level of cells and below. Instead, he believed that the creative potentials in matter had nothing to do with consciousness or mind but could be explained in *purely physical* terms as natural products of dissipative complex dynamic structures.

Prigogine's study of dynamic systems established the importance of a handful of interrelated concepts, such as intrinsic *self-organization* (meaning that systems tend to organize themselves into higher orders of complexity) and *emergence* (appearance of higher orders of complexity through self-organization). These insights led him to understand time as an irreversible arrow, creating complexity and plurality out of a primordial unity. His work explains how higher orders of complexity can spontaneously arise in complex unstable systems; in other words: *order arises from disorder.* Rather than the determined, ordered mechanism of the clockwork universe, life oscillates on the edge of chaos between order and disorder. In this way, Prigogine's work invites us to revisit the ancient intuition that all is flux and to consider that the promise of certainty is an illusion. Prigogine referred to the radical changes brought about by complexity science as "probabilistic revolution."[9]

Just as the Copernican-Brunian revolution would eventually remove us from the center of the universe to an orbit within an inconspicuous solar system, the probabilistic revolution shifts our perception, perhaps even more fundamentally, from being to becoming. For centuries, materialism has described us as physical, deterministic objects. Now the probabilistic revolution requires us to reimagine ourselves as chaotic (or "chaordic") processes in a web of irreversible complexity, in which every living being is constantly in the process of *becoming* through self-organization, emergence, and interdependence. Edgar Morin calls this revisioning of the universe as a complex cosmos *chaosmos*.

IMMANENCE AND COEMERGENCE

Fritjof Capra describes consciousness as "not a transcendent entity, but manifest within an organic living structure" through a process called *immanence,* which means "construction from within."[10] In systems theory, this tendency toward construction from within—the ability for an organism to self-organize—is called *autopoesis.*

Humberto Maturana and Francisco Varela, both Chilean biologists and the main theorists in the Santiago School, developed the theory of autopoesis through studying chemical systems. They observed that these systems tended to maintain and reproduce themselves through internal networks. Their studies led them to conclude that living systems are "discrete self-producing molecular networks closed in the dynamics of molecular productions, but open to the flow of molecules through them."[11] The molecular and cellular structures of living systems form a boundary around their autopoetic processes in order to maintain structural integrity of the organism. However, that boundary must be permeable enough to allow energy into the system in order to sustain it. I mentioned previously that von Bertalanffy had already described living organisms as open systems. Prigogine suggested that systems can be operationally closed but thermodynamically open, and that the arrow of time is thus irreversible for living systems because they remain open, and therefore they are never static.

Maturana and Varela expanded our understanding of simultaneously closed and open systems by describing organisms in terms of their "domains of existence": "Living systems exist in two non-intersecting domains, the domain of their components as molecular autopoietic systems, and in the domain in which they operate as organisms (totalities) in a medium that makes them possible."[12] A living system operates in two domains: one in which it is self-sustaining, creative, and operationally closed, and another in which it engages others and therefore must be thermodynamically open (meaning it can exchange energy and information with its environment).

For example, I am a system made up of systems, a self-contained whole; but in order to remain alive, I must also take in food and water and eliminate waste. Spatially, the boundaries of my human self move through a mixed living and nonliving medium (the planetary ecosphere) encountering other living organisms and inanimate objects, also structurally organized. Only by moving through this medium do I have my own unique identity as a whole, autonomous being. I could not have become what I am without my biospheric medium.

The fact that organisms consist of structures in a world of structures means we are *structurally determined*. Our structural integrity self-generates from within, and our boundaries retain that structural integrity. Our structure influences our experience and behavior, and our relationships with other structurally determined systems can affect our structure, changing it and altering our experience and behavior. Evolution can be said to take place as a result of changing relationships between structures, both living and nonliving. How our structures interact, creating congruent structural changes, creates the phenomenon that systems thinkers call *coemergence*. Maturana and Varela call this congruence *structural coupling:* "the dynamics of congruent structural changes that take place spontaneously between systems in recurrent (in fact recursive) interactions, as well as the coherent structural dynamics that result."[13] This interactive evolutionary dynamic results from *recursivity,* the perpetual mutually interacting dynamic that occurs between structural systems.

RECURSIVITY AND IMBRICATION

Two significant concepts elucidate what we mean by complexity: *recursivity* and *imbrication. Recursivity* accounts for the simultaneous states of being created and creating, of being and becoming. In cellular networks, recursive loops create the emergence of novel properties and higher levels of complexity, and the same process occurs in societies. Recursivity has created both complex societies and pluralistic unity. Morin discusses the importance of recursivity: "For all processes of self-production, and significant for understanding complexity at the human level."[14] Recursivity occurs because we are thermodynamically open systems. This two-way open/closed aspect of living organism enables exchanges of energy with other systems (that's what "thermodynamically open" means). Morin points out that we are continually compensating "for the dissipation of energy in line with the second law of thermodynamics, and this means we must take in energy from the environment. We do this by ingesting material that contains energy, and to do this we need knowledge of the environment, and in particular knowledge of the organization of the environment." Morin goes on to point out that "self-organization requires an interplay between the knowledge of how to organize the self and the knowledge of how the environment is organized."

Moving from the level of biological organisms to cognition and social networks, we also see recursive loops in action, as well as how autonomy and interdependence create culture, art, dance, and music. I would extend this beyond humans to the more-than-human world. From the waggle dance to the whale song, recursivity creates a world full of connected creativity.

Morin focuses on recursivity within human systems. He describes the hypercomplexity of recursive systems as *imbrication* (a term used to describe how roof tiles overlap). In Morin's words, the better we understand the "highly imbricated" state of humankind and the natural world, the sooner we will be able to become a planetary society. The recursivity within our own skins, between humans in society, and also with the more-than-human world, means that our relational realities overlap, creating cascades and fluctuations that will always affect us. What we do within our medium changes the medium, which, in turn, changes us.

Anthropocene perils require humans to become aware of the ever-greater imbrication of human and more-than-human systems. As our human-created systems affect even the most remote more-than-human systems, our recursive reality insists that we learn the lessons of complexity. We are not separate, but our separate thinking harms our world. As Morin puts it, "Reality is as much in connection (relationship) as in the distinction between the open system and its environment."[15] Thinking separation unravels reality, thinking connection (relationship) regenerates it.

UNITAS MULTIPLEX

In *Homeland Earth,* Morin poetically describes our *unitas multiplex*— multifaceted oneness:

> Every human being is a cosmos . . . Everyone experiences, from birth to death, an unfathomable tragedy, marked by cries of pain, orgasms, laughter, tears, prostration, greatness, and misery. Everyone harbors treasures, deficiencies, faults, and chasms. Everyone harbors the possibility of love and self-sacrifice, of hatred and resentment, of revenge and forgiveness. To acknowledge this is once again to acknowledge human unity.[16]

The complexity worldview seeks to understand what it means to live with the implications of the irreversible, chaotic processes that generate life, which create plurality out of unity, and yet remain unified by what we all share in common: for example, the cycles of impermanence, birth, and death. We all also share subjectivity, what it feels like to be a sentient being. One way or another, we all attempt to engage in inter-subjectivity, expanding our sense of self through relationship. As open/closed living systems, structurally coupled with the wider universe, we strive constantly to coexist within the *unitas multiplex*. Given the complexity of interactions, we live always surrounded by uncertainty, mystery, change, and paradox.

In an uncertain, paradoxical universe, what do we have to hang on to? How can we ever know anything with certainty when chaos seems to rule creation? Systems and complexity theory help us to navigate that frightening territory where the illusion of certainty ends and probability and paradox take over.

The systemic worldview provides a different template for solving problems. It shows us how systems create novelty and breakthroughs through structural change. Therefore, in order to facilitate change, we must change systemic structures. In order to change structures, we have to understand those structures and how they relate to each other.

In an important book, systems theorist Donella Meadows encourages listening to "the wisdom of systems."[17] She explains that in order to address systemic challenges, the best course is to listen to what the system needs in order to support its ability to self-create. She describes the main ways that systems thinkers avoid paradigm traps that lead to dysfunctional systems, focusing instead on ways to reorient systems to produce more sustainable and more compassionate outcomes.

In order to learn the wisdom of systems, we first have to identify patterns associated with certain kinds of systems. By recognizing systemic patterns, we can see how systems structurally create social systems and social structures, economic systems and economic structures, bodily systems and body structures, cell networks and cell structures. All structures have nested structures within them and simultaneously belong to larger systems of which they form parts.

Interactions between systems create the unfolding of our world. In short, we can think of evolution as the process of these systemic interactions. Given this complexity and interdependence, how do we make choices that create resilient, sustainable, and even better, regenerative systems?

Meadows describes how resilience and self-organization play major roles in sustainable systems. She defines resilience as "a measure of a system's ability to survive and persist within a variable environment."[18] Self-organization, as I have said, refers to the ability to self-create, or to generate higher orders of complexity. In other words, over time, complex systems evolve and diversify. Meadows points to one of our societal follies: sacrificing the process of self-organization for "short term productivity and stability." In other words, we hurry to impose organization in the name of progress—a huge systemic error, especially where reductionist technological innovation meets capitalist economics. Systems thinkers recognize the danger of specialization and the wisdom of transdisciplinarity, where open communication between various disciplines tends to mitigate reductionist tendencies.

How often have we heard of pharmaceutical companies releasing minimally understood products only to find that the side effects outweigh the benefits in the long run? Another example: huge chemical manufacturers that distribute chemicals without understanding their interactions with other innumerable chemicals and how they will impact the global ecosystem. Because the ideology of "progress at all costs" lies at the heart of the archcapitalist credo, modernity forges ahead using vaguely understood technology for short-term gain—only to find that it threatens everything that makes life possible and nourishing. By shifting to a systemic worldview, we can examine how well any subsystem supports the metasystem—the medium within which we become what we are and without which we cannot survive. Seeing the interplay between systems requires stepping away from reductionism, and adopting a wider perspective—a kind of metalens that can incorporate all lenses, all world views.

METASYSTEM, METAVIEW

Edgar Morin calls the systems worldview a *metaview* because it allows us to step outside our own society and culture to "see" it better, and to "avoid relativism and ethnocentrism."[19] From a different point of view, we can visualize the combinations that create structures and patterns and generate the shape of life.

In chapter 3, I wrote about metapatterns and discussed the patterns that connect and characterize life. By moving away from a reductionist view, which focuses on the smallest parts of systems, we shift toward understanding the connections between structures within systems and the relationships between systems themselves. Morin says of this crucial shift: "Reality is therefore as much in the connection (relationship) as in the distinction between the open system and its environment."[20] Thinking in terms of relationships not only helps us to recognize the need for a shift to a partnership paradigm but reorients us as observers, because we have to account for our own relationship with whatever we observe.

Objective empiricism sought to remove the observer by splitting apart the perceiving, experiencing subject from the object under investigation. But of course, if we stop to think about this, we realize such objectivity is an impossible myth. We can never completely remove the observer because, first, to observe anything we must be in some kind of relationship with it; but second, and philosophically more importantly: *empiricism means knowledge gained through experience.* If we remove the experiencing subject from scientific inquiry, no science, no knowledge would be possible. It simply cannot be done.

In chapter 5, I discussed how vexation science emerged from the idea that conquest and interrogation of nature could render up its secrets. In *The Great Instauration,* Bacon suggested that science should "harass," "vex," and "squeeze" nature, by what he called "the arts of man"—in other words, science should *torture* nature to force her to yield her secrets. Although Bacon the British empiricist is often contrasted with Descartes the French rationalist, Bacon essentially assumed the Cartesian mind-body split. The idea that science should, or even *could,* get purely objective knowledge from nature took for granted that *subject* (the experiencing scientist) and *object* (the thing being studied) could be separated.

A further consequence of this: the relationship between science (objective humans) and a separate nature (insentient world) could only be a one-way street: nature offering us endless energy and information, with us offering little or nothing in return. Vexation science and colonialism could extract knowledge and resources from nature with no concern about the consequences. Deanimated nature had no intrinsic value, purpose, or rights; it waited "out there" just to serve human needs.

If we see nature as a complex, connected creative process in which we always participate, we understand that our thoughts and relations influence what happens. We are only a small part of this dynamic and dimensional process, but the coming of the Anthropocene means that we have much knowledge-power, and the responsibility to develop greater wisdom. This view radically challenges classical empiricism (of separate subject and object) and recognizes that all of nature—including *us*—is both subjective and objective. Scientific inquiry, therefore, does not rely on "objectivity" but must expand through *intersubjectivity:* the subjectivity of the scientist interacts with the subjectivity of the animate world. Beyond that, when we view nature's connected creativity as sacred, axiology can no longer remain neutral—the touchstone of science becomes lived experience, not solely abstractions. That does not preclude scientific objectivity, but expands it through complexity consciousness.

From the perspective of complexity consciousness, every part of nature's connected creativity offers something to the metasystem—or it wouldn't have emerged in the first place. From that perspective, we might ask: what do human beings have to offer the metasystem?

In *A Pluralistic Universe,* William James cautioned, "Not to demand intimate relations with the universe, and not to wish them satisfactory, should be accounted as signs of something wrong."[21] Complexity consciousness offers us the possibility of intimacy with the universe. But this requires the ability to listen. Rejoining the great conversation means listening to nature's desires, experiences, and needs. Rather than extract the resources and secrets of a commodified, deanimated nature, we must ask questions of an animate more-than-human nature, and then *listen* to the answers—even if the answers are difficult to hear.

Finally, as Donella Meadows pointed out, we must listen to the wisdom of systems. Nature is our metasystem, and without metawisdom guiding us, we cease to be valuable to the evolution of that system. Nature will not suffer fools long. I see the metasystem as like the Hindu goddess Kali, destroyer of arrogance. Even without projecting emotional characteristics onto nature, it's easy to see that it supports those beings that serve their local system, which in turn serves the metasystem. Positivistic desires to manipulate nature's process may be just the kind of hyperordering that nature destroys—not as an anthropomorphic deity or external agent, but by the built-in dynamic discovered by systems theorists: *creative disorder*. In order to rejoin the great conversation within nature, we have to get comfortable and even intimate with chaos and uncertainty.

DIALECTIC TO DIALOGIC

When Ilya Prigogine described the probabilistic revolution, he suggested changing our epistemological toolbox from "interrogation" of nature to a "dialogue with nature."[22] This dialogic quality characterizes systems and complexity thinking. In a world where self-organization leads to emergent new properties, reductionism renders an incomplete picture of life. In order to understand nature's intelligence, systems thinkers engage in dialogic thought, assuming that the wisdom of systems underlies all of existence. Morin notes: "Complexity is also a mode of knowledge when we integrate certain principles: the principle of retroactivity, of connectivity, in a dialogical principle."[23] This principle of retroactivity incorporates the metaview I referred to earlier; the principle of connectivity acknowledges that relationships form the basis of all complex systems (both living and inorganic); and the dialogical principle synthesizes opposites.

Dialogic thinking can heal the oppositional thinking that dominates and limits the present paradigm. Rather than looking for answers
that fit current knowledge, we can begin to ask questions that shift our
understanding. Thinking outside the box becomes *thinking outside the
system that created the box*. In order to think outside our social and cultural systems, we need to hold space for duality and complexity.

From the start, back in ancient Greece, dialectic thought has dominated Western philosophy. It arose as an early attempt to deal with
duality and complexity and disparate viewpoints and opinions. Early
classical dialectic involved a confrontation between a thesis and an
antithesis (two opposing views), resulting in a synthesis that includes
and transcends both views. The contradiction between two viewpoints,
then, can lead to an entirely new thesis.

The original dialectic can be traced back to classical skepticism
and Aristotelian formal logic. German philosopher G. W. F. Hegel
(1770–1831) expanded the dialectical method into what some have
called *trialectics,* so called because any thesis and antithesis generates a synthesis. This triadic pattern turns two logical arguments into
another, third assertion. For Hegel, this synthesis supported his entire
ontological premise: absolute idealism. In *Phenomenology of the Spirit*
he described the triadic transition from subject and object, to Absolute.
Much like Plato's triad of the Good, Beautiful, and True, human
understanding strives toward this Absolute during conscious evolution.
Hegel attempted to unify rationalism and empiricism, bridging the rift
between subject and object, leading him to conclude that all is consciousness (or Spirit), and, therefore, must be approached through logic
that brings one closer to absolute truth.

Hegelian synthesis opened a new approach to understanding the
dynamic nature of reality, which, because of its emphasis on change and
evolution, led to the development of process philosophy. Whitehead
offered a major corrective to the Cartesian mind-body, subject-object
split. He united subject and object, showing how they relate to and
mutually imply each other as phases in a process. Whitehead proposed

a form of process panpsychism, whereby matter (objects) intrinsically possess mind (subjects).

Panpsychists do not believe that sentience and subjectivity exist as separate from matter (dualism), as a rare emergent property of matter (materialism), or as the universally ubiquitous source of everything (idealism). Rather they see sentience as both ubiquitous and inseparable from matter. In other words, matter/mind always go together, inseparably coupled, yet always remaining distinct phases in the process that forms reality out of the objective past and subjective possibilities. Systems theory shares with process philosophy and panpsychism the idea that *relationships* form a central and indispensable role in the formation of reality from moment to moment. From a panpsychist perspective (though not from the perspective of systems theory) those connections fundamentally exhibit some sort of "knowing." A truly dialogic conversation with nature requires the ability to synthesize, because answers often appear paradoxical as a result of simultaneous unity and complexity, order and disorder.

FROM EITHER/OR TO BOTH/AND

Oppositional duality, the tendency to think in terms of either/or— as black/white, up/down, high/low, hot/cold, good/bad, and other binaries—becomes especially pathological when applied to social hierarchies or political rhetoric such as "with us or against us." This kind of thinking influenced our metamyths, creating pernicious binaries throughout; even the idea of an external creator became male as opposed to female. But why wouldn't the creator of the universe or multiverse, if there is one, be nonbinary? Similarly, why would nature be female, rather than nonbinary? These oppositional, binary thoughts limit our ability to expand our understanding of a complex reality, and our ability to navigate a hypercomoplex world.

In *The Mystical Mind,* neuroscientists Andrew Newberg and Eugene d'Aquili, who coined the term *neurotheology,* correlate aspects of human behavior with specific brain regions. They identified seven of these regions as *cognitive operators*. For instance, they describe the "binary operator" that correlates with dualistic thinking, which allows us to "extract meaning from the external world by ordering abstract elements into dyads."[24] We use this operator to make sense of things by comparing them to other things—a useful evolutionary capacity that helps us to order information. However, social conditioning can keep humans stuck in oppositional polarities, leading to ideological dogmatism and close-mindedness. Humans are not unique in binary thinking, but we may be unique in how our binary thinking creates oppositional ideologies.

Morin advocates *dialogical thinking* as a more open-minded alternative to oppositional thinking. He points out that "the universe is not subject to the absolute sovereignty of order; it is the outcome of a 'dialogical' relationship (a relationship that is both antagonistic, concurrent, and complementary) between order, disorder, and organization."[25] Modern physics, chaos theory, and systems science all reveal that we exist in a both/and universe, and so we need nonoppositional ways of knowing and understanding reality.

A return to a more embodied, dialogical thinking and practice will better enable us to navigate complexity. Complexity consciousness gives us a dialogical, systemic worldview that unites subject and object, order and disorder, one and many in a co-creative relationship. Complexity consciousness expands us toward an appreciation of *multifaceted oneness*—the infinite expressions of connected creativity—and also the cosmic depth of each being. Complexity consciousness teaches us respect for the beautiful diversity and shared creativity within and around us. We also learn to value chaos as much as order, the unknown as much as the known, and the possibility held in uncertainty.

Like sitting with a Zen koan, complexity consciousness commits us to the practice of nonattachment to any paradigm, allowing us to be present to nature's sometimes shockingly paradoxical revelations.

Part 3

COMM-UNITY

8 CREATIVE SYNERGY
Connected Creativity

Instead of mastery over nature, the scientist's knowledge would become the synergy of humanity and nature.

HENRI BORTOFT

If we want to attain a living understanding of nature, we must become as flexible and mobile as nature herself.

JOHANN WOLFGANG VON GOETHE

When I was a child, my mother taught me a delightful game. We would go out into the mountains, the beach, or even our garden, and whatever creature we saw, we would try to imagine its experience of the world. Long before I was aware of the important philosophical nature of this game, I used my vivid young imagination to enter the unknowable worlds of many wonderful creatures. I imagined riding thermals upon the outstretched wings of a hawk, circling a rabbit below. Then becoming the rabbit, fearing the looming shadow of the circling raptor, my heart beating out of my chest, I would imagine hopping as quickly as I could toward a nearby hole, the welcoming pungent earth, dark and safe. The game was an attempt to get inside another being's experience, to know how it would feel to *be* that creature.

Children naturally play this game, and often give a voice to nonhuman beings. My daughter, at about five years old, put her ear to a tree, saying, "Trees speak very, very slowly. You have to listen for a long, long time." I remember thinking how right she was—not that we can hear trees' voices as we do human language, but that they speak a different language, a slower, deeper language that emerges out of their own adaptations, systems, and temporal scales. We are just beginning to understand their language and even their cultures. Trees, we now know, participate in communities, nurture their children, and cooperate with their kin. Trees communicate with their arboreal communities through large and intricate mycelial networks in the soil, unnoticed by most humans. The forest ground virtually tingles with nonverbal, nonlinguistic, highly complex communication and conscious interactions. This primordial form of communication supports our planetary ecosystem, and constitutes a kind of organic subterranean Internet.

If we suspend our conditioning and human sensory limitations for a moment and play the game "What is it like to be . . . ?" the world expands into a matrix of dazzling experiential textures. Using a combination of our own intuition, imagination, and learned knowledge, we could envision what it might be like to be many beings. As butterflies, we might experience the floral world in psychedelic patterns accompanied by intoxicating smells. We might yearn to taste nectar with our feet, and then eagerly drink it with our sensitive proboscis. We would seek out other butterflies in flight, softly fluttering together on the breeze in a graceful mating dance.

Or, as humpback whales, we might listen eagerly to the song of another whale reaching us from thousands of miles away as we sing our own elaborate song, receiving and transmitting messages through complex and lengthy orchestrations of our vocal range. Perhaps to attract a potential mate, perhaps to enlist the collaboration of distant friends in a search for food, we would glide through the vastness of the ocean, always compelled to sing. We would sing our alliances, rivalries, and yearning—colossal bards traversing the depths.

As canines, we might rejoice at the prospect of a walk with our human companion, knowing that in every spot of urine, or glandular marking, literally around every corner, upon every breeze, a world of information and meaning awaits. We might receive thousands of messages through what my family refers to as our canine family member's "pee mail." As dogs, we would be eager to mark and sniff the same spots, carrying on olfactory-dependent conversations, with neighborhood friends or adversaries. We might imagine all the vehicles for carrying smells: the ground, the wind, a passing garbage truck . . . all potentially conveyors of vital, or maybe just interesting, information. A dog's sense of smell, if we suddenly had it, would undoubtedly rock our worlds to the core.

Putting ourselves inside the experience of another being—a mind-expanding practice, and an intuitive and ancient way of thinking—allows us to understand more about the world around us.

Children naturally tend to play this game, prompted by an intuitive longing to connect with and understand their world. I don't think it's just a coincidence that the "what is it like to be . . . ?" game also happens to be a brilliant philosophical inquiry and epistemological tool. Given an encouraging environment, children grow into natural philosophers and tend to ask the most relevant philosophical questions. If you have been around children in their fourth or fifth year, you might hear them repeatedly ask "why?" in a seemingly infinite regress.

Small children, not yet bound by social constraints, instinctively enjoy a process of discovery, seeking the limits and boundaries of their world, letting their imaginations run wild. However, by the time Western children reach age seven, most of them "know" that trees don't speak. They have also learned that the experiences of nonhuman beings matter little to their society. In response to social conditioning, they come to believe that the more human-seeming an animal is, the smarter it must be.

But we might ask: Are humans smarter? Are human experiences more valuable than any others? Does it matter that butterflies see in ultraviolet? Does it matter that whales sing precise, lengthy, elaborate songs? Does it matter that dogs have a sense of smell ten thousand times more sensitive than that of humans? Does it matter that trees communicate through subterranean fungal networks? This chapter suggests that it matters, because the more we understand about the amazing abilities and experiences of nonhumans, the more we will have the humility we need for a participatory and partnership-oriented worldview. Enactment of sacred symbiosis and kinship requires cultural humility that extends to nonhumans.

John Muir, grandfather of the environmental movement in the West, intuited that consciousness exists throughout the natural world. He had a deep sense that nature was "endowed with sensations that we in our blind exclusive perfection can have no manner of communication with."[1] Muir's panpsychist philosophy included an extension of rights and liberty to every creature from a holistic perspective, calling all nonhumans "earth-born companions and our fellow mortals."[2] He frequently attributed sentience, and even intelligence, to nonhuman beings. He also understood other animals as people with communities and experiences of their own, to whom we are related. In 1901, in his famous collection of essays, *Our National Parks* (so poignantly relevant right now), he wrote:

> How many hearts with warm red blood in them are beating under cover of the woods, and how many teeth and eyes are shining! A multitude of animal people, intimately related to us, but of whose lives we know almost nothing, are as busy about their own affairs as we are about ours.[3]

Muir had a sense of foreboding about the industrial and scientific revolution: human worlds were rapidly losing touch with the more-than-human world, and particularly the "inherited wildness in our blood." At the height of the Darwinian revolution and the expansion of positivism beyond science into society, Muir saw the potential for danger and destruction as human society increasingly distanced itself from our common "earth-boundness" and "inherited wildness," which we share with other creatures. Biologist E. O. Wilson referred to our deeply intimate and inevitable connection to nature as *biophilia*—"the urge to affiliate with other forms of life."[4] Expanding upon this, biologist Clemens G. Arvay has made a strong argument for "the biophilia effect," the reality that our regenerative connection with the more-than-human world remains essential to human well-being. Our health and wellness literally depend upon those connections.[5]

Muir respected the scientific discoveries of his age, and longed to reconcile science and the more-than-human world. He contemplated deep time revealed in geological formations and developed a lifelong obsession with glacial ice. He saw the vastness of geological time—Earth's life story told in eons—as indicative of our relatively recent arrival in the natural world. He yearned to commune with and understand the great story of geological evolution, and inquired into our place in the grand sweep of ecology, the great web of the cosmos. Muir devoted his life to wildness, inspiring generations to embrace a feeling-based alternative to the growing dominance of positivism. Many scientists after Muir have confirmed that this embrace of the more-than-human world and wildness should not be a privilege for the few, but should become and remain a right for the many.

In the 1950s, Rachel Carson documented in detail the reality Muir could only predict. She exposed an explicit link between positivism—the assumption that science constitutes the only true knowledge, and that it alone can solve all problems—and the modern drive for unchecked progress that directly leads to the environmental problems we now face. She intuited that scientism was complicit in the potential silent spring we may yet face in the Anthropocene. Though she herself was a devoted scientist, she understood the wisdom of systemic thinking. She courageously challenged the government and other scientists with the revelation that progress could actually be killing the planet. Her act of great devotion to the Earth and all its creatures inspired the formation of the Environmental Protection Agency (EPA) and many other organizations that serve to protect and regenerate planetary ecosystems.

One of the most tragic, denial-based reactions I have seen in the Anthropocene is the dismantling of the EPA, the sale of national parks for development and drilling, and the removal of endangered species protections in the United States. At a time when we face the reality of a spring without birds, and a world without pollinators, it seems quite a shocking regression. Hence the urgent need to address the root of the problem that lies in pathologically competitive, disembodied, and oppositional thinking. These thoughts reinforce corporate and technocratic dominance, while the struggle paradigm feeds the terrible triad of archcapitalism, scientism, and technocracy. Governments of the Anthropocene could be gathering the best minds of philosophy and science to create cleaner energy and better forms of employment and income for those who would be left jobless in the transition. Instead the corporate lobbyists dig in their heels, employing the language of opposition through polarizing populist slogans to garner support for corporate myopia that in the long run, will benefit no one, especially not the people.

Scientism serves corporations and the growth-based economy, reduced to little more than a servant of market forces—profit at all costs, at the expense of social, economic, and ecological sustainability. As a result of the influence of capitalism, runaway technology lacks the wisdom of systems and the dimension of complexity consciousness.

Our human flourishing is inextricably tied to more-than-human flourishing; this is a fundamental rule of kinship. Kinship economics, politics, and science would consider sacredness as vital to survival. Rather than nothing is sacred, much is sacred. Some things are sacred to every being: air, water, soil. Other things are sacred to some beings and not others. Sacred kinship means that we respect the sacred cycles that regenerate all life, and we also respect what is sacred to each person or community (human or nonhuman).

The ability to co-create with diverse kin through complexity consciousness means cultivating what I call *creative synergy*.

FROM MASTERY TO SYNERGY

In *Physics of the Future: How Science Will Shape Human Destiny and Our Daily Lives by the Year 2100*, theoretical physicist and futurist Michio Kaku takes us on a fantastic trip into our not-too-distant future. I like this kind of scientific futurism, and enjoy thinking about wonderful inventions that could make life easier for humans (though, of course, not at the expense of other species). Kaku suggests we will finally become "masters" of nature.[6] Although I respect and admire the beautiful accomplishments of Kaku and of scientific discovery and deeply feel that human technology emerges from nature's connected creativity, I wonder that we still haven't moved beyond the myth of mastery. Science-based futurists believe that technological innovation paves our way toward utopia, but the Anthropocene forces us to face the possibility that mastery is paving our world into a bleak dystopian wasteland. Sacred futurism perceives the need for reaching beyond the dangerous dyad of mastery and progress toward the possibility offered by creative synergy.

Thinking of ourselves as masters of nature implies that we are, or even could be, somehow separate from nature. A radically different perspective, from a different epistemological lineage, accepts that humans form an integral part of the web of life. Instead of viewing ourselves as masters and overseers of nature, we can shift our perspective and attitude and see ourselves as partners in synergic relationship with all other species on our shared planet.

Physicist and Goethe scholar Henri Bortoft suggests that a more holistic scientific paradigm could support a "synergy of humanity and nature."[7] Etymologically, our word *synergy* comes from the Greek *synergos,* meaning "working together." In the chapter on entelechy, I discussed Aristotle's *energeia,* meaning "actuality," and *dynamis,* meaning "potentiality." *Energeia* derives from the Greek words *en,* meaning "in," and *ergon,* meaning "work" or "action." Aristotle (and his followers) did not separate form (*eidos* or *morphē*) from *hylē* (matter) and so avoided Plato's dualism of mind and matter. For Aristotle, unlike for

Plato, form and matter could not be separated. In Aristotelian metaphysics, form gives shape and structure to otherwise formless matter. He described a unified process, *kinesis,* whereby potentiality (*dynamis*) transforms into actuality (*energeia*). Furthermore, *kinesis* referred to *entelechy,* the completion or realization of potential (fulfilling an end goal). With this in mind, then, we could understand our word *synergy* as a kind of collective entelechy, when diverse beings, each with its own entelechy, partner in their shared future.

Bortoft's "synergy of humanity and nature" implies partnership with nature. As a collective enterprise, synergy involves empathy, mutual compassion, and connected creativity—ingredients for a future worth having.

Expanding "what it's like to be?" we might ask, what do other beings, other centers of experience, care about, desire, and need? Taking the experience, cares, desires, and needs of other beings seriously helps us to create more possible futures and fewer dystopian paradoxes.

In the previous chapter, I offered the thought that kinship helps us honor the sacred cycles we share on Earth, and also the sacred within and for diverse human and nonhuman people. Creative synergy means we recognize that sacredness is also shared across species. One of my mentors, Peter Reason, describes this:

> But it is not just humans who mark out the sacred: the pilgrimage routes and gathering places of species that migrate across the planet, the spawning grounds of great shoals of fish, the delicate spots where wrens build their nests—all these have qualities of the sacred.[8]

When we take the experiences of other beings seriously, we realize that what is sacred to them should also be sacred to us: a fundamental principle of sacred kinship.

Goethe took the experience of the more-than-human world seriously, and his theories offer an important synergetic alternative to mechanistic science. According to Bortoft:

> Goethe's organic unity is a way of seeing that includes differences. It avoids reducing multiplicity to uniformity . . . it also avoids fragmenting reality into sheer multiplicity. It allows the uniqueness of the particular to appear within the light of the unity of the whole.[9]

In his best-known scientific work, *The Metamorphosis of Plants,* Goethe approaches plant biology from a different position than the positivist scientific paradigm. Instead of emphasizing reduction, calculation, and rational analysis, he proposed that we can better understand living organisms by using intuition. Rather than viewing a plant as an assemblage of parts, he viewed it as growing from an unseen, archetypal *Urorgan,* or "primal organ" (similar to contemporary biologist Rupert Sheldrake's idea of morphic fields). Goethe, who anticipated and influenced the work of Bergson and Whitehead, claimed that the organic inner movement of the whole plant, from which "parts" manifested, could not be viewed, or calculated, with the analytical mind. Rather than viewing organic movement according to a set of coordinates, he described the unfolding of organisms as a relational process, unintelligible by the analytical mind alone. Goethe saw what Bortoft calls the "omnipotential" or "dynamical" form, the "coming-into-being" of a plant (reminiscent of Aristotle's entelechy).

Goethe elucidated the idea of "multiplicity in unity" as a fundamental characteristic of organic life. In short, he presented a holographic view of the natural world, where each being (or part) contains something of the whole. Through his protégé Schelling, Goethe's ideas on morphology and transmutation influenced Darwin's *Origin of Species.* In fact, in the third edition of *Origin,* Darwin names Goethe as one of the originators of the "transmutation" view.[10]

Alarmed at the mechanization of science and nature following Newton's revolutionary mathematical breakthroughs in physics, Goethe offered an *organic* alternative for understanding nature. Whereas Newton emphasized *quantification,* Goethe proposed a "science of qualities."

DELICATE EMPIRICISM

In chapter 5, I discussed the rise of Romanticism in reaction to positivist science. Romantic scholars such as Goethe gave voice to growing concerns about positivism and the widespread belief among scientists that quantitative analysis alone could provide understanding of reality.

Goethe, by contrast, embraced embodied experience and creativity as part of the scientific process. He realized that because every being is part of an ultimate unity, nothing can ever be truly separate from anything else. In this sense, Goethe could be considered an early proponent of relational and holographic thinking, and founder of what would become participatory theory. He insisted that observation inevitably implied *participation*—scientists could not stand back from nature and examine it without interacting with it. For Goethe, all of life and reality formed an interrelated, dynamic whole, in which each part holographically reflected the whole. He advocated *delicate empiricism* in contrast to objective empiricism, recognizing that no true separation exists, or could exist, between subject and object, and that the disposition of the observer toward the observed affects the observer's perception. Goethe's work explicitly challenges the reigning reductionist paradigm—where a whole is assumed to be nothing but the sum of its parts; instead, Goethe noted that in addition to its parts, every whole system also contains relationships between its constituent parts.

Relationships among parts of a whole form synergies, where contributions of the parts combine to add new qualities to the whole system. Living systems in particular manifest these dynamic, synergistic relationships. However, reductionism (analyzing wholes exclusively in terms of their parts) misses the profound contributions of synergies to the processes of life. If we go along with reductionist assumptions, we cannot experience the rich dynamic and interrelatedness of complex systems. Consequently, we make choices based on the fallacy of separation, which Whitehead called the "fallacy of misplaced concreteness."

Whitehead emphasized the error of confusing mere conceptual

abstractions for actual concrete reality. The idea of separateness (the premise of reductionism) exists only as an abstraction, a concept; by contrast, we can *feel* the actual reality of relationships. Abstractions remove us from participation, and thereby separate us conceptually from consequences. Without making the investment of relationships, we perceive ourselves as free of the burden of responsibility: corporations can dump toxic waste into the ocean, and individuals dump toxic household chemicals down the drain. As discussed in the chapter on complexity, systems thinkers call this *bounded rationality*—where actors are removed from the consequences of their actions. They fail to see the metaview or to understand that their actions inevitably affect the whole system. The metaview helps us to understand the greater picture of the metasystem. Thinking through the lens of metaview and metasystem means thinking synergy.

CONTEXTUAL ATTITUDE AND LIVING THINKING

Craig Holdrege, a Goethean scientist and founder-director of the Nature Institute, has devoted his life's work to exploring Goethe's delicate empiricism—a departure from the standard, mainstream embrace of objective empiricism and what he calls "object thinking." Holdrege points out: "Through a lack of critical reflection, reductionism perpetuates itself and ignores the roots of responsibility within the human being."[11] He considers adopting a perspective of wholeness as crucial, reorienting toward what he calls a "contextual attitude."

This contextual attitude emerges from understanding that "organisms actually interpenetrate" and that "even the whole earth can be considered as further dimensions of organisms." Because of the interpenetration of organisms, we find ourselves always and irreducibly *contextualized*—embedded thoroughly in our environment—and, therefore, our tiniest footprint affects the whole in some unforeseen way. Holdrege teaches Goethean thinking to scientists and educators in order to awaken this vital awareness of context-sensitive relationship.

In *Thinking Like a Plant: A Living Science for Life,* Holdrege advocates a shift in human consciousness that expands our current object thinking to more plantlike thinking: "Such flexibility of thought that our ideas were no longer rigid, static, and object-like, but grew and when necessary, died away."[12] He calls this more flexible, participatory cognition "living thinking," which "transcends the dichotomies of man-nature, subject-object, and mind-matter." Employing delicate empiricism, Holdrege discovered that it is plants' ability to metamorphose that makes them so successful. They adapt well, better than many animal species, accounting for the immense diversity of the plant world.

Holdrege describes the metamorphic wisdom of flora, which clearly cycle through periods of "transformation, expansion, and contraction." In fact, every being in the natural world attunes to this rhythmic dance, oscillating between ebb and flow. Because we tend toward object thinking, we tend to "hold onto ideas as fixed entities." In other words, ideas become objectified and solidified, and we commit the fallacy of misplaced concreteness. However, if we allow our consciousness to unfold *organically,* through process thinking, we are less likely to cling to ideas that no longer serve us or to mistake ideas for reality. We would naturally open to the creativity of the present by opening to our own lived experience, rather than imposing cognitive constructs on reality. Based on a Goethean view of plants, Holdrege asks an important question: "How can we learn to make our actions increasingly organic and less haphazard?" I believe the answer can be found by honoring the widespread sentience teeming in the world around us.

In the title of his famous 1974 essay, Thomas Nagel posed a penetrating philosophical question: "What is it like to be a bat?"[13] He argued that solely reductionist (objective) approaches to understanding the subjectivity of another creature ultimately fail to render a complete understanding of their experience. We might ask, then, what non-reductionist approaches could complement science toward a better understanding of what it's like to be another creature? What could that better understanding of another being's experience teach us? We might ask how we can become flexible enough in our thinking to learn from the experience of another being so seemingly different from us. When we open up to such inquiry—*by engaging with the presence of other sentient beings*—we soon come to realize the value of flattening the hierarchy of species that we have imposed on the world. Human exceptionalism puts us at the top of a vertical hierarchy, but synergy places us within a flattened hierarchy, although not in the center; rather, context situates us in that more flexible hierarchy. This means nonhuman creativity can teach us essential lessons about how to live. This creative synergy already pervades biomimicry, but we can extend creative synergy by letting other beings teach us, not only how they create technology, but also how they create culture. Synergy means that we include the insights of many beings in the way we shape the future.

SUPERHUMAN

Nonhumans everywhere, on every scale, possess powers that have always sparked the creative imagination of humans. Our earliest creation stories cast animals in the role of gods and goddesses, supernatural beings that transcend our understanding, or malevolent forces sent to harm us. These god-creatures include Anubis, the jackal god, gatekeeper of the afterlife, and Bastet the cat, goddess of war, in ancient Egypt; and Hindu gods such as the elephant-headed Ganesha, remover of obstacles, and Hanuman, the monkey god of devotion and strength. Among the Aboriginal people of Australia, Eingana, the dreamtime snake, gives birth to the world as the mother of all beings. Among the Haida, we find the orca whale as the ancient protector of humankind. In the modern West, superheroines and superheroes often possess the extraordinary abilities of insects and animals—for example, Cat Woman, Spider-Man, and Wolverine. We infer that when these amazing abilities are combined with human intelligence, they can be used for the greatest good or the worst evil.

We tend to see these nonhuman abilities as powerful, but not superior or even equal to human ingenuity. Anthropocentrism and human exceptionalism blind us to the remarkable intelligence of other creatures, while the myth of mastery compels us to exploit them, or their abilities, to benefit our species. As we awaken to the reality that other species possess skills way beyond human abilities, such as *bioluminescence* (communication through light), *echolocation* (locating objects through sound), *magnetoreception* (the ability to detect magnetic fields), *seismic communication* (conveying information through mechanical vibrations of the substrate), and countless others, our sanest response must be humble curiosity and reverent wonder. Creative synergy requires humility, the ability to listen deeply, and the embrace of radically different ways of knowing. As scientific research reveals creativity, intelligence, and sentience on many scales, we would be truly unwise to close ourselves to diverse teachings. Creative synergy offers us new ways to flourish together in the Anthropocene.

GREEN GENIUS:
THE WISDOM OF CONNECTIONS

Many humans view themselves as the dominant species on the planet, but in *Brilliant Green,* plant neurobiologists Stefano Mancuso and Alessandra Viola point out: "Earth is an ecosystem inarguably dominated by plants . . . much more advanced, adaptable, and intelligent beings than we're inclined to think." Mancuso and Viola identified in plants not only all five of what we consider human senses, but also an additional fifteen that humans lack. For instance, plants see by perceiving and seeking light; smell by receiving and releasing biogenic volatile organic compounds; and touch and hear through using the ground as a vector, and conductor, for sound. Plants did not develop specific, localized sensory organs, but experience their world throughout their entire organism. They also have senses we can hardly imagine, such as an internal hygrometer to measure humidity, the ability to "sense gravity and electromagnetic fields," and to "recognize trace amounts of chemical elements important or harmful to its growth."[14] Imagine if we could directly sense harmful toxins in our environment; we wouldn't have to trust the FDA and other powerful government agencies that supposedly watch out for us. Instead, we could simply sense what would make us ill—a highly useful superhuman power that plants already possess.

Recent research offers us the potential to understand the inner world of plants. Entomologist Richard Karban at the University of California, Davis, studies plant defense communication, and offers us the insight that plants recognize and respond differently to kin.[15] Plants communicate in a coded language of VOCs (volatile organic compounds) that interdisciplinary studies are attempting to render intelligible to humans. We may soon be able to understand and even speak the language of plants.

In *The Hidden Life of Trees,* forester Peter Wohlleben offers us a better understanding of arboreal communities and individuals. He tells the tale of his conversion from conventional forester, aligned to the commodification of trees, to an awakening as a participant in the community of the forest. He offers enchanting and scientifically supported stories about tree language, life, and even love:

> Under the canopy of the trees, daily dramas and moving love stories are played out. Here is the last remaining piece of Nature, right on our doorstep, where adventures are to be experienced and secrets discovered.[16]

Science has just begun to reveal a plant world full of collaborations, communication, creativity, and kinships. We know now that trees not only participate in communities but also cooperate with their kin and nurture their young. Trees and shrubs even have a circulatory "heartbeat" that is too slow for humans to perceive. Many of the qualities we fail to perceive about trees affirm my daughter's intuition that trees speak too slowly for us to hear. Many beings live in temporalities much slower than ours, giving them the impression of being static. But the wisdom of plants and trees is the wisdom of connections. Their collaborative creativity unfolds sometimes over many seasons, or generations.

As our awareness of plant and tree individuals (abilities, feelings, intelligence, senses) and cultures (community and cooperation) expands, we may find that these ancient beings who make up the most biomass on the planet have something to teach us about survival strategies, collaborative creativity, and kinship. Biologist and writer David George Haskell, in *The Songs of Trees,* offers us profound insight into tree wisdom, "To listen to the trees, nature's great connector, is therefore to learn how to inhabit the relationship that gave life its source, substance and beauty."[17]

What can the genius of plants and trees teach us about collaboration, kinship, longevity, and the wisdom of slow thinking?

MUSHROOMS: MASTERS OF SYNERGY

In the beginning of this chapter I described the underground mycelial network that conveys information through the earth, much like the Internet in human communication. This transfer of information through immense subsurface mycelial networks plays a crucial role in our planetary ecosystem in ways we have just begun to understand.

In *Mycelium Running: How Mushrooms Can Help Save the World,* mycologist Paul Stamets proposes that mycorestoration can help restore ecological health. He describes the evolutionary strategy of "mycelial architecture . . . so pervasive that a single cubic inch of topsoil contains enough fungal cells to stretch more than eight miles if placed end to end . . . moving through subterranean landscapes like cellular waves."[18] This dynamic network carries and filters microbes and sediment, which nourish plants and also provide nourishment for myriad organisms. Stamets explains that mycelia have adapted to help regulate ecology by responding to debris with these mycelial "waves." He points out that humans create huge fields of debris often beyond our ability to remediate; we have become "ecological disrupters" challenging the "immune systems of our environment." We have essentially pushed the ecosystem beyond its carrying capacity. Stamets proposes that mycelial ingenuity could restore balance to our ecosystem, overtaxed by human waste. Human technology has seriously disrupted planetary systemic health requiring a palliative that perhaps only ancient and widespread mycelium networks can provide. Can we learn the true mastery of synergy from fungi: how to partner in the regeneration of our living planet?

Stamets proposes that we might be able to offset and "regulate the flow of nutrients" through mycorestoration. He proposes multiple ways of partnering with mycelia in order to restore balance. These include *mycoremediation:* mycelia can digest toxic wastes and pollutants; *mycofiltration:* mycelia can reduce silt and pathogens from agricultural runoff; *mycopesticides:* mycelia can control insect populations; and *mycoforestry* and gardening: mycelia play a vital role in topsoil restoration. "Enlisting fungi as allies, we can offset the environmental damage inflicted by humans by accelerating organic decomposition of the massive fields of debris we create—through everything from clear-cutting forests to constructing cities." Stamets describes many superpowers of mushrooms and how they can remedy environmental damage—from individual organisms to the entire ecosystem. He also points out that fungi outnumber plants about six to one in biological diversity, and that the mycelium kingdom contains between one and two million species. Stamets persuasively argues that we depend utterly on the superpowers of mycelial networks and that we can work with them to regenerate damaged planetary systems. He advocates learning the wisdom of fungi and "partnering" or "running with" mycelium. What can mycelium teach us about how to shift from mastery to creative synergy?

If fungi outnumber plants by a factor of six, and plants outnumber humans, then we may legitimately question the assumption that humans qualify as our planet's dominant species. If winning the game of domination means losing the game of partnership, and partnership enhances evolutionary survival, how does domination benefit us? In terms of networking, partnership, and strategy, mycelia and plants exhibit greater flexibility and adaptability.

The superpowers of mycelia allow them to squeeze eight miles of their network into one cubic inch of topsoil. They can turn toxic waste and pathogens into nutrients. Mycorrhizal mushrooms transport nutrients to many species of trees and connect acres of forest through dense networks of cells, creating healthy forests and in turn a healthy planetary atmosphere. Recent research reveals that some fungi can even eat plastic and can prevent and cure a variety of diseases. Typically we place fungi and plants at the bottom of the food chain, at the bottom of the evolutionary hierarchy, but these kingdoms of life populated our planet long before we evolved and may remain long after we are gone. These ancient and well-adapted organisms truly dominate the Earth— especially when we take account of their diversity, the amount of land they occupy, and their evolutionary success. In the Anthropocene, the mycelia teach us resilience.

In *The Mushroom at the End of the World: On the Possibility of Life in Capitalist Ruins,* anthropologist and ethnographer Anna L. Tsing describes the teachings of the matsutake mushroom as "its willingness to emerge in blasted landscapes" and "explore the ruin that has become our home." She offers us some ideas emerging from her ethnographic studies of mushroom culture and the human culture surrounding it. She also offers the metaphor of mushroom: From the mushroom cloud to the fungi that may survive these "blasted landscapes," the mushroom teaches us about living with "precarity." The Anthropocene's precarious futures mean understanding how to be radically curious about what these new ruinous landscapes offer us. "Precarity is the condition of being vulnerable to others. Unpredictable encounters transform us; we are not in control, even of ourselves."[19] Mushrooms, literally and metaphorically, can teach us about living in the Anthropocene: that precarity offers us a new way of relating to each other.

What can fungi teach us about the regenerative powers of resilience and synergy in the ruinous landscape of Anthropocene?

BEE BRILLIANCE

Bees have always been sacred to humans; our legends and stories celebrate the little winged creatures as symbols of abundance and prosperity. From the Minoan Potnia, called "Pure Mother Bee," to the Mayan god Ah-Muzen-Cab, bees have been seen as symbols of power because they are essential to life. Ancient people recognized their brilliance long before modern science began to investigate it.

Our apian allies have always been revered for their creativity, ingenuity, and crucial role in the health of the ecosystem. The hexagonal shape they use in their combs is one of the most resilient structural forms known. Scout bees communicate complex information and locations through the waggle dance, using pheromones to create a sort of map for their hive mates. Bees can also recognize faces of allies and enemies and can even communicate those to their hive mates. Beyond that, they have also been shown to possess emotions, and even get depressed.[20] A recent study also revealed that bees can not only understand math but the sophisticated concept of zero.[21]

Any beekeeper will tell you that beehives have their own personalities and that their bees know them. This deeply felt bond between keeper and hive finds expression in an ancient tradition called "telling the bees," in which someone tells the bees about events taking place in their keeper's life, or of his death, so that the bees can celebrate or mourn with them.[22] There exist many anecdotes in which bees attended the funerals of their keepers. Whether or not these stories can be validated, they remain valid recognitions of how bees have coevolved with humans. Our lives are deeply intertwined.

Bee brilliance cannot be disputed any longer, as we understand more about their complex cultures and cognition and recognize how much bee culture remains deeply entangled with other animal cultures, including our own. What can bee brilliance teach us about complexity-based living strategies and the vital lesson of interdependence?

CETACEANS: COMPLEXITY CONSCIOUSNESS

Great controversy still surrounds animal creativity and intelligence. Many cling to human exceptionalism, fearing the immense implications of nonhuman intelligence and sentience. It shakes the very foundations of our society; we would have to rethink so many systems (and I believe we are already beginning the process). Many scientists now recognize the complex intelligence of various nonhuman species and call for these changes. Some would even expand beyond exceptionalism to recognize that many nonhuman species possess not only sentience, but also culture and language. In *The Question of Animal Culture*, biologists Kevin Laland and Bennett Galef describe the ancient roots of the idea of animal culture, noting that Aristotle first provided evidence of social learning of songs in birds. We have intuited the reality of animal culture for a very long time, but rejected it because it does not align with mastery and progress practices. After all, eating, enslaving, and experimenting on other people with cultures, though not foreign to humans (conquest, genocide, holocaust), seems unpalatable to supposedly awakened humans. Humans are beginning to react in many ways to new revelations about nonhumans, on a spectrum ranging from vitriolic denial to militant and dogmatic antihumanism. Either approach presents issues of great complexity that must be considered as we transition away from practices based upon human exceptionalism. Awakening to diverse creaturely cultures requires the application of complexity consciousness.

The debate about animal culture heightened following reports of Japanese researchers in the 1950s and 60s who made the radical claim that many animal species possess their own cultures. In *Gene, Mind, and Culture* (1981), Charles Lumsden and E. O. Wilson proposed that "10,000 species, including bacteria" have some kind of culture. Laland and Galef point out also that more and more scientists now take the possibility of nonhuman animal culture seriously: "Over the past two decades there has been a profound change in the frequency with which scientists who write about population specific behaviors in animals refer to them as 'culture.'"[23]

A growing number of ethologists and other biologists accept that many nonhuman species exhibit forms of cultural behavior. Laland critiques arguments against animal culture as "anthropocentric bias." Clearly if we have a constructed bias against widespread sentience and intelligence, then we will be reluctant to envision how it might express itself.

In *The Cultural Lives of Whales and Dolphins,* cetacean biologists Hal Whitehead and Luke Rendell propose a strong argument for cetacean culture based on research conducted over many decades. They begin by identifying the key attributes that identify culture in cetaceans: technology, cumulative culture, morality, culturally transmitted and symbolic ethnic markers, and the cultural effect on reproductive fitness. The authors note that their critics say they define culture too broadly, preferring to focus definitions of culture on abstract and phenomenological concepts such as "meaning." But as Whitehead and Rendell state: "Meanings in cetacean culture . . . are not accessible to us."[24]

Whitehead and Rendell have opted for a looser, simpler, and less anthropocentric definition of culture. They separate cultural attributes into three main categories: *definitely culture, likely culture*, and *plausibly culture*. In the *definitely* category, they define the strongest evidence for cetacean culture as the songs of the humpback whale. The songs change in the two modes the authors describe as "evolutionary" and "revolutionary"—changing slowly over time, yet sometimes completely within a relatively short period. Because of this, they cannot be studied adequately through laboratory research. The authors point out that the key to attribution of culture lies in the fact that the humpback whale song "changes greatly within the lifespan of the individual." Whitehead and Rendell believe that different dialects of pulse-calls among different communities of killer whales exhibit signs of culture. Research reveals that these calls "vary between pods, clans, and communities."

The second category, *likely* evidence for cultural transmission, consists of vocal and nonvocal behavior in large matrilineal whale groups, the copying of foraging behavior in killer whales and dolphins, strong evidence of differing dialects among sperm whales, and the possible transmission of migration routes from mother to calf in humpback and beluga whales. While the third category, *plausible* evidence, consists of case studies that don't indicate variations in social learning, nevertheless, observations indicate plausible cultural transmission and therefore do merit investigation. Species in this category include bottlenose dolphins, who engage in cooperative feeding techniques and also exhibit different dialects.

Studies of language in cetaceans reveal that dolphins may communicate not just in clicks, whistles, and other vocalization, but in sonar holograms. Researchers have long known that cetaceans use sonar and echolocation, but recently, using new technology, a team of researchers has expanded this observation to include sonopictorial representation.

Until recently, the idea of sonopictorial "sight" was considered mere conjecture. But a research team led by Jack Kassewitz of Speakdolphin in Miami, Florida, recorded dolphin echolocation sounds reflecting off several objects. They discovered that the reflected sounds actually do contain sonopictorial images. When dolphins "heard" replays of the recorded sounds, they identified the objects with 86 percent accuracy— evidence that they experience and understand echolocation sounds as kinds of "audio pictures." Kassewitz then replayed the sound pictures to a dolphin at another location and the second dolphin also identified the objects with high accuracy, confirming that dolphins possess sonopictorial communication. British team member Stuart Reid later imaged the reflected echolocation sounds using CymaScope technology that enables researchers to see the sonopictorial images created by the dolphins. Reid reports that they resemble ultrasound images seen in hospitals. We can plausibly conclude from this that dolphins may communicate in pictures, transmitting what they see to other dolphins. If so, then dolphins not only possess both language and culture but abilities that surpass human abilities.

Indeed, using new technology and methodology, researchers reveal not only that some nonhuman species possess communicative abilities comparable to ours, but that in many cases their abilities may surpass ours. The cetacean brain has a complex neocortex (the area responsible for self-awareness and emotions). Lori Marino, neuroscientist and president of the Whale Sanctuary Project points out that the limbic system of an orca is "so large it erupts into the cortex to form an extra paralimbic lobe."[25] Based upon her extensive research, Marino suggests that "It may be that many cetacean species have achieved a level of social-emotional sophistication not achieved by other animals, including humans."[26] Marino, who has dedicated her career to researching the intelligence and sentience of cetaceans, advocates for the personhood of dolphins and whales based upon the clear evidence for their cognitive and social complexity and self-awareness, "Because dolphins see themselves in mirrors, it means that in some ways, their minds work the way ours do. They know who they are."[27]

They know who they are. They are people with complex abilities we cannot yet fathom—complex, cultural people who could teach us something when we are ready to learn. Recently, scientists, researchers, and many others observed an orca mother carrying her dead calf for six days toward the San Juan Islands where she met a pod of orca females. After she arrived, she and the other orca females gathered at the mouth of the cove, and then circled continuously from sunset into the moonlight, following the path of the moon. The scientists involved agree that the orca was expressing grief, and many of the onlookers perceived a distinctly ceremonial aspect to the circular motion around the moonbeam.[28] Researchers and activists also perceive her tragic vigil as a message to humans, as the orcas face increasingly low survival rates of their offspring, signaling the possibly immanent extinction of their kind due to human-generated pollution and the effects of climate change on ocean ecosystems. These immensely intelligent, complex orca and other cetacean societies may be asking us for assistance, or perhaps their rituals have nothing to do with us. Whatever the case, these stories remind us of our entangled kinship in a continuum of consciousness.

We cannot ignore the message in the recent vigil of the orca mother and her ceremonial gathering around the moonbeam-lit waters of the San Juan Islands cove, a sacred place for their kind. We cannot deny their cognitive and cultural complexity, and the possibility that they possess a cosmology story and spirituality of their own. We are not the only animal on this planet capable of self-awareness. We would be foolish to believe dogmatically that we are the only animal capable of ritual, story, and a sense of the sacred. Complexity consciousness requires us to remain humbly curious about the complexity of other beings.

What could cetaceans teach us about complexity consciousness?

CORVID CREATIVITY AND PLAY

Crows, ravens, and jackdaws—birds notorious in legends, fairy tales, and horror stories—make up the genus *Corvus* of the family Corvidae. Though infamous in Western culture as the familiars of witches and wizards, many ancient origin stories and myths portray crows and ravens as powerful creators, mischievous tricksters, and sage guides. Given their repeated appearance in our earliest cosmologies, humanity would do well to intuit the significance of their high intelligence and creativity to our own evolutionary path.

These days, we know that crows have complex cognition, such as facial recognition, tool use, and regional dialects; they even engage in mysterious funerary rituals when kin pass away. Recent viral videos on social media show them engaging in apparent play behaviors, "snowboarding" down slanted snow-covered roofs and car windows, swinging from branches, and even playing ball. Kaeli Swift, researcher at the School of Environmental and Forest Sciences at the University of Washington, lists the "Big Seven" of play identification, all significant because of seemingly purposeless activities:

1. Object play (*manipulating things for no reason*)
2. Play caching (*hiding inedible objects*)
3. Flight play (*random aerial acrobatics*)
4. Bath play (*more activity in water than necessary to get clean*)
5. Sliding down inclines (*snowboarding, sledding, body sliding*)
6. Hanging (*hanging off branches but not to obtain food*)
7. Vocal play (*you know how kids go through that phase when they talk to themselves a lot? The crow version of that.*)[29]

Swift points out that no one can satisfactorily answer why crows play, but suggests: "Learning about their peers, gaining new experiences in a low-risk way, honing their stress response, and growing their big brains, all seem like a good excuse to have a bit of fun to me." This reminds me of how play functions as a key ingredient in human innovation. C. G. Jung once said, "The creation of something new is not accomplished by the intellect but by the play instinct."[30] The more humans understand that play forms an essential part of creativity, the more we realize the vital role creativity plays in our survival and flourishing. Like any highly intelligent and creative being, crows intrinsically possess the gift of play.

As urban crows interact frequently with humans, they begin to adopt typically human games, such as ball playing. In *In the Company of Crows and Ravens,* John Marzluff, a professor of wildlife science, relates the story of Japanese researcher Reiko Kurasawa, who noticed that jungle crows (*Corvus macrorhynchos*) near a tennis court in Tana, Japan, seemed to emulate tennis playing by standing on either side of and bouncing balls off the net. Marzluff sees stories like these as "stunning" examples of the "beginning of cultural transmission across species"—demonstrating a "cognitive ripple" phenomenon. He goes on to say: "If ball-playing spreads among crows by social learning, then we could conclude that crow culture had adopted an aspect of human culture."[31] Essentially, cultural transmission occurs from humans to crows. However, cultural transmissions work both ways. In *Gifts of the Crow,* Marzluff describes how profoundly this interspecies relationship forms an evolutionary two-way street: "As crows affect our culture . . . we affect their ecology, evolution, and culture. We are co-evolving, each shaping the other to varying degrees."[32] We live with the crows as partners in both our wild and urban ecosystems, and they live inside our consciousness—interspecies companionship linked in a web of sentience.

After many decades researching crow behavior, Marzluff suggests that crows:

> provoke and remind us how foolish it is to assume an all-knowing human ascendancy over nature. . . . The birds will remain to soothe our urban souls, stimulate new artisans and dreamers . . . and provide future generations of people with wisdom to maintain healthy ecosystems on our planet.[33]

Corvids remind us that play forms an essential element of life: when we stop being creative and playful, we soon perish. Ethologist and animal advocate Marc Bekoff, in *The Emotional Lives of Animals,* suggests that play "isn't an idle waste of time. Play is essential for an individual's mental and physical well-being."[34] Psychologist Mihaly Csikszentmihalyi describes the importance of play: "Play is grounded in the concept of possibility."[35] Play transmits novel forms of behavior that could generate new possibilities for planetary evolution as a whole. We must keep playing to embody our possible futurity.

The coevolution of certain corvid species and humans reminds us that we do not create in a species vacuum. Interspecies creativity has always been an evolutionary reality; forgetting this would be an evolutionary mistake. We must learn compassionate and conscious interspecies play toward collective futurity.

Futurity requires creative synergy and interspecies play. What can corvids teach us about creative synergy and the importance of play?

Corvids have been known to gather around their dead and carry out elaborate displays that seem to us like funerary rites. Scientists who study them caution us not to misinterpret their behavior through anthropomorphizing them. They suggest that a better explanation might be that corvids are gathering to learn about the death and avoid danger. However, Bekoff suggests that there is no reason to doubt that corvids are mourning; continuity means that many creatures share the emotional ability to grieve for their lost kin.[36] I would also suggest that humans often ask questions surrounding the death of someone they know in the interest of learning what they might avoid. We are capable of grieving and wishing to stay alive at the same time.

I began chapter 4 by describing my love for the dawn chorus of birds; that chorus calls me into connection and commitment to care for our shared world, come what may. In his powerful book *Flight Ways,* environmental philosopher Thom van Dooren tells stories of the extinction and mourning of and with our winged coevolutionary kin; we coevolved, and we are ultimately entangled in our extinction. In the chapter "Mourning Crows," van Dooren describes how the mutuality of our finitude opens us to other mutual realities.

> Mourning offers us a way into an alternative space, one of acknowledgement of and respect for the dead. In this context, mourning undoes any pretense toward exceptionalism, instead drawing us into an awareness of multispecies continuities and connectivities that make life possible for everyone.[37]

Just as corvids and humans coevolved, we may face coextinction. We share grief and sorrow, and humans can also grieve with other species, as they cease to exist. The "alternative space" of interspecies grief becomes a shared sacred space of futurity.

Corvid grief teaches us that we are not alone in our feelings of sorrow related to loss. How can corvids teach us about shared grief? How can we become more compassionate toward nonhumans, knowing they also experience the pain of loss? Corvids feature in many creation stories about our beginnings; might our shared stories with crows and ravens teach us to live with the perils of the Anthropocene?

TARDIGRADE TENACITY

The dictionary definitions of *tenacity* vary from "the quality of being able to hold on or grip firmly" to "the quality of continuing to exist." The tardigrade, more commonly known as a water bear or moss piglet, seems better at holding, gripping, and existing than most other creatures. Some of the over twelve hundred species of *Tardigrada* are about 600 million years old. They hang on to existence through their remarkable ability to form a *tun,* or dessicated ball, when their environment lacks adequate moisture—what scientists call *anhydrobiosis.*[38] This process is also called *cryptobiosis,* meaning "hidden life." Much as some larger creatures form balls to protect themselves, these tiny arthropods can remain dormant, possibly for decades, through slowing their metabolism down almost to a halt. Scientists have exposed them to temperatures over 300 degrees and under 400 degrees Fahrenheit, and have even sent them into space.[39] Tardigrades can survive just about any environmental challenge. Moss piglets (my favorite name for them) are not only seriously tenacious, but incredibly adorable; with their four pairs of legs and tubular mouth, they have enchanted the world (or at least some of us).

One quality that enchants us most about tardigrades may be their ability to survive apocalypse, which has been confirmed by scientists who study them.[40] In the Anthropocene, that seems a most welcome quality in the face of earthquakes, eruptions, fires, floods, and tornadoes. We are beginning to recognize that even if we apply regenerative technologies to the many perils of Anthropocene Earth, nothing will ever be the same as it was in the relatively temperate Holocene. Earth species will face the challenge of adapting to new conditions or ceasing to exist, evidenced by the mass extinction events taking place everywhere. Adaptations require not only biomimicry that changes human systems, but also biomimicry that regenerates all the nonhuman systems and the ecological assemblages that humans depend upon. We may also find that the tardigrade genome embellishes our own with new human-enhancement technology, but the touchstone of compassion must apply: how can HET make us more compassionate? Can we also be compassionate to tardigrades in our efforts to understand them?

Humans must learn how to regenerate water systems in an impending water crisis, or learn the lesson of anhydrobiosis. We have not adapted the ability to remain dormant through weather extremes, but we will undoubtedly have to learn how to conserve energy and even to slow down our collective metabolism to live with less. We will need to develop the tenacious wisdom of the tardigrade.

What can the tardigrade teach us about tenacity in the face of extreme and volatile conditions?

Awakening to creative synergy, can we begin to see how the brilliance of superorganisms, compassionate creativity, complexity consciousness, curiosity, play, and resilience fit together as an evolutionary strategy?

FROM CHASM TO CONTINUITY

In *Are We Smart Enough to Know How Smart Animals Are?* primatologist Frans de Waal presents a thorough argument that closes the imagined chasm between human and nonhuman animal consciousness. He discusses the work of a twentieth-century German biologist and grandfather of biosemiotics, Jakob von Uexküll, who described the nonhuman animal's experience of the world as their *Umwelt,* or "surrounding world." De Waal suggests that although we can never actually know what it is to be like a bat, or any other creature (including another human), we can imagine the *Umwelten* of other beings as a way of pushing beyond the limitations of our human perspective.

De Waal points out that this attempt to transcend our own Umwelt and project ourselves into others must become part of the interspecies researcher's method. Rather than using pure analysis, or purely sensory observation, the researcher must understand the subject under investigation by using imagination based in empathy in an attempt to understand the experience of another being. He cites instances in which the results of an experiment were affected by the behavior—or, even more subtly, by the biases—of the researcher, which, in turn, affects the result of the experiment. In other words, tests set up according to the anthropocentric paradigm implicitly assume—and thereby "confirm"—the superiority of humans.

De Waal offers an alternative to this anthropocentric methodology. An unbiased (or at least *less* biased) researcher might ask: "What sort of experiment . . . would do justice to the animal's special anatomy and abilities?"[41] Rather than assuming an animal doesn't "get the problem," a more precise and accurate statement would be the researcher doesn't "get" the test subject. The anthropocentric researcher did not explore "what is it like to be a . . .?" and accordingly adapt the experimental method to the animal's particular Umwelt. "A good experiment doesn't create a new and unusual behavior but taps into natural tendencies," de Waal emphasized. Rather than create arbitrarily unnatural and difficult situations for the animal subject, de Waal encourages interspecies researchers to respect that animal's nature, tendencies, physical structure, and abilities—and to design experiments accordingly.

The more researchers respect and empathize with their nonhuman cousins, the more their research reveals that attributes we tend to think of as especially human turn out to be widespread in nature. For decades, de Waal has gathered evidence of facial recognition, empathy, altruism, self-awareness, inferential reasoning, referential signaling, and metacognition in other primates and in nonprimates. He also discusses what he calls *perspective taking,* or the ability to put oneself in another's shoes. De Waal says this capacity goes hand-in-hand with empathy—as a "biological imperative." He also cites evidence for *targeted helping*—assisting others based on an assessment of their situation. Cetaceans and primates, for example, engage in this behavior.

Rather than emphasizing scientific objectivity, this more humane approach takes account of the subjective experience of both observer and subject, and their relationship. Researchers who adopt this approach continue to expand our appreciation for sentience and intelligence in other species.

De Waal discusses the *cognitive ripple effect* based on the fact that cognitive achievements spread like ripples in a pond. The more researchers become aware of this, the more the potential of making interspecies connections expands. De Waal says: "It would be a true miracle if we had the fancy cognition that we believe we have while our fellow animals had none of it." As we become cognizant of how many nonhuman animals surpass even what we consider human-specific attributes, we begin to view them through a different lens.

De Waal describes a young male chimp named Ayamu, who shocked the scientific community in 2007 by displaying a photographic memory that far surpasses any human's, including a British memory champion. Surprised, even disturbed, by the outcome of this experiment, the scientists tried to come up with some other explanation, but could not. Once in a while, a startling occurrence can knock us out of our comfortable and narrow paradigm. Ayamu's display of "superhuman" memory serves as a cautionary reminder.

De Waal identifies what he calls *neocreationism*—a subtle kind of quasi-religious fundamentalism that accepts evolution, but not continuity. He points out that this brand of evolution aims to justify the idea that a chasm separates human and nonhuman consciousness. But the continuity of Darwinian evolution implies that a continuum of intelligence exists among species. To claim otherwise warps the evidence of evolution. Nonetheless, because of "humans are special" fundamentalists, we must deal with the continuity versus chasm problem, sometimes called Wallace's Problem.

Alfred Russel Wallace, who is credited with developing a theory of evolution more or less at the same time as Darwin, saw continuity among nonhuman animals, but he believed that continuity abruptly stopped at human consciousness. To Wallace, the human mind qualified as the exception to the Darwinian notion of utilitarian traits. The only explanation he offered involved divine influence. De Waal addresses this problem by pointing out that many species have larger brains, with more neural connections, than human brains. Even complex frontal lobes, supposedly the hallmarks of human intelligence, occur, larger and more complex, in other species. Given this, de Waal asks whether, therefore, we should consider those species more conscious than us? "All in all, neural differences seem insufficient for human uniqueness to be a foregone conclusion anymore," he says.

In light of de Waal's thoughtful argument, we can appreciate how the assumed chasm exists more as an artifact of human bias and lack of imagination and empathy than as any true gap between humans and other species. The continuum of intelligence, from simpler to more complex organisms, does not imply a hierarchy of dominion. Instead, it suggests a branching system of differential intelligence, expressed in each species' ability to creatively adapt to the changing circumstances of its particular ecological niche and Umwelt. Instead of viewing ourselves as more intelligent, we just happen to possess intelligence adapted to the specific needs of our species. Our brains do not make us more conscious; they make us *differently* conscious. We are just one expression of consciousness in nature's potentially infinite matrix of intelligence.

EMBODIED ENVISIONING

De Waal cites Goethe's discovery of the miniscule piece of human jawbone, the *os intermaxillare,* thought only to be present in nonhuman animals, as another datum refuting the chasm theory. Considered a primitive skeletal structure by Enlightenment scientists, the presence of this tiny bone in humans helped Goethe affirm the continuity between animal species. Goethe's interest in the human/nonhuman continuum went beyond morphology (the shapes or forms of organisms); he also challenged the dominant mechanistic ontology of his day.

Any worldview that separated humans from the rest of nature, he realized, would give humans an assumed right to exploit the natural world. (History has proven him correct.)

Goethe's panpsychist leanings led him to envision the divine as embodied throughout the natural world. He also believed that nature's diversity expressed a deeper unity underlying all species. His embodied ontology—so different from the abstracted, cerebral thinking of British empiricism—provided the philosophical soil in which his scientific theory grew. Despite Goethe's profound insights—and his strong cautions against the increasing mechanization of his age—his science of qualities did not win over enough scientists or philosophers. Instead, British empiricism, and the mechanistic-quantitative worldview it entailed, won the day.

Nevertheless, a renewed interest in Goethean science has influenced research methodologies in the last few decades. Many of the biologists, primatologists, cetacean researchers, and others mentioned in this chapter agree that enlightened animal research requires not only empathy but also the desire to leave one's own Umwelt in an imaginative attempt to step into the world of other species.

De Waal describes true empathy as "other-oriented" and urges researchers to evaluate nonhuman species through an other-oriented lens. A Goethean worldview shifts from object thinking toward living thinking, which incorporates the biological imperative of empathy—as well as the evolutionary imperative of creativity, converging into what I have called *ethical imagination*. The ethical imagination seeks, above all, synergy with nature by taking seriously the embodied experience and entelechy of all beings.

Although "what is it like to be any other sentient being?" cannot be answered except by the organism in question, developing ethical imagination requires that we actively consider the experience of other beings. By employing ethical imagination, we not only push beyond our limited worldview and discover the Umwelten of other beings; perspective taking and empathic action also support the desires and needs of other sentient beings. De Waal emphasizes the *embodied* nature of ethical imagination, and that it involves the ability to attune to each other.

Subjectivity remains a private affair. We can only imagine another's experience, leading to many current planetary problems; remember the utopian paradox. If we possessed a hive mind, like the bees, or a network brain, like mycelium, we would likely avoid many of the challenges that arise from our inability to step into the minds of others. Superorganisms hold much wisdom for living with the perils of the Anthropocene. In *Teeming: How Superorganisms Work to Build Infinite Wealth in a Finite World,* revolutionary biologist Tamsin Woolley-Barker tells us, "superorganism insects are collaborative savants" and that we could learn from them how to become better collaborative creatives. She suggests, "As superorganism apes, we have the unique ability to imagine the futures we want, dream our collective dreams, and reverse-engineer them together."[42] Creative synergy incorporates many forms of creativity and many knowledge systems. It invites us to embrace superorganism superpowers toward shared dreams that will shape the future.

ATTUNEMENT AND ENCOUNTER: ENCHANTED EPISTEMOLOGY

Creative synergy involves developing the ability to tune into, or attune to, others, especially other species. Ecological critic Timothy Morton suggests that many of our discourses at the moment are about how we are "transitioning to caring about nonhumans in a more conscious way." Part of this transition entails an attunement to the infinite inner nature of *other,* which almost leaps out at us if we are available. Stephan Harding describes this kind of phenomenon through *encounter,* when the essence of the muntjac deer extends toward him. I have also experienced this sensation of reciprocal feeling through attunement and encounter, as a being's otherness enchants me with its depth and mystery. Morton puts it beautifully when he says, "The not-me beckons, making me hesitate."[43] Attunement and encounter offer us embodied, enchanted experiences of *other*. This kind of experiencing stops our ordinary, Cartesian consciousness from obscuring the dimensional aspect of reality rejected by our previous paradigm.

Epistemology is a way of knowing, so *enchanted epistemology* is a way of knowing beyond the prosaic world we are taught to perceive. Enchanted epistemologies offer us a way to see the real magic in the world—the connectedness, creativity, and complexity everywhere. Attunement and encounter are both enchanted epistemologies because they restore that magical aspect that has been chopped out of our knowledge system by the occidental schism, Occam's razor, and Hume's guillotine. Real magic doesn't preclude scientific discovery or ordinary ways of knowing; it expands them. Real magic means that the world is still full of possibility beyond the march of progress, that deeper music is still available to us through expanded ways of knowing.

RESPECT AND RECIPROCITY

Philosopher Ludwig Wittgenstein famously said, "If we could talk to a lion, we couldn't understand him."[44] Wittgenstein meant that the lion would be unintelligible to us because humans and lions have different frames of reference for meaning. The human and lion Umwelten are different, so the meaning they make may be different. However, unintelligibility doesn't preclude sharing meaning such as joy, grief, play, and sorrow. Anyone who has had the companionship of a nonhuman person knows them to not only feel but also, most likely, tune into the feelings of their humans perhaps better than humans tune into them. Canines and felines, for example, can sense body language and mood, and may even smell body chemistry for cues to what you think and feel. Some have the ability to detect cancers, and some can even detect imminent death. Beyond that, they communicate constantly in ways we don't yet understand, sometimes because of our sense of human exceptionalism, sometimes because we depend upon other senses to make meaning, and in some cases, perhaps, because it might painful to hear what they have to say. What nonhumans say to us may have immense implications for our societal practices.

Nonhuman animal eyes, windows to their souls, are not merely mirrors, but deep opaque pools of infinity with inexhaustible meaning and mystery. More and more we understand other animals to be creative, emotional, intelligent beings with cultural lives and language. Not only do nonhuman animals possess cultural lives and language, but they also have personalities, perhaps even at the smallest scales. In fact, personality may be an evolutionary strategy of nature's connected creativity. In his insightful new book, *Mousy Cats and Sheepish Coyotes: The Science of Animal Personalities,* biologist John A. Shivik offers us the profound revelation that "personality exists in all animal species, and that behavioral variation is a fundamental force that enables evolution."[45] Even at the smallest scales, personality pervades nature as an aspect of connected creativity.

These revelations compel us to respect our nonhuman kin not only as family, but as diverse subjective selves with unique personalities. *Respect* derives from the Latin *re-,* "back" and *spectare,* "to look." Donna Haraway discusses deconstructionist Jacques Derrida's important book *The Animal That Therefore I Am,* in which he begins with a meditation on his cat, who gazed at his nakedness one day. His reflections, which challenge Descartes's *cogito,* also challenge human exceptionalism, yet they never turn back to the cat's Umwelt. Haraway points out that he comes to "the edge" of respect, but fails to "become curious about what the cat might actually be doing, feeling, thinking, or perhaps making available to him in looking back at him."[46] Respecting nonhuman people means looking back with compassionate curiosity and cultural humility, to ask what they might feel, mean, and think. Respect also means understanding how much that relationship makes available to us and how we might aid them through our attunement. This kind of respect requires reciprocity: we would seek to become intelligible to the lion, or the cat, or any nonhuman person we encounter. We would seek to learn *their* language instead of always asking them to learn ours.

Respect for the more-than-human world requires a transition to reciprocal relations with nonhuman kin. Creating reciprocal relations means asking ourselves how we might listen better to their desires, experience, and needs. We may not speak the same verbal language, but we share much nonlinguistic (and even some linguistic) meaning: we speak, create, dream, fun, joy, love, play, and much more. We can relate to each other because we share feeling and thoughts, as well as many of the same vulnerabilities. We share precarity, and we share the existential predicament of finitude and impermanence. We share much by way of cosmological origin, DNA, cognitive continuity, and the fact of being earthlings. If we have so much in common, we can certainly share world building, always remembering that we may have very different desires and needs. A simple practice in reciprocal respect would be letting our canine family walk us. I do this with my furry family member; she takes me for a walk, so she can pick up and drop off her pee-mail in a leisurely fashion, lingering over scents as I would messages or news online. I also realize that the precision of how and where she leaves her messages most likely has to do with her ability to sense the magnetic poles of the Earth.[47] I shift my attention from what I want from her and what is convenient to me to what she wants. I also realize that her wants in life may be due to her extrasensory abilities. Imagining what it would be like to have those extra senses helps me to understand how to respect her as another person with unique abilities, desires, and needs. This simple shift converts mastery to synergy and revives our sense of kinship. Many opportunities are arising now for interspecies connected creativity, as we ally toward a better shared future.

Some questions we might ask ourselves as we commit to synergy: How can we respect our nonhuman kin, with all their extrasensory abilities and unique personalities? How do we look back and answer their gaze? How do we become more intelligible to them, learn their language? How do we find out what they feel? Think? Want? How can we love them the ways they want to be loved?

We always participate in the complex, connected process that we call *nature,* but, as I have previously suggested, *how* we participate matters. Creative synergy's combination of diverse and enchanted epistemologies provides us with better forms of participation than our own. Christian de Quincey writes about the *cosmic organism* that unites all matter through feeling: "Terrestrial nature is itself an embodied node in the larger ecology of cosmic processes."[48] Creative synergy reinforces our kinship with the greater planetary ecology, the Earth node of cosmic process, by tuning us into the many other frequencies on that dazzling planetary spectrum of creativity.

Our ability to be other-directed as individuals and as a species directly relates to our survival. Relationship (kinship, symbiosis, and synergy) forms a critical and sacred aspect of being and becoming together. Our embrace of diverse creativity, embodied experience, and expanded knowledge systems offers us a possible realm of futurity in the Anthropocene. Our world shrinks, literally and metaphorically. That shrinking sphere means also migrating populations of many species, many human and nonhuman people needing refuge in a volatile world. Population grows and development expands, even into protected wilderness. What terrain is left? I would suggest that it is a realm beyond conquest, beyond mastery, and beyond progress: the realm of interspecies intersubjectivity. As we incorporate the lessons of complexity, symbiosis, and synergy, we must find a way into the future that includes many dreams, many stories, and many voices.

In the next and final chapter I will offer thoughts on how we might embark on a journey together into the sacred space of shared futurity: entirely uncertain, but full of *real magic.*

9 SACRED FUTURISM
Radical Enchantment

We are called to be the architects of the future, not its victims.

BUCKMINSTER FULLER

Let us put our minds together and see what life we can make for our children.

CHIEF SITTING BULL

How many civilizations have risen and fallen on our planet? How many species have lived and died in our solar system? How many species have formed, lived, thrived, and advanced, only to expire, in our galaxy? How many technologically advanced civilizations in the universe created their own demise by depleting their resources, or succeeded and evolved to immense complexity, only to be wiped out by some unforeseen cataclysm? How many civilizations have evolved past anything we could imagine, and exist presently as beyond our comprehension? The Drake equation, a probabilistic argument used to determine the number of active and communicative extraterrestrial civilizations in the Milky Way galaxy, was theorized by Frank Drake in 1961. Though Drake's original estimates have been modified since that time, he began an important dialogue that offered an alternative to the implausible anthropocentric notion that humans are the only advanced civilization in our galaxy, let alone our universe. Since that dialogue began, it seems much more likely that many other life forms and civilizations, some far more advanced than ours, populate the universe. With the recent discovery of exoplanets similar to our own within our galaxy, the probability increases that we are not alone even within our tiny corner of the vast universe.

We do know for sure that universal forces create births and deaths, ebbs and flows, oscillations, cycles, epochs, and ages, and give rise to earthlings—and, most likely, to many other life forms unrecognizable to us. From our narrow perspective, we can only conjecture what might be going on elsewhere in the universe. Shamans and visionaries, artists and scientists, poets and physicists, have attempted to transcend the limitations of human consciousness and reach into a realm of possibility beyond the known.

Current images of possible futures tend to be highly polarized. Science fiction paints shining utopias and bleak wastelands, peaceful and harmonious planetary societies or war-torn, chaotic dystopian hordes of cannibals and postapocalyptic mutants. As a child, my imagination covered a spectrum of possible futures, both hopeful and terrifying: dreams of bright futures in deep space mingled with dark nightmares of a nuclear apocalypse.

Science fiction and speculation occupied my adolescent imagination as the line between science fiction and scientific theory grew thin with advances in technology. Increasingly, whatever could be imagined eventually became real. I began to suspect that our imaginations had a lot to do with our future. I realized that the impossible becomes possible given enough time. What we only imagine now may yet come to pass; what we imagine matters more than we think. Not only does *what* we imagine for our future matter, but *how* we imagine it may be even more important.

In the face of climate change, overpopulation, mass extinctions, cyclical catastrophic events, near-Earth asteroids, religious wars, terrorism, nuclear proliferation, superbugs, and potentially malevolent AI, our imaginations seem about as capable of addressing our problems as a wet match in a hailstorm. Some scientists caution that even if we shift away from fossil fuels, biodiversity will not recover for thousands of years. More hopeful discourses suggest that rapid technological shifts could salvage the future and even create an advanced civilization. Whatever the case, the Anthropocene marks the end of a golden age of delusion, the beginning of a humbling unknown.

Sacred futurism views all these stories as powerfully interactive. Our ability to embrace uncertainty with imagination, compassion, and hope affects our role in the unfolding universal story. Joanna Macy has called this the time of the "Great Turning," and invokes the powerful metaphor of three rivers: "Now, in our time, these three rivers—anguish for our world, scientific breakthroughs, and ancestral teachings—flow together" to help us face the unknown.[1] Transformation tends to converge what we consider disparate: birth and death, old and new, despair and hope. Tension between opposites creates the warp and woof of life's mysteries. Nature requires us to tolerate this tension, and as we learn to flow with it, we discover the essence of transformation.

NATURE'S TERMS AND COSMOGENESIS

Author Kurt Vonnegut said in a famous letter to the future: "It (nature) has not only exterminated exquisitely evolved species in a twinkling, but drained oceans and drowned continents as well." He went on to suggest that in the face of such incredible forces, such unpredictability, and the constant possibility of annihilation

> are not those who promise ultimate victory over Nature through perseverance in living as we do right now, but those with the courage and intelligence to present to the world what appears to be Nature's stern but reasonable surrender terms:

1. Reduce and stabilize your population.
2. Stop poisoning the air, the water, and the topsoil.
3. Stop preparing for war and start dealing with your real problems.
4. Teach your kids, and yourselves, too, while you're at it, how to inhabit a small planet without helping to kill it.
5. Stop thinking science can fix anything if you give it a trillion dollars.
6. Stop thinking your grandchildren will be okay no matter how wasteful or destructive you may be, since they can go to a nice new planet on a spaceship. That is *really* mean, and stupid. And so on. Or else.[2]

Vonnegut furnished that perspicuous list in 1988, but humans continue to resist living by nature's terms. Anthropocene nature challenges our resistance. We continue to think that science can fix everything if we give it a trillion dollars. Science can indeed fix many things, but it cannot fix or alter nature's terms. Those terms are nonnegotiable. Life is complex, and nature's terms are simple. We cannot reduce complexity, but we can expand our own creativity to include, first and foremost, a better understanding of those terms. In this hypercomplex age, we need to use our creativity to inquire more deeply into nature's terms and how we honor and respect them.

In *The Universe Story*, visionary cosmologists Thomas Berry and Brian Swimme describe their adaptation of Albert Einstein's cosmological principle, which states that, on a large scale, the universe exhibits homogeneity and isotropy, operating according to the same physical laws throughout.[3] In addition, the cosmogenetic principle claims that evolution of the universe involves three key characteristics: *differentiation, autopoiesis,* and *communion.*

Berry and Swimme describe the tendency for all systems in the universe to generate a cascade of ever-expanding complexity through symmetry-breaking differentiation. As this cascading process continues, higher orders of increasing complexity self-organize, and new systems with new capacities emerge. Although the universe's complexity expands in a dazzling kaleidoscopic of patterns, everything remains related, interconnected, and in deep communion—the sacred fundament of cosmic evolution.

Nature's planetary terms relate to how the cosmogenetic principle expresses itself through Earth and its inhabitants. All beings, each a minicosmos or microcosm, operate according to these principles.

Vonnegut uses the phrase "surrender terms," which implies that nature stands as a formidable enemy to whom we must raise a white flag. Instead of "surrender," I prefer the idea of *acceptance*. We would do well to accept nature's terms—regarding them as an opportunity for transformation, by choosing to participate in the process, knowing that nature, while formidable and irreducible, also displays generous and wonderful complexity. If we attempt to reduce complexity, we end up disconnected from the flow of cosmic unfolding. Complexity can be met only with active and intentional communion as we encounter each ambiguous, even perilous, moment with curiosity, humility, and inquiry.

ARCHITECTS OF COMPLEXITY

In the 1960s, Buckminster Fuller gave a powerful call to the world: "We are called to be the architects of the future, not its victims." To this he added an equally powerful and provocative challenge: "[to] make the world work for 100 percent of humanity in the shortest possible time through spontaneous cooperation without ecological damage or disadvantage to anyone."[4]

This crucial question requires a shift to a new way of thinking that I have discussed in this book so far: partnership instead of domination, and synergy instead of mastery. Using the insights of panpsychism and complexity thinking, this book aims to augment Fuller's vision by establishing a sacred foundation for futurism. In the spirit of embodied envisioning and sacred futurism, I ask: *How can we make the world work for as many sentient beings as possible in the shortest possible time through synergic creativity, minimizing ecological damage or disadvantage to any species?*

Does this seem naïve, idealistic, radical? Synergic creativity thrives on inquiry, especially radical inquiry. The word *radical,* after all, comes from Latin *radix,* or "root." In order to face insurmountable problems, we must ask the most impossible-seeming questions, which dig deeply into our existential roots. To secure a sacred future, we need to ask radical questions such as *what kind of future will support the well-being of all species' cultures?* How might different answers to these questions coexist and support each other? The answer lies in our ability to tolerate, and even embrace, complexity. We have to recognize that all nonhumans and humans share the same cosmological origin—and that we become through differentiation, self-creation, and are reunited through communion. Communion requires the ability to connect and co-create through complex consciousness, so that we might see the real magic in each other and the world. This expanded, or enchanted, epistemology offers us that possibility. I call the radical revisioning of our world that offers us that greater possibility of futurity *radical enchantment.*

Philosopher Freya Mathews describes the panpsychist worldview as "enchanted," meaning that we live in a landscape of intersubjectivity. She suggests that we are "permeable" to other subjectivities, and that permeability leaves us open to cotransformation.[5] Similarly, ethnographer Anna Tsing offers the idea that encounters are "indeterminate; we are unpredictably transformed." She suggests that "radical curiosity beckons."[6] Radical enchantment combines complex consciousness, the enchanted worldview, and radical curiosity toward navigating a hypercomplex futurity that offers unexpected opportunities for cotransformation.

Edgar Morin cautions that we tend to think of futures in terms of either/or because of oppositional rather than inclusive thinking. He explains that uncertainty, complexity, and the dynamic nature of living systems means that what seems impossible becomes paradoxically possible.

> We are . . . faced with the unheard of paradox in which realism becomes utopian and the possible becomes impossible. However, this paradox also tells us that there is a realistic utopia, and that there is a possible impossible. The principle of the uncertainty of reality is an opening in both realism and the impossible.[7]

If we give up because our current utopian visions elude us and allow ourselves to become paralyzed by dystopian nihilism, we become the victims of the future. What if, instead, we imagine how to synthesize the complexity of the world not through reducing it, but using synergic creativity, guided by both/and thinking? Where we crave certainty, we cultivate curiosity—about ourselves, each other, and our world. We transform *with* the world while learning how the world could be, transcending our fears in courageous communion. Transform, commune, and evolve. That is no guarantee, but it is a possibility.

THE UTOPIAN PARADOX: NOWHERE PLACES AND HAPPY PLACES

Sir Thomas More, humanist, philosopher, lawyer, and devout Catholic, was a Tudor court statesman known for brutal torture of Protestant heretics, and eventually executed by Henry VIII for conscientious objection to the Act of Succession. Before his reign as chancellor, however, Moore coined the word *utopia* in 1516 in a controversial work of that name. *Outopos,* or "nowhere," is a play on words on the Greek *eutopos,* or "happy place." Little did he suspect how this text would shape the Western narrative.

Some scholars see More's work as either a philosophical inquiry into a purely humanistic society or as an Epicurean inquiry into pleasure as the guiding principle.[8] Others see it as a satire poking at the implausibility of either scenario. Whatever the case, he began a lasting Western preoccupation with utopia, and with whether any such collective happy place could exist at all.

Discussing the range of philosophical ideas on this subject would take several volumes, so I will just say that a happy place might be different for every being, and that perhaps the only happy place comes about only through intersubjective alignment—a collective *moment*, not a place. An amphibian might consider a boggy, wet pond its happy place, or a cetacean, the cold, dark depths of the ocean. In their version of the Geneva Convention, canines would undoubtedly ban baths as unnecessarily cruel. Every creature might build a different version of utopia. If sentience exists throughout nature, but Umwelten vary significantly, then my happy place would be very different from yours, even if we belong to the same species, come from the same culture, or live in the same family. Complexity thinking doesn't seek to reduce experience to a single common denominator, but asks us to inquire into how diverse experiences and knowledge should guide communal world building. If we begin to connect diverse concepts and reconcile apparent opposites, we can build more flexible and resilient societies in the face of hypercomplexity.

Any utopian ideology that seeks to reduce complexity through narratives based on domination will quickly become dystopian. We need to recognize a key difference between mastery and synergy: Whereas mastery creates a closed loop of suffocating dogmatic thinking, synergy encourages connection, consideration, and co-creativity toward transformation. Instead of being stuck in a closed, static loop, we open to the transformative spiral of lived and shared inquiry. In order to create a better world for many species—not just the best of all possible worlds for a dominant group of humans—we have to develop transformative inquiries.

Happy places cannot be created by mastery of nature or abstract governance. If utopia doesn't exist anywhere, then *eutopia,* the happy place, exists right here and now in the sacred spaces of attunement and encounter and in enchanted epistemologies. A future of happy places shared by humans and nonhumans emerges out of a radically enchanted present.

FROM TECHNOMAGIC TO SYNERGIC SCIENCE

Social philosopher William Irwin Thompson warned: "A science that never learns is not science, it is superstition, a new kind of primitive technomagic."[9] Rather than reduce technological innovation to inventing useful things or to solve problems, we must continuously inquire into whether things *are* truly useful, not just to humans, but to the whole, and whether solving immediate problems may create bigger problems. Technomagic can be viewed as a kind of evil eye to ward off our phantoms, and soothe our fear of the unknown, but it produces temporary solutions with long-term problems. In contrast, a learning science matures into a less dogmatic, more spiritual endeavor that seeks to embrace the deeper patterns of the universe over time. Where technomagic operates through blind intelligence and dogmatic ideology, real magic flows out of the fluid and flexible, connected creativity of nature.

In his prophetic book *Future Shock,* Alvin Toffler described a necessary shift from technocratic planning to "social futurism." He pointed out that *econocentric* technocracy cannot support the complexity of our rapidly changing society. Technocrats, he says, suffer from "econo-think" and consequently from myopia. The technocratic society attempts to solve multiple, complex problems with economic solutions and quick fixes. "Every society faces not merely a succession of probable futures, but an array of possible futures, and a conflict over *preferable* futures."[10] Toffler argues that social futurism addresses preferable future options through the "art of futurism." This ties into the concept of synergy versus mastery, and of a learning science rather than technomagic. Technocracy uses technomagic to control an uninformed, poorly educated population that has lost the ability to think critically. However, a learning science, based on the art of futurism, supports creative synergy through a considered inquiry into *preferable* futures.

Our current environmental circumstances require us to embrace the radical and critical notion that *technology should serve the planetary ecosystem,* not the other way around. Synergic science tempered with sacred futurism would free itself from dogmatic bias and escape corporate domination. Science freed from corporate enslavement and societal dogmatism could manifest the best innovations of ethical imagination and compassionate creativity, which are essential to a preferable future. If we value our scientists—some of the hardest-working people I know—we will want them to have the funding they need to support ethical and compassionate research, not research biased toward their corporate benefactors.

BIOMIMICRY: NATURE AS TEACHER

The Biomimicry Institute defines biomimicry as "an approach to innovation that seeks sustainable solutions to human challenges by emulating nature's time-tested patterns and strategies." The institute describes its motivating insight:

> Nature has already solved many of the problems we are grappling with. Animals, plants, and microbes are the consummate engineers. After billions of years of research and development, failures are fossils, and what surrounds us is the secret to survival.[11]

This powerful sentence sums it up well: "Failures are fossils, and what surrounds us is the secret to survival." Attunement to nature's principles awakens us to simple, but crucial, rules we can mimic and use to design human environments. Whereas our rigid constructions and ideologies fossilize us, literally and figuratively, nature's principles are based on flexibility and adaptability. *The Biomimicry Resource Handbook* defines six main principles of life used in biomimicry: (1) evolve to survive; (2) adapt to changing conditions; (3) be locally attuned and responsive; (4) use life-friendly chemistry; (5) be resource-efficient; (6) integrate development with growth.[12]

1. *Evolving to survive* means continually incorporating and embodying information. Rather than evolving through ideological

abstractions (e.g., survival of the fittest or anthropocentricism) that lead to conquest and domination, we use our embodiment, our senses, and our imagination to collaborate in the continuum of sentience.

2. *Adapting to changing conditions* means responding appropriately to dynamic contexts. Instead of reductionism and control, we adapt by becoming as flexible as nature herself.

3. *Being locally attuned and responsive* means integrating ourselves into the environment. We awaken to the needs of our local community and environment—human and nonhuman.

4. *Using life-friendly chemistry* means, as common sense tells us, that chemistry should not harm the chemist or the well being of the larger environment.[13] Although many species create toxins to ward off potential predators or threats, they create only as much as needed, with as little toxicity as possible to themselves.

5. *Being resource-efficient* means that we do not consume more than we can produce, we recycle materials, and we conserve energy.

6. *Integrating development and growth* means that we grow and develop by building structures on stable, ecology-sustaining platforms, from the bottom up, using nested hierarchies.

In *The Dream of the Earth,* Thomas Berry suggests that we need to relearn our "capacity for listening to what the Earth is telling us"—the only way to face our "dangerous future." He adds that we alone do not determine our future; instead, our future depends on "the entire Earth in the unity of its organic functioning."[14]

According to the modern paradigm, ideas come from human brains. However, from a panpsychist perspective, ideas circulate intersubjectively throughout the noosphere. We constantly share collective ideas; no idea arises in a vacuum, or through a special conduit from above. Rather, creative thoughts ripple through an infinite ocean of consciousness. Good ideas tend to repeat themselves in different forms, on different scales, to coordinate ecosystems within one cosmic organism. The principles of biomimicry express nature's diverse, collaborative creativity and guide us to produce elegant and functional designs.

Epistemologist Alfonso Montuori describes the kind of creativity needed to navigate uncertainty and complexity in our times: "A collaborative, contextual, complex creativity will be a vital ingredient in coping with the present and creating the future."[15] He explains that the model of the lone genius belongs to the mechanistic age—that our hypercomplex age requires us to revise the notion of creativity itself.

Many scientists now advocate the transition to new methodologies that include the touchstone of compassion. Marc Bekoff describes the revelation of contemporary scientists that more humane research renders better science: "Research that harms animals often produces misleading data."[16] Just as traditional objective inquiry often harms humans by attempting to reduce the complexity of lived experience, it also harms nonhumans. We might expand our understanding of the complex world by transitioning to methods that incorporate the researcher into the research, understanding that what hurts the subject may also in some way hurt the research—and possibly the researcher.

We might ask: how can we transition toward the sacred space of compassionate curiosity and inquiry?

Participatory Action Research (PAR) and More-Than-Human Participatory Action Research are new approaches that incorporate the researcher into the research, as co-subject. Peter Reason and Hilary Bradbury suggest that PAR is not so much a "methodology as an orientation toward inquiry that seeks to create participative communities of inquiry."[17] They cite the qualities of "engagement, curiosity and question posing" as critical to addressing significant ecological and social issues.

PAR in More-Than-Human Worlds seeks also to address significant ecological and social issues. Michelle Bastian, Owain Jones, Niamh Moore, and Emma Roe suggest that an "ecologicalization of knowledge is an essential step in moving away from the Enlightenment philosophies of rational, self-aware humans in a machine-like world" and "taking the more-than-human world seriously as a research participant."[18] This "taking seriously" of diverse human and nonhuman experience and creativity offers us the chance of a future through connected creativity. PAR offers a crucial reorientation of our attitude of inquiry essential to the enactment of creative synergy.

Transdisciplinarity offers another crucial strategy offering dimensionality to research, theory, and applications. Transdisciplinarity emerged out of the collaboration of systems thinkers, scientists, social scientists, philosophers, and other researchers interested in more transformative research. Alfonso Montuori describes transdisciplinarity as an "altogether different way of thinking about knowledge, knowledge production and inquiry."[19] Transdisciplinarity shifts our thinking about thinking by allowing many disciplines to combine insights and to produce knowledge with the understanding that the inquirer is a participant. Beyond that, the inquirer must develop the ability to take a metaparadigmatic viewpoint, cultivate complexity thinking, and balance creativity with critical thinking.

The shift away from extreme specialization toward transdisciplinarity integrates different approaches to problem solving by reaching beyond the limits of any one methodology or epistemology. Futurist and psychologist Jennifer Gidley sees transdisciplinarity as a shift toward a more "planetary, postformal, and integral society."[20] She describes such approaches as "enactments" of new ways of thinking and knowledge patterns. Gidley also discusses a possible "post-disciplinary age," which blurs the lines between arts, humanities, crafts, and sciences. Learning categories will transcend Aristotle's ontology of categorization and separation, and become more fluid and integrated. As we evolve to become more flexible in our consciousness, we will become better builders of synergistic societies and environments that support the continuity and longevity of diverse planetary life. Participatory and transdisciplinary research push us beyond the myths of mastery and progress toward creative synergy.

EARTH JURISPRUDENCE

In *Wild Law: A Manifesto for Earth Justice,* environmental attorney and governance expert Cormac Cullinan presents a lucid account of why our governance has led to environmental catastrophe, and calls for an immediate implementation of "Earth Jurisprudence."

He describes the emergence of capitalism and private ownership out of a philosophical worldview that rapidly erodes civilization and our ecosystem. He indicts the myopic delusion that places greater importance on the human world, the "homosphere," than on the planet itself. "Constitutions, laws, and the judgments that interpret them . . . express and reflect our idea of what law is and ought to be, and what societies believe in and aspire to." Because our framework of governance derives from flawed ideas and values, our legislation system reflects similar fundamental flaws.[21]

Cullinan cites the Declaration of Independence as an example of flawed thinking because it assumes the perspective of Cartesian dualism. The Declaration considers animals (and some people) as objects, ineligible for the guaranteed right to life, liberty, and the pursuit of happiness. However, he asks, what if the Declaration had said that "all *creatures*" were created equal? A constitution that guaranteed the rights of all beings would have generated an entirely different set of laws. Current society cannot imagine how this could work; it simply *assumes* that our laws must support a homocentric framework.

Cullinan quotes legal philosopher Philip Allot:

Society cannot be better than its idea of itself. Law cannot be better than society's idea of itself. Given the central role of law in the self-ordering of society, society cannot be better than its idea of law.[22]

If we want a better society, we need a better worldview. If we want a better worldview, we need to rethink our thoughts. Cullinan points out that, according to judicial law, most beings, and the planet itself, qualify as objects without rights. "Most beings are, under the governance of our jurisprudence 'objects' or 'property' of a human or artificial 'juristic person' such as a company, or could at any moment become owned." He examines how corporatocracy has shaped jurisprudence since the 1844 Joint Stock Companies Act, when an early attempt to limit corporate rights was overruled. He describes the culmination of unbridled corporate growth:

> In our 21st-century world, fictional, incorporeal beings are given enormous, largely unfettered powers to dominate and exploit every aspect of Earth. These corporations and other juristic persons have no emotions, consciences, values, ethics, or ability to commune with other members of the Earth community.[23]

Corporate disregard for the rights to the Earth community demonstrates what happens when we reject diverse experience and sentience in favor of abstract ideologies and entities. We need to put our ecological needs first, because ensouled matter cannot flourish without meeting those needs. Our complex, multilayered ecological needs cannot be reduced to basic human needs—because our needs are always embedded in a complex web of relationships. Unfortunately, a society that considers most beings (including people) as mere objects and views corporations as "juristic persons" more real and deserving of rights than actual sentient beings, minimizes the legal options for defending the rights of nature. Disconnected from the embodied processes that express life's sacred principles, the corporate "person" puts profit before people and planet. An Earth-oriented jurisprudence puts life's embodied principles before incorporeal abstractions.

Cullinan explains that before considering Earth jurisprudence, we must understand what lies outside it, or, from a systemic point of view, we must take a metaview. He explains that any Earth jurisprudence must be based on the cosmogenetic principle, or the "Great Jurisprudence," those universal laws that bind all of us through systemic complexity and cycles of transformation.[24]

Diverse connections form the sacred, creative matrix that generates life. Any society that impedes ecological connectedness also impedes the sacred principles of the universe. Above all, Earth jurisprudence supports planetary ecological synergy—within a larger sacred relationship to the cosmic organism. A future that embodies and enacts the sacred depends on laws that protect those sacred relations, processes, and principles of life.

SYNERGIC LAW

Fritjof Capra and international and comparative-law expert Ugo Mattei propose that the ideas of law and ecology have been separated by the same Cartesian paradigm that separated humans from nature. They advocate a return to law that supports communal ecological flourishing:

> We must rethink our human laws and their relationship with the laws governing the ecology of a living planet . . . putting the commons and a long-term vision at center stage.[25]

Capra and Mattei propose three effective strategies to create this shift: "disconnecting law from power and violence; making community sovereign; and making ownership generative."[26]

The first strategy would revise oppressive laws created as abstractions by centralized, distant authorities that have no relevance to real communities. Ecological law would "oppose professional interests whose profit stems from alienating the law from its makers, users, and interpreters." The second strategy would revise laws, created by the "rhetoric of modernity," that treat private property as an eternal "despotic domain." Through ecological governance, the community stands sovereign over the individual or state, just as the commons becomes more important than private property. Logically, the life of a community must have places to flourish. The commons serves as the place of connection and collective empowerment—essentially, a sacred space of synergic creativity. The third strategy would make ownership "generative" in order to preserve the commons and facilitate intergenerational stewardship of *commoning*.

Capra and Mattei discuss business journalist Marjorie Kelly's studies of new ownership models. They quote her claim that we are at the beginning of an "ownership revolution." They list her examples, such as Denmark's wind guilds and nonprofits in Latin America, which are forming solidarity economies to "protect communities and ecosystems."[27] In the last few hundred years, legal institutions that protect private ownership and state sovereignty have grown "extractive" and become the dominant model, what Capra and Mattei call the "algal blooms" of human laws. Ecological law would support the flow of synergic creativity, and consequently, planetary health. I would call laws that support this flow *synergic laws*.

Above all, Capra and Mattei stress the importance of ecoliteracy for all members of society, but especially for jurists. Indeed, we need ecoliteracy, and the knowledge it brings, in order to live with nature on nature's nonnegotiable terms, and we need to generate synergic laws that apply global jurisprudence in local contexts.

COSMOPOLITICS

What do social justice, ecofeminism, and ecojustice have in common? All these forms of activism fight injustice created by the myths of mastery, mad objectivity, and progress. Slavery created by the madness of mastery still pervades our societies. Sex slavery remains a reality everywhere; on the Internet and in homes all over the planet, chattel slavery extends into the contemporary United States in the form of the prison industrial complex, which warehouses whole populations of humans still suffering from the intergenerational trauma of enslavement. Corporations routinely enslave populations for profit. Marginalized populations, who suffer most from mastery myth and its narratives, would benefit most from synergy. Synergy does not put profit before people; nor does it put an abstracted "environment" before people. Rather synergic society uses contextual intelligence to stay in touch with diverse lived experience through cultural humility and listening, and asks how we can make things work for as many people (nonhuman and human) as possible.

Ecopoet and activist Drew Dellinger recently wrote about the "ecological King." He observes that Martin Luther King Jr.'s later speeches and writings became more oriented toward interconnectedness. In his famous 1967 Christmas Eve Sermon, he suggested, "We are all caught in an inescapable mutuality." Dellinger says of King's cosmological and ecological insights, "his holistic vision led him to emphasize the connections between racism, militarism and economic injustice, and to see continuities across social movements."[28] This movement toward the intersection between social justice, ecofeminism, and ecojustice synergizes our ability to fight the corporate-owned neoliberal governments responsible for oppression in the contemporary world.

Donna Haraway invokes ecofeminist Isabelle Stengers's formulation of cosmopolitics, saying that "decisions must take place somehow in the presence of those who will bear their consequences."[29] This requires contextual understandings of how social and ecojustice intersect. Synergic cosmopolitics would focus on how relationships between systems can regenerate both systems through connected creativity.

PERMACULTURE PRINCIPLES

In an increasingly urbanized global population, we will need to understand how to synergize artificial and natural environments, resisting the temptation to expand into wild spaces. I envision ecological urbanity and wild law converging to create truly green cities with incentives to conserve wild places.

Permaculture expert Toby Hemenway writes engagingly about shifting our concepts of urban and suburban spaces. In his extensive research, he began to realize that permaculture had less to do with pristine verdant landscapes, however much he loves them, and more to do with discovering the principles of a regenerative, restorative way of life that applies to every landscape. He says of this: "We search for the principles that generate life's resilience, immense productivity, diversity, interconnectedness, and elegance." He asks not just how we feed ourselves but how we can "meet all of our needs . . . how do we build . . . use water and energy, feel secure, make decisions, solve problems, sustain ourselves, develop policies, live together?"[30] Permaculture principles involve more than simply greening and regenerating our objective world, but all of our *intersubjective* relationships. We need to honor the inherent sacredness of the sentient, ensouled matter that composes our world through kinship, symbiosis, and synergic practice.

I see signs of a growing desire to apply nature's principles as an extension of the sacred into our embodied experience. We build our cities inefficiently, disconnected from the deep patterns of nature. Other species, however, also build cities—and do so much more efficiently. For example, ants build labyrinthine underground structures with highways connecting circular chambers, and termites build complex infrastructures with ventilation systems. Bees build immense hives with remarkable sustainable integrity. All these city builders use and reuse benign building materials. For better or for worse, cities emerge on different scales as a natural extension of sentient creativity and biological reproduction. How, then, can we build cities that transcend the industrial age's ever-growing footprints of pollution? That great challenge lies in store for a new generation of designers, architects, and city planners—to accommodate exploding populations as they expand and meet in hypercomplex urban spaces.

Western civilizations built cities according to principles of central authority, stratified hierarchy, patriarchy, and a separation between humans and the natural world. A shift to synergic societies would place greater importance on the commons and communal creativity. It would aim to reintegrate the connected creativity of nature into our lives, liberating us to be more independent. How different from our current dependence on capital, and the network of laws designed to protect the powerful! In a synergic society, we would feel more connected to each other as humans and also to the more-than-human world. Not only would the average person understand how to grow her or his own food and cultivate medicinal plants, but food-bearing and medicinal trees and plants would grow throughout cities, indoors and outdoors, improving the quality of the environment. Money doesn't grow on trees, but food and medicine do!

SYNERGIC SOCIETY AND BIOPHILIC GOVERNANCE

In chapter 8 I discussed the vital push beyond human exceptionalism toward a recognition of diverse and immense nonhuman intelligence and sentience. I also discussed the vast mycelium networks that connect trees and facilitate communication in forests. Modernity's fallacious belief that trees are insentient vegetation, to be used solely as building material or fuel, has resulted in massive deforestation, atmospheric deterioration, and rapid climate change. But research in the last several decades confirms that we simply cannot ignore our relationships with trees and plants, which are so vital to our well-being: living without that connection puts our own survival at risk.

Dr. Roger Ulrich, professor of architecture at the Center for Research at Chalmers University in Sweden, has engaged in decades of research on how gardens and plants in building design contribute to a healthy society.[31] In one study, he discovered that recovery times for hospital patients with garden views were significantly shorter than for those facing brick walls. They also had less anxiety and needed less pain medication. In 2001, Frances Kuo and Bill Sullivan of the University of Illinois Human-Environment Research Laboratory studied how the residents of Robert Taylor Home, one of the largest housing projects in Chicago, performed in their daily lives based on the amount of contact they had with trees. He reported that crime rates were 56 percent lower in the areas with trees and greenery, compared with concrete, barren areas.[32]

Kuo also studied the relationship between environment and child behavior, indicating positive correlations between greenery and children's psychological health.[33] These few examples illustrate societal awakening to the essential connection between humans and flora. Some societies consider that connection essential. In Japan, for example, many now practice *shinrin-yoku,* or "forest bathing," as essential for well-being.

Thomas Berry's tenth principle of Earth jurisprudence states:

Humans have not only a need for, but also a right of, access to the natural world to provide for the physical needs of humans and the wonder needed by human intelligence, the beauty needed by human imagination, and the intimacy needed by human emotions for personal fulfillment.[34]

All humans need to cultivate this connection. Modern industrialism created many cities in which only those at the top of the hierarchy have access to green places, while people who serve those at the top live in barren, concrete, industrialized wastelands. In a synergic society that values diversity, all humans have access to the natural world. This access through connection to the more-than-human world anchors us in meaning, wonder, and biophilia, and inspires us to protect it.

A sense of belonging to something deeper and greater than any one creed or culture can only be reinforced by sharing this connection through kinship, symbiosis, and synergic society. Connectedness offers us a way to share not only the beauty and wonder of our world's cycles of death and regeneration, but also the sorrows and tragedies that inevitably come with those cycles. We have not been kicked out of a garden, we are not alone in an insentient world, we are not in a struggle for dominance; we are kin in all our diversity and expression.

Ecopoet Mary Oliver's poem "Wild Geese" conveys the immediacy of an animate world that continually beckons us, offering us a sense of belonging:

calls you to the wild geese, harsh and exciting—
over and over announcing your place
in the family of things.[35]

A synergic society relates to the humans and nonhuman world as *family,* and the way we relate to our world shapes the structure of our laws and society. Permaculture principles and ecological law would guide the flow of right relationship in a synergic society. Similarly, ecological design principles and building codes would compel designers to think in terms not only of sustainability but also of building relationships between diverse beings. If the sacredness of relationship lies at the basis of our worldview, biophilic creativity transforms into an expression of familial love. Can we imagine a future in which our governance expresses and supports biophilia? Can we imagine a future as *family*?

SACRED LANDSCAPES AND SACRED SPACES

I have always loved wild places and considered them sacred, and I experience immense grief watching those places dwindle and be destroyed. Wild places, as more-than-human expressions of connected creativity, more than symbolize the sacred: *they nurture and feed it.* When we return to that expression of nature, we return to our primordial selves. In wilderness, the din of ego quiets, and we can hear the sacred pulse of the great conversation. We cease our preoccupation with constructed reality and feel part of a greater reality. We need to preserve our wild places, care for them, and love them because of this sacred pulse, vital to our own authentic selves.

Many people in this industrialized, urbanized world never enjoy the sacred experience of wilderness. Children growing up in urban and suburban landscapes exhibit the symptoms of what John Muir once cautioned against: the loss of "inherited wildness." I see these as symptoms of a systemic suppression of biophilia, but my work as an environmental educator has revealed to me that young people need and want these connections. I have seen children who have never experienced more-than-human ecosystems marvel at them and long to come back. I have seen the healing held in communal gardens that green concrete places, reviving the heart of community. Biophilia lives everywhere, not only in wild places, but rather in the wild aspect of the self that needs nurturing. Biophilia lies in the heart of everyone, waiting to awaken when set free from the prisons (literal and metaphorical) of mastery-made society. Earth jurisprudence and ecoliteracy would seek to create communal experiences to reawaken biophilia, regenerating inner and outer sacred landscapes. I am inspired by recent projects such as pollinator gardens in correctional facilities—a powerful embodied metaphor for regeneration.

As the human population increases, and the planet becomes more urbanized, we need to fiercely protect our remaining wilderness against the temptation to overdevelop. We also need to discover how the greening of urban landscapes, and attunement to sacred kinship, can support inner wildness and biophilia while also promoting balanced investment in preservation and conservation. A *sacred city* would not only operate on the principles of ecology and synergic law, but also on the vital principles of permaculture, a way of living that connects us with more-than-human creativity. The sacred landscape within and between beings and the sacralization of the world remain inextricably related and interdependent.

Sacred space between subjects must also be a vital domain of sacralized futurity. As societies and species overlap, we may form new creative alliances. This immanent prospect requires that we learn to cultivate kinship in unexpected ways. Donna Haraway suggests that *worlding with* many species requires "making oddkin." She suggests that "we require each other in unexpected collaborations and combinations, in hot compost piles."[36] If we think in terms of creative synergy and permaculture principles, we understand how vital intra- and interspecies collaboration is to our present. Any possible futures must emerge out of these synergic relationships, these "sacred spaces" between beings. Emergent stories about interspecies creativity and connections are not fairy tales, but reality, and are full of real, practical magic and enchanting mystery.

PLANETARY PEDAGOGY AND
SYNERGIC INQUIRY

At the beginning of this chapter, I quote the legendary spiritual leader and warrior of the Hunkpapa Lakota Chief Sitting Bull, who suggested: "Let us put our minds together and see what kind of life we can make for our children." Sitting Bull said this as he faced the systemic genocide of his people and the annihilation of his culture at the hands of European colonialism. He considered it of utmost importance that the collective imagination of his people rally toward the well-being of future generations.

Almost two hundred years later, the same paradigm that attempted to annihilate the Hunkpapa Lakota has annihilated biodiversity and cultural diversity, and threatens to annihilate our entire planetary ecosystem—jeopardizing the future of every child on the planet. How, then, do we engage our synergic creativity to imagine a future worth having for the next generations, however few or many they might be? It begins with how we educate our children now.

In *Pedagogy of the Oppressed* (1970), Paulo Freire described the biophilia-killing effects of modernity's educational paradigm. He compared conventional education to the banking system, where teachers "deposit" knowledge into students for withdrawal later on in the workforce. This "necrophilic" model thrives on systemic control:

> The banking concept of education . . . based on a mechanistic, static, naturalistic, spatialized view of consciousness . . . transforms students into receiving objects . . . attempts to control thinking and action, leads women and men to adjust to the world, and inhibits their creative power.[37]

Unfortunately, many of the world's educational systems still conform to this model. Students memorize rote information in order to pass examinations, and an excess of homework excludes the development of their own interests and creative purpose. Critical thinking, an activity that encourages challenging the status quo, is rarely taught in traditional, public educational settings. Students who think differently and learn differently from the majority often suffer in these environments; they are warehoused in special-education programs, or they eventually drop out altogether. The high dropout rate, combined with expensive college tuition fees, exacerbates the situation by feeding into the prison-industrial complex. This truly vicious cycle scores the United States low on the global educational scale (fourteenth out of forty countries) and highest in the world on the scale of persons incarcerated per capita. In this scenario, the future bends toward those who can afford it through privilege or status.

In order to create a synergic educational environment that can deal with hypercomplexity, we must begin with the premise that diversity powers ecological creativity. A lack of biodiversity indicates a problem in an ecosystem. Similarly, inability to deal with diversity in an educational system indicates an even greater underlying problem.

Futurist Charles M. Johnston described these as the *separation fallacy,* the *unity fallacy,* and the *compromise fallacy.* In *Cultural Maturity: A Guidebook for the Future,* he discusses our tendency to get stuck in one of these three fallacies. He explains that the separation fallacy occurs when differences polarize, causing oppositional dualities. The unity fallacy fails to acknowledge differentiation in favor of oneness and sameness, causing false symbiosis. The compromise fallacy seeks an extreme middle ground rather than true integration.[38] Each fallacy impedes true intersubjective alignment and integration, which depend on the ability to integrate differences and to see differences as opportunities to grow and learn.

In banking-style education, the separation and compromise fallacies reduce students to objects through institutional separation, or forces a middle ground without attempting authentic integration. Progressive schools, on the other hand, see their model as the paragon of authentic harmonious oneness—the unity fallacy. However, for the most part, private progressive schools celebrate diversity in abstraction, but have little practice in what it means to actually integrate diverse experiences. Our current major social challenge requires *integration in action,* not the copout of intellectual abstractions. Sacred futurism, likewise, requires that we teach our children how to understand and integrate their embodied experiences through authentic opportunities for inter-subjective alignment.

In their brilliant book *Synergic Inquiry*, Yongming Tang and Charles Joiner transcend the fallacies of separation, compromise, and unity through a unique methodology that seeks to identify a pattern "that is so important that it has the potential to integrate the divergent perspectives that normally compete."[39] This "pattern," the cosmogenetic principle, expresses itself throughout nature: *differentiation, autopoiesis,* and *communion.* Their methodology facilitates greater understanding between people and helps them reflect on their own reactions to others' differing perspectives; through that reflection, they expand their awareness. Rather than reaching forced consensus (the compromise fallacy), we can learn to experience another's subjectivity in an intersubjective practice called *difference holding,* and conclude the practice with *difference transcending.* Using this method, difference becomes a potent creative ally to the transformational process. I advocate this method as a fundamental part of a complex pedagogy.

Planetary pedagogy integrates diversity and supports creative synergy, similar to the idea of growing together. I would add that if we do grow together, we also *learn* together. Christian de Quincey says that ultimately "meaning, not mere mechanism, becomes the connection between beings."[40] When intersubjectivity becomes a valid principle of education, diverse subjectivities open to, and become meaningful for, each other. School becomes a sacred space to have relationships, to grow together, while learning the wonders of the relational cosmos. Planetary pedagogy implies education based on partnership dynamics and relational principles; it teaches children the wisdom articulated by Thomas Berry and Brian Swimme in *The Universe Story,* that "the universe is a communion of subjects rather than a collection of objects."[41] The practice of communion between subjects, or intersubjective alignment, constitutes a necessary part of a curriculum for generating and sustaining a biophilic society.

Planetary pedagogy assumes as an axiom that we are deeply, intrinsically, connected to the entire universe, and, therefore, to each other. Using this sacred premise, growing children feel encouraged to nurture their entelechy, and grow together. Berry and Swimme observe: "The primary purpose of education should be to enable individuals to fulfill their proper role in this larger pattern of meaning."[42] Contrary to the oppressive banking model that controls and defines people as objects to be used, biophilic pedagogy encourages children to become their authentic, creative selves in an atmosphere of curiosity, inquiry, and compassion.

Planetary pedagogy supports community through a sustained effort to *commune*. It recognizes and affirms our relationships exist within an infinite and eternal cosmic heritage, and the preciousness and purpose of every sentient being.

A planetary pedagogy supports teachers who commit themselves to lived inquiry. Teachers who grow with their students, learning from their lived experience, may literally learn how to teach through them. As an environmental educator, I often struggle to make conservation interesting to kids disconnected from the more-than-human places. I have to learn *from them* how to *teach them,* using teachable moments that often teach me so much that I didn't know. Teachers who want to engage their students in a hypercomplex world must constantly actualize their own entelechy and continue learning; engagement is reciprocal. In *Teaching to Transgress,* cultural critic Bell Hooks calls teachers to self-actualize to better "create pedagogical practices that engage students, providing them with ways of knowing that enhance their capacity to live fully and deeply."[43] Living fully and deeply requires a shift from alienated apathy or cutthroat competitiveness toward engaged connected creativity.

COSMIC CURRICULUM
AND RADICAL ENCHANTMENT

Planetary pedagogy emphasizes the *cosmic curriculum*—based on the premise that we are not a collection of objects in a machine, but communing *subjects* within universal patterns orchestrated by synchronicity. From this perspective, relationships between students (and teachers) matter as much as what the students study.

The cosmic curriculum incorporates both/and thinking into learning, expanding awareness through multiple epistemological lenses. How does math relate to music? How does physics relate to poetry? How do dreams relate to scientific discovery? Embracing multiplicity-in-unity, students can be encouraged to visualize connections between multiple subjects, enriching meaning, and augmenting teachable moments. This approach to education begins with the intention for human children to grow into flexible and fluid thinkers who know how to engage the world critically and contextually—and creatively. Empiricism meets empathy. Critical thinking meets creativity. Logic meets love. Hooks speaks powerfully on this idea in *Teaching Community,* "Love . . . is the foundation on which every learning community can be created."[44]

Contrary to traditional pedagogy, a cosmic curriculum would include nonhuman cultures and plant wisdom through a Goethean methodology and enchanted epistemologies. Children would learn not only to care for nonhuman beings, but to respect their Umwelt and unique intelligence, asking what those beings might know that we don't. A cosmic curriculum, based on communion, seeks to understand different experiences as important information about our universal process, our growing together. It also seeks to radically enchant the world by offering a dimensional view of life. It involves both critical and creative thinking that incorporates our experience of the imaginal realm into our lessons.

Dream sharing and other natural alterations of consciousness, such as meditation and visualization, play an important role in the cosmic curriculum. Children naturally feel connected to the imaginal realm, and both children and adults receive important information through different states of consciousness. Western culture sees the constructed perspective of ordinary reality as more real than any other state of consciousness. Because of this, in traditional educational settings, a teacher might admonish a child for daydreaming, and sharing a dream would be considered irrelevant to academic instruction. But in many indigenous cultures, dream sharing forms an important part of community life. Dreams come as gifts from another realm to guide our waking life. In some cultures, dreams take on the status of primary reality, with waking life a secondary reality. In the cosmic curriculum, a teacher might ask students, "What are you dreaming about?" A planetary pedagogy invites active imagination into the classroom in order to integrate the imaginal realm into daily learning objectives.

Carrying sacredness into the future depends on our children's ability to imagine a world from the perspectives of compassionate curiosity, complex consciousness, embodied envisioning and radical enchantment. Through this embodiment and expansion, the connected creativity of nature lives on in them, as well as in all the other children of the more-than-human world that now depend upon this crucial shift.

FUTURE SACRED

A future worth having demands a commitment to the cultivation of sacred relations through kinship and symbiosis. As our beginnings flowed out of an alliance between archenemies—prokaryotes and archeobacteria—our greatest achievements and advancements as a species result from co-creating to face adversity. The Anthropocene magnifies that need to ally in compassionate, complex, and connected creativity to face great adversity on many scales, for many species, in many contexts.

Our future sacredness expands through our embodied experience and imagination, our shared joys and sorrows, grief and hope. Our future sacredness takes shape in the radical enchantment of now through kinship, symbiosis, and synergy. Our future sacredness lies beyond the dreamless sleep of modern myths, in the shared awakening dreams of children, who learn the real magic that creates the world: the sacred space of connection between all beings.

NOTES

CHAPTER 1. MIND IN NATURE

1. Bar-On, Phillips, and Milo, "Biomass Distribution on Earth."
2. Müller, trans., *Rig Veda,* 10.129.
3. Loy, *World Is Made of Stories,* 29.
4. Thorpe, trans., *Edda Sæmundar Hinns Frôða,* 21.
5. Quoted in Bateson, *Ecology of Mind.*
6. Combs, *Radiance of Being,* 250.
7. Feynman, *Value of Science,* 13.
8. Deloria, *God Is Red,* 285.
9. Kohn, *How Forests Think,* 134.

CHAPTER 2. ENTELECHY

1. Curd, *Legacy of Parmenides,* 77.
2. Plato, *Phaedo,* 99a–d; in Bluck, trans., *Plato's Phaedo,* 122.
3. For a discussion of entelechy, see Joe Sachs, "Aristotle: Motion and its Place in Nature," Internet Encyclopedia of Philosophy, accessed June 24, 2018.
4. Aristotle, *Physics* 2.8; in Barnes, ed., *Complete Works of Aristotle,* 1:341.
5. Hwan-Chen, "Different Meanings of the Word *Energeia,*" 56–65.
6. Leibniz, *Monadology.*
7. Strickland, *Leibniz's Monadology,* 16–17.
8. Schonfeld, *Philosophy of the Young Kant,* 40.
9. Schopenhauer, *World as Will and Representation,* 164.
10. De Quincey, *Radical Nature,* 254.
11. Yoke Ho, *Li, Qi, and Shu,* 5.

12. Yoke Ho, 6.

13. Robinet, *Taoism,* 6–7.

14. Jung, *Synchronicity,* 96–98.

15. Bohm, *Wholeness and the Implicate Order,* 16.

16. Lovelock and Margulis, "Atmospheric Homeostasis by and for the Biosphere," 1–2.

17. Nagel, *Mind and Cosmos,* 130.

18. Houston, *Hero and the Goddess,* 62.

CHAPTER 3. METAPATTERNS

1. Bateson, *Mind and Nature,* 6–8.

2. Volk, *Metapatterns.*

3. Campbell, *Power of Myth,* 111.

4. Jung, *Collected Works, Vol. 11: Psychology and Religion,* para. 88.

5. Eliade, *Patterns in Comparative Religion,* 452.

6. Volk, *Metapatterns,* 18.

7. Volk, 30.

8. Mircea Eliade, "Symbolism of the Centre," in Eliade, *Images and Symbols,* 48–51.

9. Jung, *Memories, Dreams, Reflections,* 196.

10. Volk, *Metapatterns,* 100.

11. Gregory Cajete. "Tracking a Myth: The Concentric Rings of Indigenous Education," quoted in Native Knowledge: Circles of Life website, accessed June 24, 2018.

12. Koestler, *Ghost in the Machine,* 45.

13. Wilber, *Sex, Ecology, Spirituality.*

CHAPTER 4. SENTIENCE

1. Haraway, *Staying with the Trouble,* 80.

2. Shivik, *Mousy Cats and Sheepish Coyotes,* 68.

3. Berry, *Great Work,* 46.

4. The Cambridge Declaration on Consciousness was written by Philip Low and edited by Jaak Panksepp, Diana Reiss, David Edelman, Bruno Van Swinderen, Philip Low, and Christof Koch. The declaration was publicly proclaimed in Cambridge, UK, on July 7, 2012, at the Francis Crick Memorial

Conference on Consciousness in Human and non-Human Animals, at Churchill College, University of Cambridge. See http://fcmconference.org /img/CambridgeDeclarationOnConsciousness.pdf.

5. Marzluff and Angell, *Gifts of the Crow,* 33.

6. Miller, *Reproductive Biology and Phylogeny of Cetacea,* 5.

7. Whitehead and Rendell, *Cultural Lives of Whales and Dolphins,* 39.

8. Marino et al., "Cetaceans Have Complex Brains for Better Cognition."

9. Albertin et al., "Octopus Genome," 220–24.

10. Montgomery, *Soul of an Octopus,* 115, 141.

11. Brenner et al., "Plant Neurobiology," 413–19.

12. Pollan, "The Intelligent Plant."

13. Latour, *Facing Gaia,* 70.

14. Haraway, *Staying with the Trouble,* 11.

15. Diogenes Laertius, I.23–24, in Diogenes, *Lives of Eminent Philosophers,* 25.

16. Plotinus, *Enneads,* fifth ennead, first tractate, section 2.

17. Bruno, *Expulsion of the Triumphant Beast,* 235.

18. Bruno, *Cause, Principle, and Unity,* 42–44.

19. Strickland, *Leibniz's Monadology,* 132–34.

20. Goethe, *Scientific Studies,* 6.

21. Woodward, "Fechner's Panpsychism," 367–86.

22. Fechner, *Little Book of Life after Death,* xiii.

23. Hamilton, "Ernst Mach and the Elimination of Subjectivity," 127.

24. De Quincey, *Radical Nature,* 138–39.

25. Skrbina, *Panpsychism in the West,* 132.

26. Quoted in Richardson, *William James,* 92.

27. Schiller, *Riddles of the Sphinx,* 443.

28. De Quincey, *Radical Nature,* 154.

29. De Quincey, *Radical Nature,* 162.

30. Whitehead, *Process and Reality,* 88.

31. Skrbina, *Panpsychism in the West,* 250–51.

32. Skrbina, *Mind That Abides,* 378.

33. Tarnas, *Cosmos and Psyche,* 17.

34. Harding, *Animate Earth,* 18.

35. Mathews, *For Love of Matter,* 78.

36. De Quincey, *Radical Nature,* 77.

37. Abram, *Becoming Animal,* 269.

CHAPTER 5. OPPOSITIONAL DUALITY

1. Cutler, "Explaining the Rise in Youth Suicide," 219–70.
2. Bacon, "Of Heresies."
3. Berry, *Great Work,* 82.
4. Montaigne, "An Apology for Raymond Sebond," 401.
5. Firpo, *Il processo di Giordano Bruno.*
6. Merchant, "Francis Bacon and the 'Vexations of Art,'" 551–99.
7. Quoted in Bierman, "Science and Society in *The New Atlantis,*" 492–500.
8. Merchant, "'The Violence of Impediments,'" 731–60.
9. Plumwood, *Feminism and the Mastery of Nature,* 23.
10. Fredrick Douglass, Speech at the Civil Rights Mass-Meeting Held at Lincoln Hall, Washington, DC, Oct. 22, 1883. Accessed August 15, 2018, TeachingAmericanHistory.org.
11. Bacon, *Great Instauration,* 8.
12. Maul, "Walking Backwards into the Future," 15–24.
13. Parry, *Original Thinking,* 19.
14. Parry, 9.
15. Holton, "Johannes Kepler's Universe," 342.
16. Descartes, *Philosophical Essays and Correspondence,* 42–43, 69, 73, 138, 270–71, 276.
17. Alexander Pope, *An Essay on Man: Epistle I,* lines 289–92, Representative Poetry Online, University of Toronto Libraries, accessed August 15, 2018.
18. Hobbes, *Leviathan,* 14.
19. Laplace, *Philosophical Essay,* 107–8.
20. Wordsworth, "The World Is Too Much With Us."
21. Wellmon, "Goethe's Morphology of Knowledge," 153–77.
22. Goethe, *Faust,* 26.
23. Goethe, *Scientific Studies,* 16.
24. Goethe, 14.
25. Montaigne, "On Pedantry," 125.
26. Goethe, *Scientific Studies,* 24.
27. Maxwell, "Introductory Lecture on Experimental Physics," 241.
28. Bentham, "Of the Principle of Utility," chapter 1, paragraph 1.
29. Huxley, "Agnosticism," 768.
30. Bowler, *Evolution,* 104–5.
31. Quoted in Hale, *Political Descent,* 12.

32. Hale, 171.

33. Spencer, *Principles of Biology,* 444–45.

34. Spencer, 340–41.

35. Eisler, *Chalice and the Blade,* 157.

36. Huxley, "Struggle for Existence and Its Bearing upon Man."

37. Eisenstein, *Ascent of Humanity,* 419.

38. Loy, "Avoiding the Void," 176.

39. Haraway, *Staying with the Trouble,* 35.

CHAPTER 6. SYMBIOSIS

1. Latour, *Facing Gaia,* 254.

2. De Quincey, *Radical Knowing,* 150.

3. Margulis, *Symbiotic Planet,* 130.

4. Kropotkin, *Mutual Aid,* 9.

5. Goethe, *Scientific Studies,* 15.

6. Darwin, *Formation of Vegetable Mould,* 97.

7. Loye, *Darwin's Lost Theory,* 32.

8. Loye, 25.

9. Todes, *Darwin without Malthus,* 45–53.

10. Todes, 65.

11. Todes, 105.

12. Kropotkin, *Mutual Aid,* 44.

13. Darwin, *Descent of Man,* 130.

14. Kropotkin, *Mutual Aid,* 18.

15. Sapp, *Evolution by Association,* 45, 46.

16. Sapp, 59.

17. Margulis, *Symbiotic Planet,* 25.

18. Sapp, *Evolution by Association,* 49.

19. Loye, *Rediscovering Darwin.*

20. Darwin, *Descent of Man,* 74.

21. Teilhard, *Phenomenon of Man,* 264–65.

22. In Tsing et al., *Arts of Living on a Damaged Planet,* M51–53.

23. Margulis, *Symbiotic Planet,* 30.

24. Quoted in "Lynn Margulis," Wikipedia, last updated June 20, 2018.

25. Margulis, *Symbiotic Planet,* 32.

26. Margulis and Guerrero, "Two Plus Two Equals One," 51.

27. Margulis, *Symbiotic Planet,* 120.

28. Harding, *Animate Earth,* 168.

29. Hyde, *Gift,* 120.

30. Thomas, *Old Way,* 241.

31. Tutu, *No Future without Forgiveness,* 33.

32. Eisler. "Conscious Evolution," 196.

33. Rolling, "Pedagogy of the Bereft."

34. Eisler and Montuori, "Partnership Organization," 13.

35. Bollier, *Silent Theft,* 38.

36. Capra, "Evolution," 46.

37. Eisler, *Real Wealth of Nations,* 188.

38. Margulis, *Symbiotic Planet,* 31.

CHAPTER 7. COMPLEXITY CONSCIOUSNESS

1. Morin, *On Complexity,* 103.

2. Morin, *Homeland Earth,* 41.

3. Lao Tzu, *Tao Te Ching,* 45.

4. Morin, *On Complexity,* 21.

5. von Bertalanffy, *Robots, Men and Minds,* 57.

6. Plato, *Cratylus,* accessed August 17, 2018, The Internet Classics Archive.

7. In Graham, *Texts of Early Greek Philosophers,* 159.

8. Prigogine, *End of Certainty,* 26.

9. Prigogine, 132.

10. Capra and Luisi, *Systems View of Life,* 143.

11. Maturana, "Autopoiesis, Structural Coupling, and Cognition," 3–4, 5–34.

12. Maturana, 6.

13. Maturana, 16.

14. Morin, "Complex Thinking for a Complex World," 9.

15. Morin, *On Complexity,* 11.

16. Morin, *Homeland Earth,* 41.

17. Meadows, *Thinking in Systems,* 178.

18. Meadows, 76.

19. Morin, *On Complexity,* 91.

20. Morin, *On Complexity,* 11.

21. James, *Pluralistic Universe,* 33.

22. Prigogine, *End of Certainty,* 57.

23. Morin, "Complex Thinking for a Complex World," 19.

24. D'Aquili and Newberg, *Mystical Mind*, 52, 55.

25. Morin, "A New Way of Thinking," 10–14

CHAPTER 8. CREATIVE SYNERGY

1. Muir, *Thousand Mile Walk to the Gulf*, 358.

2. Muir, 26.

3. Muir, *Our National Parks*, 16.

4. Wilson, *Biophilia*, 85.

5. Arvay, *Biophilia Effect*.

6. Kaku, *Physics of the Future*, 11.

7. Bortoft, *Wholeness of Nature*, 115.

8. Reason, *In Search of Grace*, 62.

9. Bortoft, *Wholeness of Nature*, 247.

10. Richards, "Did Goethe and Schelling Endorse Species Evolution?"

11. Holdrege, *Beyond Biotech*, 122.

12. Holdrege, *Thinking Like a Plant*, 1.

13. Nagel, "What Is It Like to Be a Bat?" 435–50.

14. Mancuso and Viola, *Brilliant Green*, 77–78.

15. Karban et al., "Kin Recognition Affects Plant Communication."

16. Wohlleben, *Hidden Life of Trees*, 245.

17. Haskell, *Songs of Trees*, xi.

18. Stamets, *Mycelium Running*, 10.

19. Tsing, *Mushroom at the End of the World*, 3, 20.

20. Bekoff, *Why Dogs Hump and Bees Get Depressed*, 149.

21. Howard et al., "Numerical Ordering of Zero in Honey Bees," 1124–26.

22. Horn, *Bees in America*, 137.

23. Laland and Galef, *Question of Animal Culture*, 7.

24. Whitehead and Rendell, *Cultural Lives of Whales and Dolphins*, 204.

25. Madison Montgomery, "Still Think Humans Are the Most Intelligent Animals? Here's Why Whales and Dolphins Have Us Beat," One Green Planet website, July 8, 2017.

26. WDC (Whale and Dolphin Conservation), "Scientific Evidence for Whale and Dolphin Rights," accessed August 17, 2018.

27. Morell, "Lori Marino."

28. Bagby, "Southern Resident Orca Still Carrying Her Deceased Baby."

29. Swift, "Corvid Curiosities."

30. Jung, *Collected Works, Vol. 6: Psychological Types,* 123.

31. Marzluff and Angell, *In the Company of Crows,* 175, 198.

32. Marzluff and Angell, *Gifts of the Crow,* 198.

33. Marzluff and Angell, *In the Company of Crows,* 302.

34. Bekoff, *Emotional Lives of Animals,* 100.

35. Csikszentmihalyi and Bennet, "Exploratory Model of Play," 45–48.

36. Bekoff, *Emotional Lives,* 21.

37. Van Dooren, *Flight Ways,* 126.

38. Weronika et al., "Anhydrobiosis in Tardigrades," 577–83.

39. Jönsson et al., "Tardigrades Survive Exposure," R729–31.

40. Smith, "These 'Indestructible' Animals."

41. De Waal, *Are We Smart Enough?,* 15.

42. Woolley-Barker, *Teeming,* 34, 288.

43. Morton, *Being Ecological,* 71, 119.

44. Wittgenstein, *Philosophical Investigations,* 190.

45. Shivik, *Mousy Cats and Sheepish Coyotes,* 168.

46. Haraway, *When Species Meet,* 20.

47. Hart et al., "Dogs Are Sensitive," 80.

48. De Quincey, *Radical Nature,* 262.

CHAPTER 9. SACRED FUTURISM

1. Macy, *Coming Back to Life,* 14.

2. Kurt Vonnegut, "Ladies and Gentlemen of AD 2088." Advertisement, *Time* magazine, 1988.

3. Swimme and Berry, *Universe Story,* 66.

4. In Zang, *Buckminster Fuller,* 125.

5. Mathews, *For Love of Matter,* 18.

6. Tsing, *Mushroom at the End of the World,* 47, 144.

7. Morin, *Homeland Earth,* 108.

8. Greenblatt, *Swerve,* 35.

9. Thompson, *American Replacement of Nature,* 125.

10. Toffler, *Future Shock,* 460.

11. Biomimicry Institute website, "Biomimicry 101: What Is Biomimicry?," accessed June 21, 2018.

12. Baumeister, *Biomimicry Resource Handbook,* 33.

13. Baumeister, 57.

14. Berry, *Dream of the Earth,* 23.

15. Montuori, "Beyond Postnormal Times," 223.

16. Bekoff, *Emotional Lives,* 147.

17. Reason and Bradbury, *Sage Handbook of Action Research,* 1.

18. Bastian et al., *Participatory Research in More-Than-Human Worlds,* 1, 11.

19. Montuori, "Five Dimensions of Applied Transdisciplinarity."

20. Gidley, "Globally Scanning for Megatrends of the Mind," 1041.

21. Cullinan, *Wild Law,* 58.

22. In Cullinan, 58.

23. Cullinan, 64.

24. Cullinan, 79.

25. Capra and Mattei, *Ecology of Law,* 12.

26. Capra and Mattei, 131.

27. Capra and Mattei, 145.

28. Drew Dellinger, "The Ecological King: A Vision for Our Time," originally published on IONS: Institute of Noetic Sciences, January 16, 2017.

29. Haraway, *Staying with the Trouble,* 12.

30. Hemenway, *Permaculture City,* 2.

31. Ulrich, "Effects of Gardens on Health Outcomes," 27–86.

32. Kuo and Sullivan, "Environment and Crime in the Inner City," 343–67.

33. Faber and Kuo, "Is Contact with Nature Important?," 124–40.

34. Thomas Berry, "The Ten Principles of Earth Jurisprudence," Rightsofnature .org, accessed June 21, 2018.

35. Oliver, *Devotions,* 347.

36. Haraway, *Staying with the Trouble,* 4.

37. Freire, *Pedagogy of the Oppressed,* 77.

38. Johnston, *Cultural Maturity,* 401–5.

39. Tang and Joiner, *Synergic Inquiry,* 47.

40. De Quincey, *Radical Nature,* 263.

41. Swimme and Berry, *Universe Story,* 243.

42. Swimme and Berry, 256.

43. Hooks, *Teaching to Transgress,* 22.

44. Hooks, *Teaching Community,* 137.

BIBLIOGRAPHY

Abram, David. *Becoming Animal: An Earthly Cosmology.* New York: Pantheon, 2010.

Albertin, Caroline A. et al. "The Octopus Genome and the Evolution of Cephalopod Neural and Morphological Novelties." *Nature* 524 (2015): 220–24.

Aristotle. *Physics,* book 2. Translated by R. P. Hardie and R. K. Gaye, accessed June 23, 2018, The Internet Classics Archive.

Arvay, Clemens G. *The Biophilia Effect.* Boulder, Colo.: Sounds True, 2018.

Asimov, Isaac. *The Golden Door: The United States from 1876 to 1918.* Boston: Houghton Mifflin, 1977.

Bacon, Francis. *The Great Instauration.* Edited by Jeremy Weinberger. Hoboken, N.J.: Wiley-Blackwell, 2016.

———. "Of Heresies." In *Sacred Meditations.* Radford, Va.: Wilder, 2012.

Bagby, Cali. "Southern Resident Orca Still Carrying Her Deceased Baby, Update." *San Juan Journal,* July 27, 2018.

Barnes, Jonathan, ed. *The Complete Works of Aristotle: The Revised Oxford Translation.* Princeton, N.J.: Princeton University Press, 1984.

Bar-On, Yinon M., Rob Phillips, and Ron Milo. "The Biomass Distribution on Earth." *Proceedings of the National Academy of Sciences* 115, no. 25 (June 19, 2018): 6506–11.

Bastian, Michelle, Owain Jones, Niamh Moore, and Emma Roe, eds. *Participatory Research in More-Than-Human Worlds.* London: Routledge, 2017.

Bateson, Gregory. *Mind and Nature: A Necessary Unity.* New York: Hampton Press, 2002. Originally published in 1979.

Bateson, Nora, dir. *An Ecology of Mind: A Daughter's Portrait of Gregory Bateson.* Oley, Pa.: Bullfrog Films, 2010. DVD, 60 min.

Baumeister, Dayna. *Biomimicry Resource Handbook: A Seed Bank of Best Practices*. Missoula, Mont.: Biomimicry 3.8 Publishing, 2014.

Bekoff, Marc. *The Emotional Lives of Animals: A Leading Scientist Explores Animal Joy, Sorrow, and Empathy—and Why They Matter*. Novato, Calif.: New World Library, 2007.

———. *Why Dogs Hump and Bees Get Depressed*. Novato, Calif.: New World Library, 2013.

Bentham, Jeremy. "Of the Principle of Utility." In *An Introduction to the Principles of Morals and Legislation*. Oxford: Clarendon Press, 1907. First published 1789.

Berry, Thomas. *The Dream of the Earth*. Berkeley, Calif.: Counterpoint, 1988.

———. *The Great Work: Our Way into the Future*. New York: Random House, 1999.

Bierman, Judah. "Science and Society in *The New Atlantis* and Other Renaissance Utopias." *Publications of the Modern Language Association* 78, no. 5 (Dec. 1963): 492–500.

Bluck, Richard. *Plato's Phaedo: A Translation*. New York: Routledge & Kegan Paul, 1955.

Bohm, David. "A New Theory of Relationship of Mind and Matter." *Philosophical Psychology* 3, no. 2 (1990): 271.

———. *Wholeness and the Implicate Order*. New York: Routledge, 1980.

Bollier, David. *Silent Theft: The Private Plunder of Our Common Wealth*. London: Routledge, 2003.

Bortoft, Henri. *The Wholeness of Nature: Goethe's Way toward a Science of Conscious Participation in Nature*. Hudson, N.Y.: Lindisfarne, 1996.

Bowler, Peter J. *Evolution: The History of an Idea*. Berkeley: University of California Press, 2003.

Brenner, Eric D., et al. "Plant Neurobiology: An Integrated View of Plant Signaling." *Trends in Plant Science* 11, no. 8 (2006): 413–19.

Bruno, Giordano. *Cause, Principle, and Unity (De la causa, principio, et uno)*. Edited by R. Blackwell and R. DeLucca. Cambridge, UK: Cambridge University Press, 1998.

———. *The Expulsion of the Triumphant Beast*. Translated by Arthur D. Imerti. Winnipeg, Manitoba: Bison Books, 2004.

Campbell, Joseph. *The Power of Myth*. New York: Random House, 1998.

Capra, Fritjof. "Evolution: The Old View and the New View." In *The Evolutionary Outrider*, edited by David Loye. Westport, Conn.: Praeger, 1998.

———. *Uncommon Wisdom: Conversations with Remarkable People*. New York: Bantam, 1988.

Capra, Fritjof, and Ugo Mattei. *The Ecology of Law: Toward a Legal System in Tune with Nature and Community*. Oakland, Calif.: Berrett-Koehler, 2015.

Capra, Fritjof, and Pier Luigi Luisi. *The Systems View of Life: A Unifying Vision*. Cambridge, UK: Cambridge University Press, 2014.

Combs, Allan. *The Radiance of Being: Understanding the Grand Integral Vision; Living the Integral Life*. St. Paul, Minn.: Paragon House, 2002.

Csikszentmihalyi, Mihaly, and Stith Bennet. "An Exploratory Model of Play." *American Anthropology* new series 73, no. 1 (1971): 45–48.

Cullinan, Cormac. *Wild Law: A Manifesto for Earth Justice*. White River Junction, Vt.: Chelsea Green, 2011.

Curd, Patricia. *The Legacy of Parmenides: Eleatic Monism and Later Pre-Socratic Thought*. Princeton, N.J.: Princeton University Press, 1998.

Cutler, David M., Edward L. Glaeser, Karen S. Norberg. "Explaining the Rise in Youth Suicide." In *Risky Behavior among Youths: An Economic Analysis*, edited by Jonathan Gruber, 219–70. Chicago: University of Chicago, 2001.

D'Aquili, Eugene, and Andrew B. Newberg. *The Mystical Mind*. Minneapolis, Minn.: Fortress Press, 1999.

Darwin, Charles. *The Descent of Man*. London: Penguin Classics, 2004.

———. *The Formation of Vegetable Mould through the Action of Worms, with Observations on Their Habits*. New York: D. Appleton & Company, 1896.

Deloria, Vine, Jr. *God Is Red: A Native View of Religion*. Golden, Colo.: Fulcrum, 2003. Originally published in 1973.

De Quincey, Christian. *BlindSpots: Twenty-One Good Reasons to Think before You Talk*. Rochester, Vt.: Park Street Press, 2015.

———. *Radical Knowing*. Rochester, Vt.: Park Street Press, 2005.

———. *Radical Nature: The Soul of Matter*. Rochester, Vt.: Park Street Press, 2010.

Descartes, René. *Philosophical Essays and Correspondence*. Edited by Roger Ariew. Indianapolis, Ind.: Hackett, 2000.

De Waal, Frans. *Are We Smart Enough to Know How Smart Animals Are?* New York: Norton, 2016.

Diogenes Laertius. *Lives of Eminent Philosophers*. Translated by R. D. Hicks. Cambridge, Mass.: Loeb Classical Library, 1972.

Eisenstein, Charles. *The Ascent of Humanity*. Harrisburg, Pa.: Panenthea Press, 2007.

Eisler, Riane. *The Chalice and the Blade*. New York: Harper & Row, 1988.

———. "Conscious Evolution: Cultural Transformation and Human Agency." In *The Evolutionary Outrider*, edited by David R. Loye, 191–207. Westport, Conn.: Praeger, 1998.

———. *The Power of Partnership: Seven Relationships That Will Change Your Life*. Novato, Calif.: New World Library, 2002.

———. *The Real Wealth of Nations*. Oakland, Calif.: Berrett-Koehler, 2007.

Eisler, Riane, and Alfonso Montuori. "The Partnership Organization: A Systems Approach." *OD Practitioner* 33, no. 2 (2001): 11–17.

Eliade, Mircea. *Images and Symbols*. Translated by Philip Mairet. Princeton, N.J.: Princeton University Press, 1991.

———. *Patterns in Comparative Religion*. Lincoln, Neb.: Bison Books, 1996.

Faber, A. Taylor, and F. E. Kuo. "Is Contact with Nature Important for Healthy Child Development? State of the Evidence." In *Children and Their Environments: Learning, Using, and Designing Spaces*, 124–40, edited by Christopher Spencer and Mark Blades. Cambridge, UK: Cambridge University Press, 2006.

Fechner, Gustav Theodor. *The Little Book of Life after Death*. York Beach, Maine: Red Wheel/Weiser, 2005. Originally published by Little, Brown in 1904.

Feynman, Richard P. "The Value of Science." *Engineering and Science* XIX (1955): 13–15.

Firpo, Luigi. *Il processo di Giordano Bruno*. Napoli: Scientifiche Italiane, 1949.

Freire, Paulo. *Pedagogy of the Oppressed*. New York: Bloomsbury, 2012.

Gidley, Jennifer. "Globally Scanning for Megatrends of the Mind: Potential Futures of Futures Thinking." *Futures* 42 (2010): 1040–48.

Goethe, Johann Wolfgang von. *Faust*. Translated by Martin Greenberg. New Haven, Conn.: Yale University Press, 2014.

———. *The Metamorphosis of Plants*. Cambridge, Mass.: MIT Press, 2009.

———. *Scientific Studies*. Edited and translated by Douglas Miller. New York: Suhrkamp, 1988.

Graham, Daniel W., ed. and trans. *The Texts of Early Greek Philosophers: The Complete Fragments and Selected Testimonies of the Major Pre-Socratics, Part 1*. Cambridge, UK: Cambridge University Press, 2010.

Greenblatt, Stephen. *The Swerve: How the World Became Modern*. New York: Norton, 2012.

Hale, J. Piers. *Political Descent: Malthus, Mutualism, and the Politics of Evolution in Victorian England.* Chicago: University of Chicago Press, 2014.

Hamilton, Andy. "Ernst Mach and the Elimination of Subjectivity." *Ratio* 3, no. 2 (1990): 117–35.

Haraway, Donna J. *Staying with the Trouble: Making Kin in the Cthulucene.* Durham, N.C.: Duke University Press, 2016.

———. *When Species Meet.* Minneapolis: University of Minnesota Press, 2008.

Harding, Stephan. *Animate Earth: Science, Intuition, and Gaia.* White River Junction, Vt.: Chelsea Green, 2006.

Hart, Vlastimil, Petra Nováková, Erich Pascal Malkemper, Sabine Begall, Vladimír Hanzal, Miloš Ježek, Tomáš Kušta et al. "Dogs Are Sensitive to Small Variations of the Earth's Magnetic Field," *Frontiers in Zoology* 10, no. 1 (2013): 80.

Haskell, David George. *The Songs of Trees: Stories from Nature's Great Connectors.* New York: Viking, 2017.

Hemenway, Toby. *The Permaculture City: Regenerative Design for Urban, Suburban, and Town Resilience.* White River Junction, Vt.: Chelsea Green, 2015.

Hobbes, Thomas. *Leviathan.* Edited by Charles William Eliot. Cambridge, Mass.: Harvard Classics, 1909.

Holdrege, Craig. *Beyond Biotech: The Barren Promise of Genetic Engineering.* Lexington: University of Kentucky Press, 2010.

———. *Thinking Like a Plant: A Living Science for Life.* Great Barrington, Mass.: Lindisfarne, 2013.

Holton, Gerald. "Johannes Kepler's Universe." *American Journal of Physics* 24, no. 5 (1956): 340–51.

Hooks, Bell. *Teaching Community: A Pedagogy of Hope.* New York: Routledge, 2003.

———. *Teaching to Transgress: Education as the Practice of Freedom.* New York: Routledge, 1994.

Horkheimer, Max, and Theodor Adorno. *Dialectic of Enlightenment.* Stanford, Calif.: Stanford University Press, 2002.

Horn, Tammy. *Bees in America: How the Honey Bee Shaped a Nation.* Lexington: University of Kentucky Press, 2006.

Houston, Jean. *The Hero and the Goddess.* New York: Ballantine, 1992.

Howard, Scarlett R., Aurore Avarguès-Weber, Jair E. Garcia, Andrew D. Greentree, and Adrian G. Dyer. "Numerical Ordering of Zero in Honey Bees." *Science* 360, no. 6393 (June 2018): 1124–26.

Huxley, Thomas Henry. "Agnosticism." *The Popular Science Monthly* 34, no. 46 (April 1889).

———. "The Struggle for Existence and Its Bearing upon Man." Written in 1888. First published in London by Popular Science, 1889.

Hwan-Chen, Chung. "Different Meanings of the Word *Energeia* in the Philosophy of Aristotle." *Philosophy and Phenomenological Research* 17, no. 1 (Sept. 1956): 56–65.

Hyde, Lewis. *The Gift: Creativity and the Artist in the Modern World.* New York: Vintage, 1983.

Irving, Sarah. "'In a Pure Soil': Colonial Anxieties in the Work of Francis Bacon." *History of European Ideas* 32 (2006): 249–62.

James, William. *A Pluralistic Universe.* Lincoln: University of Nebraska Press, 1996. Originally published in 1909.

Johnston, Charles M. *Cultural Maturity: A Guidebook for the Future.* Seattle: ICD Press, 2015.

Jönsson. Ingemar K., Elke Rabbow, Ralph O. Schill, Mats Harms-Ringdahl, and Petra Rettberg. "Tardigrades Survive Exposure to Space in Low Earth Orbit." *Current Biology* 18, no. 7 (2008): R729–31.

Jung, C. G. *The Collected Works of C. G. Jung, Volume 6: Psychological Types.* Princeton, N.J.: Bollingen, 1976.

———. *The Collected Works of C. G. Jung, Volume 11: Psychology and Religion.* Princeton, N.J.: Bollingen, 1958.

———. *Memories, Dreams, Reflections.* Translated by Richard and Clara Winston. New York: Vintage, 1989.

———. *Synchronicity: An Acausal Connecting Principle.* Translated by R. F. C. Hull. Princeton, N.J.: Princeton University Press, 1973.

Kaku, Michio. *Physics of the Future: How Science Will Shape Human Destiny and Our Daily Lives by the Year 2100.* New York: Anchor, 2012.

Karban, Richard, Kaori Shiojiri, Satomi Ishizaki, William C. Wetzel, and Richard Y. Evans. "Kin Recognition Affects Plant Communication and Defence." *Proceedings of the Royal Society B: Biological Sciences* 280, no. 1756 (February 13, 2013).

Koestler, Arthur. *The Ghost in the Machine.* London: Arkana, 1967.

Kohn, Eduardo. *How Forests Think: Toward an Anthropology beyond the Human.* Berkeley: University of California Press, 2013.

Kropotkin, Peter. *Mutual Aid.* London: Forgotten Books, 2008. First published 1902.

Kuo, Frances, and William Sullivan. "Environment and Crime in the Inner City: Does Vegetation Reduce Crime?" *Environment and Behavior* 33 (May 2001): 343–67.

Laland, Kevin, and Bennett Galef, eds. *The Question of Animal Culture.* Cambridge, Mass.: Harvard University Press, 2009.

Lao Tzu. *Tao Te Ching.* Translated by Gia-Fu Feng and Jane English. New York: Vintage, 2011.

Laplace, Pierre-Simon. *A Philosophical Essay on Probabilities.* Translated by Frederick Wilson Truscott and Frederick Emory. New York: Cosimo Classics, 2007.

Latour, Bruno. *Facing Gaia: Eight Lectures on the New Climatic Regime.* Medford, Mass.: Polity, 2017.

Leibniz, Gottfried Wilhelm. *The Monadology.* Translated by Robert Latta, 1896.

Lovelock, James E., and Lynn Margulis. "Atmospheric Homeostasis by and for the Biosphere: The Gaia Hypothesis." *Tellus* 26 (1974): 1–2.

Loy, David R. "Avoiding the Void: The Lack of Self in Psychotherapy and Buddhism." *Journal of Transpersonal Psychology* 24, no. 2 (1992): 151–80.

———. *Lack and Transcendence: The Problem of Death and Life in Psychotherapy, Existentialism, and Buddhism.* Ithaca, N.Y.: Prometheus, 1996.

———. *The World Is Made of Stories.* New York: Simon & Schuster/Wisdom, 2010.

Loye, David. *Darwin's Lost Theory: Bridge to a Better World.* Carmel, Calif.: Benjamin Franklin, 2007.

———. ed. *The Evolutionary Outrider.* Westport, Conn.: Praeger, 1998.

———. *Rediscovering Darwin.* Pacific Grove, Calif.: Romanes Press, 2018.

Macy, Joanna. *Coming Back to Life.* Gabriola Island, BC: New Society, 2014.

Mancuso, Stefano, and Alessandra Viola. *Brilliant Green.* Washington D.C.: Island Press, 2013.

Margulis, Lynn. *Symbiotic Planet: A New Look at Evolution.* New York: Basic Books, 1999.

Margulis, Lynn, and Richard Guerrero. "Two Plus Two Equals One: Individuals Emerge from Bacterial Communities." In *Gaia 2,* edited by William Irwin Thompson, 50–61. Hudson, N.Y.: Lindisfarne, 1991.

Marino, Lori, et al. "Cetaceans Have Complex Brains for Better Cognition." *PLOS Biology* 5, no. 5 (2007): e139.

Marzluff, John M., and Tony Angell. *Gifts of the Crow.* New York: Simon & Schuster, 2012.

———. *In the Company of Crows and Ravens*. New Haven, Conn.: Yale University Press, 2005.

Mathews, Freya. *For Love of Matter: A Contemporary Panpsychism*. Albany: State University of New York Press, 2003.

Maturana, Humberto. "Autopoiesis, Structural Coupling, and Cognition: A History of These and Other Notions in the Biology of Cognition." *Cybernetics and Human Knowing* 9 (2002): 3–34.

Maul, Stephan M. "Walking Backwards into the Future." In *Given World and Time: Temporalities in Context,* edited by Tyrell Miller, 15–24. Budapest: CEU Press, 2008.

Maxwell, James Clerk. "Introductory Lecture on Experimental Physics." In *The Scientific Papers of James Clerk Maxwell,* volume 2, edited by W. D. Niven, 241–43. Mineola, N.Y.: Courier Dover, 2003.

Meadows, Donella H. *Thinking in Systems*. White River Junction, Vt.: Chelsea Green, 2008.

Merchant, Carolyn. "Francis Bacon and the 'Vexations of Art': Experimentation as Intervention." *The British Journal for the History of Science* 46, no. 4 (2013): 551–99.

———. "'The Violence of Impediments': Francis Bacon and the Origins of Experimentation." *Isis* 99 (2008): 731–60: http://nature.berkeley.edu /departments/espm/env-hist/articles/90.pdf.

Miller, Debra Lee. *Reproductive Biology and Phylogeny of Cetacea: Whales, Porpoises and Dolphins*. Enfield, Australia: Science Publishers, 2016.

Montaigne, Michel de. "An Apology for Raymond Sebond" and "On Pedantry." In *The Complete Works,* translated by Donald M. Frame. New York: Everyman's Library, 2003.

Montgomery, Sy. *The Soul of an Octopus*. New York: Atria, 2015.

Montuori, Alfonso. "Beyond Postnormal Times: The Future of Creativity and the Creativity of the Future." *Futures* 43 (2011): 221–27.

———. "Five Dimensions of Applied Transdisciplinarity." *Integral Leadership Review* (2012).

Morell, Virginia. "Lori Marino: Leader of a Revolution in How We Perceive Animals." *National Geographic* website, May 29, 2014.

Morin, Edgar. "Complex Thinking for a Complex World: About Reductionism, Disjunction, and Systemism." *Systema* 2, no. 1 (2014): 14–22.

———. *Homeland Earth: A Manifesto for the New Millennium*. Cresskill, N.J.: Hampton Press, 1999.

———. *On Complexity*. Cresskill, N.J.: Hampton Press, 2008.

———. "A New Way of Thinking." *Unesco Courier: Secrets of Complexity,* February1996, 10–14.

Morton, Timothy. *Being Ecological*. Cambridge, Mass.: MIT Press, 2018.

Muir, John. *Our National Parks*. Boston: Houghton, Mifflin, 1901.

———. *A Thousand Mile Walk to the Gulf*. Memphis, Tenn.: General Books, 2012.

Müller, Max, trans. *The Rig Veda*. London: Oxford University Press, 1869.

Naddaf, Gerard. *The Greek Concept of Nature*. Albany: State University of New York Press, 2005.

Nagel, Thomas. *Mind and Cosmos: Why the Materialist Neo-Darwinian Conception of Nature Is Almost Certainly False*. New York: Oxford University Press, 2012.

———. "What Is It Like to Be a Bat?" *The Philosophical Review* 83, no. 4 (October 1974): 435–450.

Narby, Jeremy. *The Cosmic Serpent*. New York: Tarcher, 1998.

Niven, W. D., ed. *The Scientific Papers of James Clerk Maxwell*. Mineola, N.Y.: Courier Dover, 2003.

Oliver, Mary. *Devotions: The Selected Poems of Mary Oliver*. New York: Penguin, 2017.

Parry, Glenn Aparicio. *Original Thinking*. Berkeley, Calif.: North Atlantic Books, 2015.

Plotinus. *The Enneads*. Translated by Stephen McKenna. New York: Larson Publications, 1992.

Plumwood, Val. *Feminism and the Mastery of Nature*. London: Routledge, 1993.

Pollan, Michael. "The Intelligent Plant." *The New Yorker,* Dec. 23, 2013.

Prigogine, Ilya. *The End of Certainty*. New York: Free Press, 1996.

Reason, Peter. *In Search of Grace: An Ecological Pilgrimage*. Alresford, Hants, UK: Earth Books, 2017.

Reason, Peter, and Hilary Bradbury, editors. *The Sage Handbook of Action Research: Participatory Inquiry and Practice,* 2nd ed. Los Angeles: Sage, 2006.

Richards, Robert J. "Did Goethe and Schelling Endorse Species Evolution?" Lecture, Western Ontario University, Ontario, Canada, May 2011.

Richardson, Robert D. *William James: In the Maelstrom of Modernism: A Biography*. New York: Mariner, 2006.

Robinet, Isabelle. *Taoism: Growth of a Religion*. Translated by Phyllis Brooks. Stanford, Calif.: Stanford University Press, 1997.

Rolling, James Haywood, Jr. "Pedagogy of the Bereft: Theorizing an Economy of Profitless Exchange and Social Development." Unpublished paper, Syracuse University, 2014.

Sapp, Jan. *Evolution by Association*. Oxford: Oxford University Press, 1994.

Schiller, Ferdinand. *Riddles of the Sphinx: A Study in the Philosophy of Evolution [1891]*. Translated by F. C. Scott. Ithaca, N.Y.: Cornell University Library, 2009.

Schonfeld, Martin. *The Philosophy of the Young Kant: The Precritical Project*. New York: Oxford University Press, 2000.

Schopenhauer, Arthur. *The World as Will and Representation*. Translated by E. J. F Payne. Mineola, N.Y.: Dover, 1969.

Shivik, John A. *Mousy Cats and Sheepish Coyotes: The Science of Animal Personalities*. Boston: Beacon Press, 2017.

Skrbina, David, ed. *Mind That Abides: Panpsychism in the New Millennium*. Amsterdam: John Benjamins, 2009.

———. *Panpsychism in the West*. Cambridge, Mass.: MIT Press, 2005.

Smith, Casey. "These 'Indestructible' Animals Could Survive a Planet-Wide Apocalypse." *National Geographic* website, April 23, 2018.

Spencer, Herbert. *The Man Versus the State*. London: Forgotten Books, 2018. First published in 1884.

———. *The Principles of Biology*, vol. I. London: Williams and Norgate, 1864.

Stamets, Paul. *Mycelium Running: How Mushrooms Can Help Save the World*. Berkeley, Calif.: Ten Speed Press, 2005.

Strickland, Lloyd. *Leibniz's Monadology: A New Translation and Guide*. Edinburgh, Scotland: Edinburgh University Press, 2014.

Swift, Kaeli. "Corvid Curiosities: Do Crows Play and Why?" Corvid Research blog, March 16, 2015.

Swimme, Brian, and Thomas Berry. *The Universe Story*. New York: HarperSanFrancisco, 1992.

Tang, Yongming, and Charles Joiner. *Synergic Inquiry*. Thousand Oaks, Calif.: Sage Publications, 2006.

Tarnas, Richard. *Cosmos and Psyche: Intimations of New World View*. New York: Plume, 2007.

Taylor, Mac C. *The Moment of Complexity: Emerging Network Culture*. Chicago: University of Chicago Press, 2001.

Teilhard de Chardin, Pierre. *The Phenomenon of Man*. Translated by Bernard Wall. New York: Harper Perennial Modern Thought Edition, 2008.

Thomas, Elizabeth Marshall. *The Old Way: The Story of the First People.* New York: Picador, 2006.

Thompson, William Irwin. *The American Replacement of Nature.* New York: Doubleday, 1991.

———. ed. *Gaia 2: Emergence: The New Science of Becoming.* Hudson, N.Y.: Lindisfarne, 1991.

Thorpe, Benjamin, trans. *Edda Sæmundar Hinns Frôða: The Edda of Sæmund the Learned,* part 1. London: Trübner, 1907.

Todes, Daniel C. *Darwin without Malthus: The Struggle for Existence in Russian Evolutionary Thought.* Oxford: Oxford University Press, 1989.

Toffler, Alvin. *Future Shock.* New York: Bantam, 1971.

Tsing, Anna Lowenhaupt. *The Mushroom at the End of the World: On the Possibility of Life in Capitalist Ruins.* Princeton, N.J.: Princeton University Press, 2015.

Tsing, Anna, Heather Swanson, Elaine Gan, and Nils Bubandt, eds. *Arts of Living on a Damaged Planet.* Minneapolis: University of Minnesota Press, 2017.

Tutu, Desmond. *No Future without Forgiveness: A Personal Overview of South Africa's Truth and Reconciliation.* New York: Random House, 1999.

Ulrich, R. S. "Effects of Gardens on Health Outcomes: Theory and Research." In *Healing Gardens: Therapeutic Benefits and Design Recommendations,* edited by C. C. Marcus and M. Barnes, 27–86. New York: John Wiley, 1999.

Van Dooren. *Flight Ways: Life and Loss at the Edge of Extinction.* New York: Columbia University Press, 2014.

Volk, Tyler. *Metapatterns.* New York: Columbia University Press, 1995.

Von Bertalanffy, Ludwig. *Robots, Men and Minds.* New York: George Brazillier, 1969.

Wellmon, Chad. "Goethe's Morphology of Knowledge, or the Overgrowth of Nomenclature." *Goethe Yearbook* 17 (2010): 153–77.

Welnicz, Weronika, Markus A. Grohme, Łukasz Kaczmarek, Ralph O. Schill, and Marcus Frohme. "Anhydrobiosis in Tardigrades: The Last Decade." *Journal of Insect Physiology* 57, no. 5 (2011): 577–83.

Whitehead, Alfred North. *Process and Reality: Gifford Lectures Delivered in the University of Edinburgh during the Session 1927–28.* New York: Free Press, 1978.

Whitehead, Hal, and Luke Rendell. *The Cultural Lives of Whales and Dolphins.* Chicago: University of Chicago Press, 2015.

Wilber, Ken. *Sex, Ecology, Spirituality*. Boston: Shambhala, 1995, 2000.

Wilson, Edward O. *Biophilia: The Human Bond with Other Species*. Cambridge, Mass.: Harvard University Press, 1984.

Wittgenstein, Ludwig. *Philosophical Investigations*. Malden, Mass.: Blackwell, 2001. Originally published 1953.

Wohlleben, Peter. *The Hidden Life of Trees: What They Feel, How They Communicate*. Vancouver, British Columbia: Greystone Books, 2016.

Woodward, William R. "Fechner's Panpsychism: A Scientific Solution to the Mind-Body Problem." *Journal of the History of the Behavioral Sciences* 8, no. 4 (1972): 367–86.

Woolley-Barker, Tamsin. *Teeming: How Superorganisms Work to Build Infinite Wealth in a Finite World (and Your Company Can Too)*. Ashland, Ore.: White Cloud Press, 2017.

Wordsworth, William. "The World Is Too Much with Us." In *The Collected Works of William Wordsworth*. East Sussex, UK: Delphi Classics, 2014.

Yoke Ho, Peng. *Li, Qi, and Shu: An Introduction to Science and Civilization in China*. Hong Kong: Hong Kong University Press, 1985.

Zang, T. K. *Buckminster Fuller: An Anthology for a New Millennium*. New York: St. Martin's Griffin, 2002.

INDEX

ABOUT THE AUTHOR

Julie J. Morley is an environmental educator, writer, and speaker on complexity, consciousness, ecology, and interspecies creativity. She studied Classics at the University of Southern California and Columbia University and has a master's in Transformative Leadership from the California Institute of Integral Studies (CIIS). She is currently a doctoral student at CIIS, focused on Interspecies Creativity with a special interest in crows, magpies, and ravens. She lives in Sebastopol, California. For more information visit her website: **www.sacredfutures.com**.